DESTINATION FACILITATION

A TRAVEL GUIDE TO TRAINING AROUND THE WORLD

EDITOR

DONNA STEFFEY

© 2018 ASTD DBA the Association for Talent Development (ATD)
All rights reserved. Printed in the United States of America.

21 20 19 18 1 2 3 4 5

No part of this publication may be reproduced, distributed, or transmitted in any form or by any means, including photocopying, recording, or other electronic or mechanical methods, without the prior written permission of the publisher, except in the case of brief quotations embodied in critical reviews and certain other noncommercial uses permitted by copyright law. For permission requests, please go to www.copyright.com, or contact Copyright Clearance Center (CCC), 222 Rosewood Drive, Danvers, MA 01923 (telephone: 978.750.8400; fax: 978.646.8600).

ATD Press is an internationally renowned source of insightful and practical information on talent development, workplace learning, and professional development.

ATD Press
1640 King Street
Alexandria, VA 22314 USA

Ordering information: Books published by ATD Press can be purchased by visiting ATD's website at www.td.org/books or by calling 800.628.2783 or 703.683.8100.

Library of Congress Control Number: 2017954651

ISBN-10: 1-56286-938-8
ISBN-13: 978-1-56286-938-0
e-ISBN: 978-1-947308-32-9

ATD Press Editorial Staff
Director: Kristine Luecker
Manager: Melissa Jones
Community of Practice Manager, Global HRD: Wei Wang
Developmental Editor: Jack Harlow
Senior Associate Editor: Caroline Coppel
Cover Design: Derek Thornton, Faceout Studio
Text Design: Francelyn Fernandez
Printed by United Graphics, Mattoon, IL

To past and future learners around the globe, with whom we collaborate and share the learning journey. Our common goal is to build bridges across cultures.

And to those back home who support and encourage us.

Contents

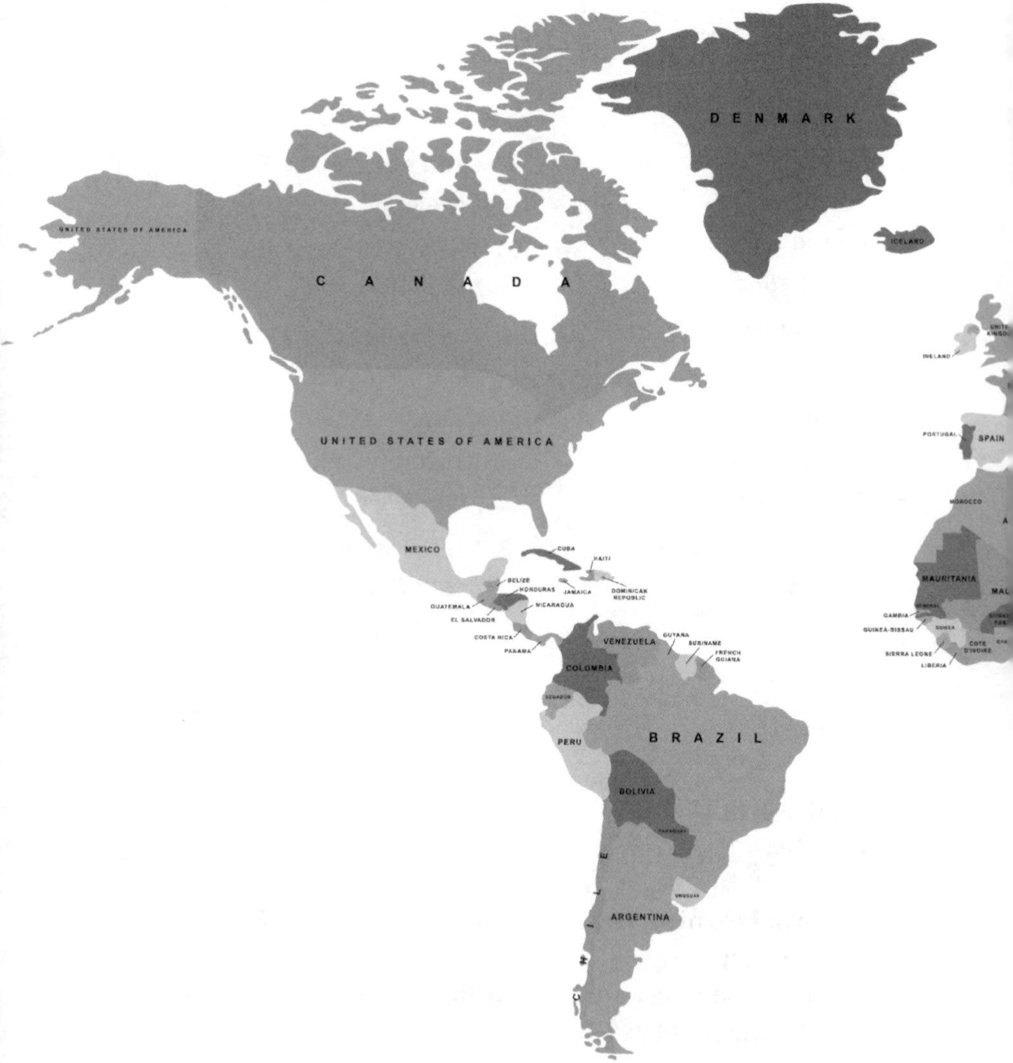

UNITED STATES OF AMERICA
C A N A D A
D E N M A R K
ICELAND
UNITED STATES OF AMERICA
MEXICO
CUBA
HAITI
BELIZE
HONDURAS
JAMAICA
DOMINICAN REPUBLIC
GUATEMALA
EL SALVADOR
NICARAGUA
COSTA RICA
PANAMA
VENEZUELA
GUYANA
SURINAME
FRENCH GUIANA
COLOMBIA
ECUADOR
PERU
B R A Z I L
BOLIVIA
PARAGUAY
URUGUAY
ARGENTINA
C H I L E
IRELAND
PORTUGAL
SPAIN
MOROCCO
MAURITANIA
SENEGAL
GAMBIA
GUINEA-BISSAU
GUINEA
SIERRA LEONE
LIBERIA
COTE D'IVOIRE

RUSSIAN FEDERATION
FINLAND
RUSSIAN FEDERATION
LATVIA
BELARUS
POLAND
UKRAINE
MOLDOVA
ROMANIA
BULGARIA
GREECE
TURKEY
KAZAKHSTAN
MONGOLIA
UZBEKISTAN
TURKMENISTAN
TAJIKISTAN
CHINA
JAPAN
SYRIA
IRAQ
IRAN
AFGHANISTAN
PAKISTAN
NEPAL
LIBYA
EGYPT
SAUDI ARABIA
QATAR
U.A.E.
OMAN
INDIA
BURMA
LAOS
THAILAND
CAMBODIA
VIETNAM
PHILIPPINES
CHAD
SUDAN
YEMEN
DJIBOUTI
SOMALIA
ETHIOPIA
SOUTH SUDAN
CENTRAL AFRICAN REPUBLIC
SRI LANKA
BRUNEI
MALAYSIA
KENYA
DEM. REPUBLIC OF THE CONGO
RWANDA
BURUNDI
TANZANIA
INDONESIA
PAPUA NEW GUINEA
SOLOMON ISLANDS
EAST TIMOR
VANUATU
FIJI
ANGOLA
ZAMBIA
MOZAMBIQUE
ZIMBABWE
MADAGASCAR
BOTSWANA
AUSTRALIA
FRANCE
SWAZILAND
SOUTH AFRICA
LESOTHO
NEW ZEALAND

Introduction

Donna Steffey

When I stepped out of the airport, everything was unfamiliar: the sounds of the taxis and blaring sirens off in the distance, the bright colors on billboards with words I couldn't understand, the unusual aromas in the air. All of it was exhilarating. When you say yes to new and different training opportunities in unfamiliar countries, you can explore new cultures, share unforgettable experiences, and be inspired by people from different countries eager to learn and share their customs.

If you are a local practitioner working for a multinational organization who designs for or delivers training to learners from around the world in the face-to-face classroom, you are working in a global classroom. However, not all talent development professionals relish waiting in long airport lines, living out of a carry-on suitcase, or being away from their families for extended periods. In today's world, you don't have to pack luggage to experience different cultures and people. If you design or deliver online learning for participants within a multinational organization, you are also working in a global classroom. Whenever we work in global classrooms, the opportunity for misunderstandings and cultural mistakes increases, which can interfere with learning transfer.

As a talent development professional, I made the choice years ago to seek out the adventure of training abroad. The opportunities can be stimulating, enriching, educational—and challenging. More than once I was caught up, unintentionally, in a whirlpool of cultural faux pas. One time it was as simple as dropping chopsticks and having the manager replace each person's eating utensils with forks. Another time, placing the wrong football image in my slides caused the class discussion to derail. Maybe the worst mistake was grossly misquoting a famous national author, which brought a burst of laughter from the crowd and embarrassment to me.

There are two great ways to gain knowledge to avoid mistakes: Experience the challenges and learn the lessons yourself, or learn from the experiences of others. *Destination Facilitation* brings together a team of talent development professionals to share their knowledge and wisdom to guide others toward productive training results. They are explorers, people-lovers, and master trainers who have all facilitated in multiple countries. This book compares needs assessments, design processes, facilitation, and classroom management techniques in different countries. Our goal: to give you the confidence and knowledge to say "yes" when opportunities to design and deliver training for people in another country arise, without having to worry about inciting an international incident.

And that starts with developing a global mindset.

Global Mindset Behaviors

The world seems to be getting smaller and more similar. Starbucks, McDonald's, and a Disney store are in just about every corner of the world. It is easy to forget, with KFC in 125 countries, whether you are ordering food in Beijing, Bangalore, or Buenos Aires. People may enjoy the same foods, but that does not mean that the same techniques, language, sense of humor, and learning styles work everywhere.

Who would think that to call someone "sir"—a polite and respectful way of addressing a man in many cultures—would be wrong in Oman? Hamza Taqi, a trainer from Kuwait, found this out while conducting a DiSC Communication workshop with a group of senior leaders in a prestigious government entity in Oman. One of the leaders asked for permission to speak. Hamza gestured with an open hand and said, "Please, sir." The room grew quiet and uncomfortable. Participants looked at each other and shared awkward smiles. The person who asked to speak blushed. Hamza had no idea what he had just said to change the mood and make his learners feel uncomfortable. During the break, Hamza asked what he had done wrong. A participant informed him that the title *sir* was used only for a member of the royal family. A title of respect that Hamza showed to all his students across the globe did not work in Oman. (Read more about his experiences in chapter 1.)

But knowing a list of protocols to follow and the taboos to sidestep in each country is not enough to help avoid international miscommunications and awkwardness. Nor is knowledge of different cultures sufficient information to create a positive learning environment for knowledge transfer to occur. It is important to be open to feedback when working internationally to notice the awkwardness of a situation and make adjustments.

> The Thunderbird School of Global Management defines global mindset as, "A set of attributes that helps people work better with individuals and organizations unlike themselves. It is the ability to understand the similarities and differences among cultures and not be paralyzed by the complexity of the differences. It is about being comfortable with being uncomfortable in different environments" (Herbert 2000).

David Livermore, president of the Cultural Intelligence Center in East Lansing, Michigan, and author of 10 books on global leadership, is an expert on the topic of global mindset, or "cultural intelligence" (CQ) as he refers to it. He defines CQ as "the capability to function effectively in a variety of cultural contexts including national, ethnic, organizational and generational" (Livermore 2011). He has worked with leaders in more than 100 countries and surveyed more than 50,000 people from every major industry and region of the world on the topic of CQ (Ang and Van Dyne 2008, 3). He used this information to create a model for better understanding global mindset or CQ (henceforth, we will use the terms interchangeably)—a set of competencies to be taught, developed, and measured. The CQ model is a new tool for approaching cultural sensitivity, racism, and cross-border effectiveness, and discovering what unites us as people rather than what separates us.

CQ consists of four interdependent competencies: drive, knowledge, strategy, and action.

CQ Drive: The Interest, Confidence, and Impetus to Adapt

Drive is the motivation behind CQ. It is about having the ambition and energy needed to persevere throughout the challenges and conflicts that come with intercultural work. Patience, flexibility, resilience, and tolerance of ambiguity are critical components of CQ drive. Drive also includes the enjoyment you experience from culturally diverse situations, as well as the tangible benefits and confidence gained from being in intercultural encounters.

My first trips abroad involved teaching for three weeks in the United Kingdom, traveling by train across England, Scotland, and Wales. I had the motivation for a first international assignment, but meeting and teaching new people each day, dragging luggage around a new country, and planning food, transportation, and lodging before GPS and cell phones all proved to be too much. It started as an exciting adventure but ended with frustration, stress, and illness. Completely exhausted, I wept openly on a train leaving London's Paddington Station during rush hour. Be sure to try that maneuver if you need to empty out a train in England, where public displays of emotion are not culturally acceptable. I wish I could tell you the trip was a complete success, but it was not.

Having the drive to do international work is not enough. It takes more.

CQ Knowledge: Understanding Intercultural Norms and Differences

CQ knowledge is the extent to which an individual understands the role culture plays in influencing how people think and behave. Culture is the deeply rooted patterns of values, customs, attitudes, and beliefs that distinguish one group from another. Having a familiarity and awareness of how cultures are similar or different is CQ knowledge. Gaining the knowledge needed to function with someone from a different culture enhances global mindset.

CQ Strategy: Being Aware of Culturally Diverse Situations and Planning Accordingly

It is great to have the drive and desire to work cross-culturally, and it makes sense to gain knowledge and understanding of another culture to be aware of the similarities and differences. However, we must be able to use our drive and knowledge to manage expected and unexpected situations adeptly. CQ strategy is about planning, when the needs assessment and thorough design outline become essential. Many international projects require us to work in different workspaces, at an inconsistent pace, and maybe in a different time zone. Very often we do not have time for reflection and to adjust our behaviors. Having a plan going into a new situation is important. Reflecting and tweaking our plan as we become immersed in the new experiences is demonstrating a global mindset.

When Kedar Vashi, from India, was invited to work in China for a second time, he had the drive and cultural knowledge from his first trip, so he was feeling confident. To Kedar's surprise, the new group was a close one, comfortable working with one another, who spoke only a little English. Kedar became reserved and formal and maintained his distance from the group. Participants offered polite smiles in response to his awkwardness. They chatted away in a language of which he understood not a word. Each time they giggled, he suspected that they'd made some snide remarks about him.

That night Kedar reflected on his experiences. He needed a strategy. Between formal and informal communication, there is a huge space called normal. So while he would still not feel comfortable being informal with them, he could at least try to be normal, like how he would be with someone new in his own office.

The next day, as people walked in, Kedar gave them a big smile, extended his hand, and said hello. At first, participants were surprised and a bit awkward. By lunchtime, Kedar decided to be a bit adventurous and join them for a Chinese lunch instead of a separate vegetarian continental lunch. When one of the participants offered Kedar a Coke, he knew his strategy was working. (Read more about his experiences in chapter 6.)

CQ Action: Using Verbal and Nonverbal Actions Correctly

CQ action is about selecting the proper measures in a culturally diverse situation. A person with a global mindset learns which actions will, and will not, improve effectiveness. Being self-aware, knowledgeable yet flexible, and able to adjust behavior quickly when the reality of the specific cultural contexts changes is important.

When Bahaa Hussein, from Egypt, was asked to teach a program in Pakistan, he was cautious to ask the right audience needs assessment questions. His first questions were about the English proficiency of the learners, because Pakistanis mainly speak Urdu. He was told that his participants understood English, which was good news.

Training with the first group on day one went fine. But there was a big surprise on day two—the second group of participants was passive, with very limited response to the engagement questions and almost zero interaction. About an hour into the presentation, Bahaa realized that the learners weren't shy. The problem was that they could not understand him, so he had to adjust his plan. He called for a break and invited an attendee from day one, who spoke both languages, to be his translator and co-facilitator. Instantly, the engagement level peaked. The pace of the session slowed down. Bahaa had selected the correct actions to improve the effectiveness of his training for this culturally diverse situation. (Read more about Bahaa's experiences in chapter 10.)

Dan DeRoche, a trainer from Canada, had a similar situation, but chose different actions. He went to China on his first international assignment. Dan's Canadian co-facilitator had done the audience needs assessment and learned that participants were fluent in English. Unfortunately, it turned out that the participants were not fluent. With no translator available, Dan called for a break. His team quickly simplified the language on their slides, thought of analogies to use for some of the more complex issues, agreed to slow down their speech, and incorporated more table group discussions. The session was slowed down, but participants recognized and appreciated the adjustments. (Read more about Dan's experiences in chapter 4.)

Both trainers incorporated the CQ competencies and demonstrated a global mindset. They had the drive for cross-cultural training, gained knowledge of the culture they were working in, created a training design plan based on a thorough needs analysis, and adjusted their actions to accommodate their learners.

Benefits of a Global Mindset

Multinational corporations employ millions of people around the world. Fortune 500 companies expect their growth to come not from domestic markets but from emerging markets. The potential talent pool of workers will come from there as well (Livermore and Van Dyne 2015). In today's environment, people are required to work with colleagues from a wide variety of backgrounds and experiences, making the workplace more complex, vibrant, and competitive. Understanding other cultures helps shape communication effectiveness in the workplace and influences how we handle conflict and make team decisions. The confluence of customer diversity and workplace diversity requires a culturally intelligent approach to talent development. And yet, a recent study done by the Economist Intelligence Unit (2014) found that 70 percent of international operations fail because of cultural differences.

Organizations need talent development professionals who can design and adapt learning content to meet the needs of increasingly diverse workforces. A diverse staff provides local insights into the intentions and concerns of a broad customer base. In today's globalized world, a global mindset is a necessary tool for every talent development professional who deals with diverse teams of employees, customers, partners, or government regulations.

The more someone demonstrates a global mindset, the more likely they are to outperform others, gain new opportunities, and experience success working in a global context. One reason for this is because individuals with a global mindset are less likely to experience burnout from their intercultural work, so they can maintain higher energy while presenting. They adjust more easily to shifting expectations and demands when working with culturally diverse colleagues face-to-face or virtually.

A global mindset allows talent development professionals to be role models. Whether they are designing an internal workshop on leading with cultural intelligence or facilitating a webinar on how to work with global teams, their global mindset will be evident. With a global mindset, talent development professionals understand the perspectives and priorities of training requesters from other regions and can develop mutually acceptable, tailored training solutions.

Deniz Şenelt Kalelioğlu, from Turkey, is an example of someone who decided to develop her global mindset. She always had a curiosity about new people and new places; "go for it" has been a long-standing career motto for her. In the last 12 years, Deniz has traveled to 80 regions of the world, delivering training in nearly 30 countries and reaching more than 100 nationalities. Deniz says that when she puts a country or international conference on her goal list, she learns as much as she can about that region's culture. She then creates a strategy for using social media and her global network to meet decision makers from that area. Then the real assessing and planning begin as Deniz creates just the right training program for her client. Deniz's career has soared with this strategy. She has a worldwide network of friends and colleagues. More important are the participant's lives she has touched with the wisdom she shares. (Read more about her experiences in chapter 14.)

Claudia Salazar, a trainer from Colombia, realized she committed a nonverbal gaffe during a train-the-trainer class she attended as a participant. Claudia describes the workshop as like the International Space Center, with 14 participants from eight countries. The learners bonded and shared meals. The final day of class ended with a pair-share walkabout. In Claudia's Latin style, she started the walk with a warm cheek-kiss greeting, hung on the arm of her Asian partner, and expressed sincere regards. Her Asian partner stiffened up and became quiet and nervous. Fortunately, both people had high CQ. When Claudia noticed his nonverbal responses, she asked him to explain the cultural differences. Both made nonverbal adjustments and remain friends to this day. (Read more about her experiences in chapter 9.)

Apply Global Mindset to the Classroom

When a talent development professional develops a global mindset, it becomes easier to demonstrate respect while navigating the global classroom. Here is a taste of some tips for applying a global mindset to the classroom:

- **Use International English when designing and delivering training.** International English is free from slang, idioms, and references that only people from one country might understand. Include photos and images that are familiar to the audience. Explain all acronyms. Don't assume that because you all work for the same organization that all participants understand the abbreviations. Cultural self-awareness will enable you to be alert to your vernacular. Consider having your materials and delivery reviewed by a local expert.

- **Vary the timing of training delivery.** Unfortunately, one time does not fit all globally. With online programs, there will be inconvenient times for the participants or instructor. Be flexible with delivery times to be fair. Consider delivering the same online class twice. Also, keep in mind holidays, break times, and even what constitutes a "weekend" across the globe. The website www.worldtimeserver.com can help.
- **Conduct a thorough audience needs analysis.** When working with a globally diverse group, be sure to ask many questions about the audience, including English competency. Also, increase CQ knowledge by learning as much as you can about the cultures of the people who will be attending training.
- **Include opening icebreakers to get to know participants.** Participants will want to get to know you too, but it's not just about background information. They'll also want to become familiar with the pace and cadence of your speaking voice. CQ strategy involves our ability to be self-aware, adjust to feedback, and flex our actions. It's important to establish trust early in training—that way, participants are comfortable with giving feedback so we can modify our behavior.

Recently, I trained in Argentina. Suggesting that participants provide feedback about my speaking pace did not guarantee they would be comfortable offering feedback. Our icebreaker involved everyone standing with their eyes closed and holding a piece of colorful paper. The instructions told participants to tear off pieces of paper to make matching snowflakes. The communication used included talking too fast, using fake words, being vague, and even whispering. We all laughed at the end as we saw our unique creations. The debrief was to create a list of all the communication errors, including participants not asking questions. Our colorful snowflakes became a tool throughout the four-day course. When they needed the pace slowed, something explained further, or just to take a break, they waved the snowflake.

How to Use This Book

Destination Facilitation is set up like a travel guide. You will find "packing tips" for bringing along a global mindset to help you prepare for the adventure ahead. Each chapter is written by an author who represents an excellent example of how to pack a global mindset. Collectively, these writers—from 15 nations—have taught in 150 countries and speak 33 languages. These talent development professionals include e-learning and technical experts, coaches, consultants, instructional designers, professors, and training directors.

There are two specific traits shared among this group of bold international collaborators. First, they are each driven by a passion for helping their organizations grow through helping others learn. Second, they have a global mindset, as demonstrated by their ability to foster connections with colleagues from around the globe in a way that transcends cultural differences and builds trust.

Review best practices in chapter 1 as you traverse the training landscape. We have found that these techniques work around the globe if you simply apply a little "local flair." Enjoy the hidden gems that only locals know about how to use humor, body language, and activities to engage learners so that they can apply knowledge and skills back on the job.

The individual country chapters all follow a similar model:

- People and Culture: Get to Know Your Audience
- Getting Started: Conduct a Needs Assessment
- Itineraries: Plan the Learning Journey
- Packing Lists: Logistics, Technology, and Resources
- Customs: Body Language Dos and Don'ts
- Climate: Create a Warm Learning Environment
- Things to Consider: Handle Classroom Challenges
- Tips and Warnings: Advice for Nonnative Trainers.

In chapter 15, you'll find techniques for designing and delivering global virtual instructor-led training, and learn the language of technology training. You'll also become familiar with detours to avoid, like poor needs assessments, introductions that fall flat, or presentation skills that don't work.

Chapter 16 wraps up with a review of global learning trends to consider in the future, including content areas, self-paced learning, gamification, mobile learning, and business simulations.

Enjoy the trip through learning trends and insights you can use to create incredible training victories with learners from around the globe. Then carry those souvenirs of success throughout your career.

About the Author

Donna Steffey is an international trainer, author, facilitator of the ATD Master Trainer Program, and adjunct faculty member at Lake Forest Graduate School of Management.

References

Ang, S., and L. Van Dyne. 2008. "Conceptualization of Cultural Intelligence." In *Handbook of Cultural Intelligence: Theory, Measurement, and Applications,* edited by S. Ang and L. Van Dyne, 3. Armonk, NY: M.E. Sharpe.

The Economist Intelligence Unit. 2014. *Values-Based Diversity Report: The Challenges and Strengths of Many.* London: *The Economist.*

Livermore, D. 2011. *The Cultural Intelligence Difference: Master the One Skill You Can't Do Without in Today's Global Economy.* New York: AMACOM.

Livermore, D., and L. Van Dyne. 2015. *Cultural Intelligence: The Essential Intelligence for the 21st Century.* Alexandria, VA: Society for Human Resource Management. www.shrm.org/foundation/news/Documents/Cultural%20 Intelligence.pdf.

Paul, H. 2000. "Creating a Global Mindset." *Thunderbird International Business Review* 42(2): 187-200.

1

Training Best Practices

Hamza Taqi

A few years ago, a group of global master trainers from nine countries met and discussed best training practices. We wondered if those best practices could be effectively used around the globe to ensure the transfer of learning. After our meeting, we kept the conversation going through social media. Our pledge was to apply the best practices in our home countries and share what worked and what did not.

Over the years, our group has celebrated training successes, as well as promotions, three new babies, and two weddings. We have also identified best training practice "adjustments" needed in various countries with people from different cultures.

This chapter discusses the eight training best practices for whomever or wherever you may train:

1. Conduct a thorough needs analysis.
2. Define the results.
3. Outline the learning journey.
4. Select a variety of delivery methods.
5. Design the training materials.
6. Plan the logistics.
7. Create a warm learning environment.
8. Provide performance support and evaluate success.

Training is a process, not an event. Talent development professionals must look more at the entire organizational system when considering solutions to performance issues—and less on their delivery. The needs analysis should begin long before any training course is delivered to solve organizational problems and continue after the learning event ends.

Practice 1: Conduct a Thorough Needs Analysis

When stakeholders request training, a comprehensive assessment of the situation becomes necessary. Talent development professionals must demonstrate agility in their needs evaluation process, and make sure it aligns with overall business goals. A needs analysis checklist will probably include:

- business-level analysis
- learning- or task-level analysis
- audience or learner analysis
- delivery or technology resource availability
- performance needs evaluation.

What our group of master trainers found interesting is that needs analysis is conducted similarly around the globe. Each region uses similar data collection methods, such as one-on-one conversations, surveys, focus groups, or examinations of historical data. Yet the tone of the conversations and questioning techniques used differs from country to country.

Asking the right questions can help talent development professionals get started with a needs analysis. Because there is variation in questioning techniques, the key is not to ask questions in any specific order. Rather, ask at least two questions from each category:

- **Business Needs:**
    - What are the business goals driving this request?
    - What outside factors or regulations are driving this need for training?
    - What will success look like for the organization?
    - What will the return on investment be for the organization if this training initiative is successful?
- **Learning Needs:**
    - What knowledge and skills do learners need to complete their job?
    - What new insights and expertise will they require for future job responsibilities?
    - What is the work environment like where employees will be performing their job?
    - What industry-specific regulations affect how and why they carry out their work?

- **Audience Needs:**
  - What knowledge, skills, or previous training has this audience received?
  - What is their expectation for how and when they will receive training?
  - What is their attitude toward training?
  - Are all participants at the same skill level?
- **Delivery Needs:**
  - What is the training budget? Is it flexible?
  - How much time is allocated for training on these skills?
  - What training resources and materials are available?
  - Is training the best solution?
- **Evaluating Performance Needs:**
  - What are employees currently doing?
  - What are the quality standards required for employees to do this job?
  - What should learners stop, start, or continue doing?
  - What difficulties do learners face when doing their job?
  - Are there any additional factors that could be hindering performance?

Be sure to ask the last question about additional factors hindering performance. Some Gulf Cooperation Council (GCC) countries—which include Bahrain, Kuwait, Saudi Arabia, and other nations in the Middle East—are less likely to share information that may make an organization look bad. Using that final indirect question may lead to new data.

For example, a GCC client I worked with had an issue with high turnover in a call center. The client decided to hire new agents who would attend an introductory program to equip them with the necessary skills. The training program included using the customer relationship management system and practicing phone etiquette. Five groups of new call center agents were scheduled to attend training; however, the program was called off after three groups. While the design and delivery of the program were deemed successful, 42 percent of the new agents left within the first month. We knew we were on the wrong track with training. HR exit interviews determined that the primary issue was the call center manager. In this case, had we asked the "additional factor" question before training was designed and delivered, the client might have been able to save lots of money by not hiring new agents or offering training.

Ultimately, a needs analysis process examines many areas and affords the opportunity for the training professional to become immersed in the work environment to determine if training, is, in fact, the right solution. This stage is crucial to address the actual problem and helps the trainer gain credibility.

Practice 2: Define the Results

Conducting a thorough needs analysis is not enough, however. Talent development professionals must be able to organize and communicate findings clearly and persuasively to get buy-in from managers.

Again, our group found that expectations of what should be included in the report vary by country. In general, some items to include in the needs analysis summary report are:

- a one-page overview or executive summary
- the purpose of the training project
- a summary of the methodology used to collect data
- a data synopsis
- recommendations, including possible outcomes, learning objectives, program delivery methods, timeframes, audience, content, and scope.

The last point is important, because trainers also need to understand business goals to be influential. In an ideal world, a company would be able to describe what employees need to know or be able to do and how that affects its overall goals. Unfortunately, that does not always happen, and trying to hit a target when it is foggy is nearly impossible. When outcomes are properly defined and necessary competencies identified, learning objectives are easier to write.

Practice 3: Outline the Learning Journey

The next phase is to define the learning experience. Trainers need to walk in their learners' shoes and imagine the learning journey. It helps them see the big picture and the details more accurately.

I treat this process as a rehearsal of my training session. Going through it in my mind helps me prepare, or sometimes allows me to change an activity. A mind map can help you capture the experience efficiently.

Here are some questions to ask that will help you outline the learning journey:

- What are the objectives?
- What content should be included?
- How should this be sequenced?
- What follow-up is needed?
- How will we measure success during the class and back on the job?

Practice 4: Select a Variety of Delivery Methods

Not every learner learns the same way, and not every trainer trains the same way, so a blended approach is best when training abroad. In fact, blended learning, the process of combining two or more delivery methods for one training solution, accounted for approximately one in five hours of training delivery globally (ATD 2015).

Here are some examples of blended delivery methods:

- Technology-based learning, such as e-learning courses or interactive videos, is effective when the training course is about technological tools learners need to use. You can also include prewritten activities that learners might encounter on the job.
- Simulation games can allow marketing, finance, sales, and customer service trainees to use computers to test

their skills. And they can meet face-to-face to discuss the outcome of the game.

- Coaching and on-the-job training is a nontechnical solution that still combines two learning methods.
- Combining pre-work reading with classroom or e-learning sessions provides a place for learners to ask questions and share experiences that inspire debate and contribute to the learning environment.

Before suggesting a blended approach, assess the organization's readiness. Consider these questions:

- What is the organization's technological infrastructure locally and globally?
- What are the audience's technical skill levels? Technical expertise varies around the globe, with mobile learning being more popular outside the United States.
- Does the topic lend itself to e-learning? Is it skills or knowledge based? How much time is needed to redesign the course for online learning?
- What is the size of the audience and what time zones would be involved in a global rollout?

To learn more about available technology, read chapter 15, "Navigating the Virtual Classroom," by Demetrice (Denise) Walker.

Practice 5: Design the Training Materials

For every hour of instructor-led delivery, a designer will spend 40-60 hours on design and development. Asynchronous e-learning can require more than 120 hours of development time (Kapp and Defelice 2009). We need to visualize the experience from our learners' point of view, but we also need to keep basic design components in mind:

- **Review local intellectual property laws.** Copyright law is different around the world, but there is a difference between using someone's specific concepts and using general ideas in materials.

- **Getting the visuals, symbols, and language right for global audiences is not always easy.** Decorum is important in some cultures, while images that show diversity are important for others: One of my clients with a global program counted the number of facial images that represented their culture on the PowerPoint slides. And symbols can mean very different things in different countries. Have a colleague from the target audience review your materials to prevent embarrassment. Visuals do matter!
- **Using fewer words and more visuals is now considered a best practice.** Make sure there are clear instructions to explain a concept or activity, but keep in mind the six by six rule: six words to a sentence, and no more than six sentences on a page or slide.

When designing participant materials, think about how learners will use them. For example, you can use not only workbooks and PowerPoint visuals, but whiteboards, polling, and job aids.

Discussion boards and blogs are great social media tools to reinforce learning and create a blended approach. You can also develop internal wikis. For example, one client of mine had a wiki for their customer service call center. Customers often called and mispronounced products, so the wiki had both the incorrect product names and the real names.

Practice 6: Plan the Logistics

Planning logistics is different around the world. Regardless, be sure to plan, pack extra resources like adapter cords and batteries, and then verify your plan again to avoid surprises on the delivery day. Use your imagination to visualize the entire event and create a checklist of tasks to do before and during the event. Here are some examples:

- **Before the Event:**
  - **Select the right venue and training requirements.** In some regions of the Middle East, only a five-star hotel

will do, while a multipurpose room is just fine for many training sessions in Japan.

  - **Think about the space needed for learning activities and class size.** Are there additional nearby spaces to use if the classroom is small? Are separate rooms required for team or group activities?
  - **Ask about available technology.** Some locations require you to purchase it with the room rental. Also, ask about the reliability of the technology.
  - **Complete material preparation and printing before arriving in a different country.** Shipped materials are often delayed in arriving at their destination because they're sitting on a dock awaiting customs inspection. Carry extra copies of all materials.
  - **If planning virtual instructor-led training, remember: bandwidth, bandwidth, bandwidth.** If you're planning to use a video, keep the video resolution as low as possible without compromising the quality. To prepare for these challenges, I recommend learners use LAN connections when available to provide a steady connection.

- **During the Event:**
  - **Agree on a schedule.** Every region differs on start and end times, the necessary length of lunch, and when to schedule breaks. The schedule can make or break the effectiveness of the training course. Moreover, creating an appropriate schedule shows your sensitivity to the region and establishes more credibility.
  - **Arrange the classroom for maximum engagement.** Keep in mind that in some areas of the Middle East, men and women use separate classrooms.
  - **Incorporate activities to match the content and the learner.** In Japan, for example, limit activities to role

plays—no games. But in Latin America, participants love any type of game.

- **Plan for what could go wrong during the event and have a plan to avoid it.** Apply a global mindset, remain flexible, and be prepared to adjust at the last moment.

Practice 7: Create a Warm Learning Environment

If preparation is on target, there will be less tension, enabling learners to focus. Be present in the training moment and remember: Talent development professionals set the stage, energy, and passion. Bad energy can affect learners; therefore, you must be conscious, alert, and active to create a positive learning environment.

Greet learners as they come in. Although you should do your research before the event, if you have no knowledge of a participant's culture, ask a question or two about their work and experiences. Implement a global mindset strategy, and the newly gained insights, to continue developing the relationship. In some cultures, it is a good idea to show vulnerability so that participants will show theirs. With other cultures, demonstrate expertise and command of the classroom situation.

For example, I recently conducted a seminar in India and asked an Indian friend to share a phrase in Hindi to use in my opening remarks. Saying, "Mumbai is small in land but its people have huge hearts" got a standing ovation, and the gesture helped the audience remain engaged.

During your opening remarks, establish credibility and caring. Practice, practice, practice, so the right tone is set for that audience. In many cultures, the correct tone will disarm any potential classroom difficulties. But with any challenge, you need to decide on the spot to take action or accept the situation and move on. Know that there are many ways to respond to challenges, and being friendly and respectful overcomes most obstacles. Each regional chapter includes specific body language dos and don'ts, along with how to handle particular classroom challenges.

Practice 8: Provide Performance Support and Evaluate Success

The learning triangle concept requires the trainer, learner, and manager to work together to reinforce ongoing performance improvement (Coates 2010). We each have a role in the follow-up support and documentation process. Here are some global tips for talent development professionals:

- Involve the manager early in the design process and development of learning objectives. Tie the design of the course back to organizational goals.
- Encourage managers to review objectives with learners before attending the course.
- Provide managers with simple post-course job aids, coaching talking points, and recommended schedules for follow-up.
- Create a buddy system for participants to hold one another accountable. Have them commit to the action plan together. Learners have a better chance at influencing one another to change work routines.
- Recommend that managers publicly recognize and reward learners doing something right, such as adapting to new behaviors and applying learning correctly.

When it comes to evaluating the success of training, use the Phillips model to measure the five levels of learning transfer:

- Level 1 measures reaction and satisfaction with the learning experience.
- Level 2 measures how much was learned based on the course objectives.
- Level 3 measures if knowledge is used back on the job and if behavior changed.
- Level 4 measures results.
- Level 5 measures return on investment.

Most organizations excel at measuring Levels 1 and 2, yet accurately measuring a training initiative's effectiveness often requires

Levels 3, 4, and 5. One idea is to incorporate Levels 3 and 4 in group meetings or coaching sessions.

To determine the necessary evaluation level, consider time, resources, and the evaluation's purpose. It's unnecessary to go to each level of measurement for every situation. For example:

- If the organization is trying to evaluate a facilitator's skills or the quality of training materials, only a Level 1 evaluation is needed.
- If regulations necessitate documentation to prove that learners know the content, a Level 2 evaluation is necessary.
- If you're trying to improve a performance problem, then a Level 3 evaluation is required to demonstrate that the behavior has changed after the course.
- For safety concerns or sales, customer service, or performance issues, a Level 4 review may be necessary to determine if results are improving.
- For any program that is costly or has high visibility with senior leadership, a Level 5 return on investment evaluation will be worth the time required.

A thorough and accurate evaluation leads to additional needs analysis and identifying results. It helps build a trustful partnership based on continuous improvement.

Conclusion

This chapter summarized the eight best training practices that became part of the master trainer discussion years ago, of which I was fortunate to be a part. The rest of the book will describe the adjustments necessary to apply these best practices in a particular country, across a region of the globe, or in person or online.

One last thought: Remember that you are dealing with people. While they can be complicated at times, if you show compassion, they will response accordingly.

About the Author

Hamza Taqi is an electrical engineer, a chartered marketer, and a workplace learning professional. Throughout his 20 years in the banking and telecom industries, he has helped developed the businesses of multinational brands like Visa, Mastercard, Nokia, Warner Bros., and Disney. He found his passion in marketing, which led him to specialize in the people development industry. As chief excitement officer for Knowledge Consulting Co., Hamza has dedicated his life to people growth. His passion for transforming mindsets by touching hearts earned him the nickname "Mr. Excitement."

Hamza is an ATD Master Trainer and Master Instructional Designer. He also has certifications in disciplines such as coaching, consulting, change management, and facilitation in synchronous learning. He is a certified facilitator for The FISH! Philosophy and an Accredited Situational Leadership II Facilitator. A subject matter expert in customer relationships and marketing, he began training at the Institute of Banking Studies in 1992.

References

ATD (Association for Talent Development). 2015. *Global Trends in Talent Development.* Alexandria, VA: ATD Press.

Coates, D.E. 2010. "Enhance the Transfer of Training." *Infoline.* Alexandria, VA: ASTD Press.

Kapp, K.M., and R.A. Defelice. 2009. "Time to Develop One Hour of Training." ATD Learning Circuits blog, August 31. www.td.org/Publications/Newsletters/Learning-Circuits/Learning-Circuits-Archives/2009/08/Time-to-Develop-One-Hour-of-Training.

2

Africa

David Brown

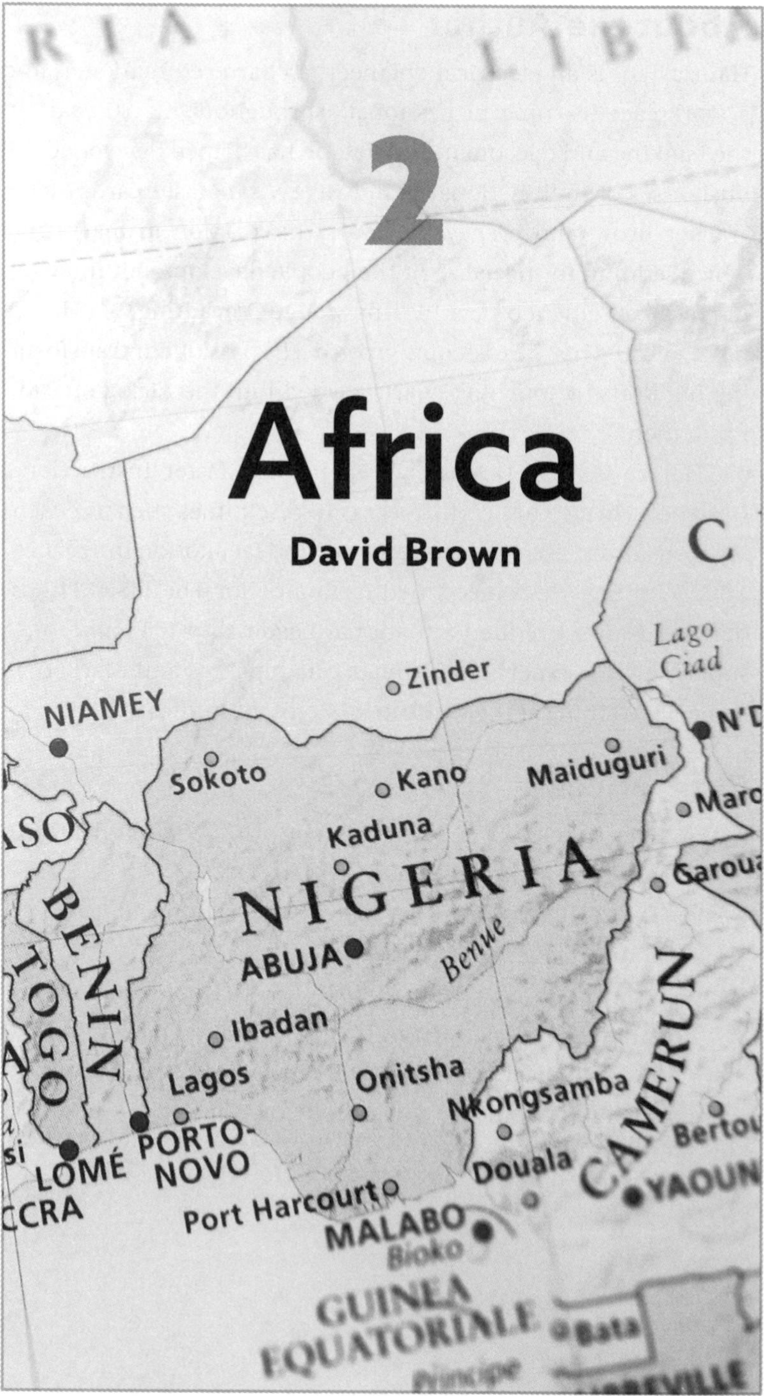

This chapter will bring you on a journey of the maps, routes, quick turns, and alleyways to cross (or avoid) in becoming a successful trainer and facilitator in Africa. Nigeria, my home, is one of 54 countries in Africa, with a population of more than 170 million. We speak more than 520 languages and have more than 300 ethnic groups. It is sometimes hard to believe that Nigeria is just one country in Africa, albeit the largest in population.

I was born to teach. Both my parents are teachers. Mum is an educator and entrepreneur; she founded a school in northern Nigeria in 1979, and named it after her mom and dad. After attending kindergarten at her school, I went to a Catholic primary school. Thinking this would be an escape from 24/7 school, I soon realized that was incorrect, because every day after official school, I went straight back to my mother's school for extra lessons. Our home felt merely like a dormitory for sleeping.

Immersion in school—its administration, methodologies, and practices—could only mean one of two things for me: hating it or loving it. I made the decision to embrace education, and I have developed courses in business intelligence, financial modeling, Microsoft Office, data visualization, reporting, presentations, and more. I have facilitated courses in 10 countries, four of them African, and I continue to learn and love training.

Throughout my career, I've learned that it's essential to build a connection and create trust in the first few minutes of interaction with any training audience. One way to make this happen almost every time is to study and align methodologies to the cultures and practices of the learners.

This chapter will primarily describe my experiences in Nigeria and West Africa. Because Nigeria has the largest population in Africa and one of the most diverse populations worldwide, it is a good proxy for all of Africa. I will also make occasional references to other countries and regions of Africa.

Chapter 2

People and Culture: Get to Know Your Audience

Africa is the most diverse continent on Earth, with nearly 2,000 languages—a third of the world's total languages. About 75 of these languages have more than a million speakers. Africa's countries were created mostly by European colonialists, who divvied up the continent with little regard for its inhabitants. This historical perspective helps international trainers make sense of why there is so much diversity across Africa.

Africa's landscape includes mountains, forests, and grasslands in regions rich with flora and fauna as diverse as its population. This beautiful continent includes the famous Mount Kilimanjaro and Mount Kenya, and holds the second largest freshwater lake in the world: Lake Victoria. Much of the region has high rainfall and a warm climate, suitable for farming and tourism alike. Each region is unique regarding the people, the state of technological advancement, and the landscape. Knowing a few key facts about this continent is critical to any learning experience.

Mount Kilimanjaro

Languages

Nigeria's population speaks many languages. English is taught in schools and used in commerce. Nigerians also speak a variant of pidgin English with local and Portuguese influences. Almost everyone in Nigeria speaks a mother-tongue language; the major ones are Hausa-Fulani, Yoruba, and Igbo, spoken in the northern, southern, and eastern regions of Nigeria, respectively.

Research by Harvard University's African Language Program breaks down African languages into four broad families: Niger-Congo, Nilo-Saharan, Afroasiatic, and Khoisan. Of the four, Niger-Congo is the biggest, and is the largest language family in the world (Mugane 2017).

Along with their indigenous languages, most Africans speak one of the following foreign languages: English, Portuguese, French, Spanish, or Arabic. When in the corporate classroom or online, recognize that the audience will be diverse, and do not assume they are acculturated to Western values, ethics, or norms. Learning styles will vary from person to person based on many demographics.

Customs and Formalities

Many American gestures mean something completely different in African nations. For example, the left hand is never used to take or pass an object; the right hand or both hands are acceptable. Also, some regions are very formal regarding greetings and behavior. In Nigeria, to demonstrate respect for an older person, squat, nod, bow, or prostrate. Most people will shake hands, but in my experience, it is better not to initiate the handshake unless the other person first extends their hand. As a young man, I extended my hand to greet an older gentleman, and the fellow reprimanded me with, "Didn't your mother teach you manners?" Keep it simple and respectful and you should be fine.

Religious and Political Preferences

Many regions of Africa have strong religious and political histories. Don't make assumptions about religious or political preferences inside or outside the classroom to avoid causing undue distress among learners.

I learned this the hard way in a class of primarily older adults, when I made the mistake of referring to a common saying of the Hausa (a major language and tribe in northern Nigeria). The saying sparked resentment in members of another major tribe, the Fulani. The mistake triggered a heated debate between a Hausa participant and a Fulani participant concerning a centuries-old tribal feud. I quickly quelled the dispute and learned a valuable lesson: Even though I grew up among Hausa and Fulani members in northern Nigeria, I shouldn't get too comfortable using their sayings and phrases, especially when not fully informed of the rich history and subtle rivalries of learners.

Nigeria is equally divided between Christians and Muslims. Therefore, it is a good idea to give a two-hour lunch break on a Friday, which will allow Muslims enough time to attend their Friday prayers in a nearby mosque. These simple actions go a long way toward building trust.

Getting Started: Conduct a Needs Assessment

Preparing to deliver training in Nigeria, and Africa in general, may be a bit challenging because of the diversity of the audience. Building trust and respect is a fundamental requirement for running an effective course. Understanding economic and workplace trends in Africa will also improve training. Start with a series of needs assessments and evaluations for the region and for the audience, whether they will be face-to-face or online. Before successfully reaching an audience, learn the location's level of technological advancement, along with managers' and learners' opinions on education and training.

In Nigeria and most of Africa, not many trainers are aware of instructional design and learning cycle models such as ADDIE or Kolb & Fry's Experiential Learning Model, respectively. Nevertheless, to get the best from your training engagement, conduct a front-end analysis (FEA) as part of your needs assessment. This significantly improves the chances of a high return on investment for the client and future work for you. FEA is a process for determining why a perceived performance gap exists and how to fix the problem (Franklin 2006). It consists of a gap or performance analysis and a root cause analysis. You may get little financial commitment from clients, so you must think creatively about cost-effective ways to conduct needs assessments. The more information you collect, the better the training experience will be for the trainer and the learners.

Assess Available Technology

The learning landscape is improving to include such platforms as webinars, social media, and mobile learning. *The Economist* (2015) estimates that the number of mobile phones in Africa will rise to 930 million by 2019, and the spread of smartphones will likely increase Internet penetration to 50 percent within seven years. In West Africa, particularly Nigeria, mobile technology is becoming more advanced as well.

There are many benefits to these media, depending on the audience's learning styles and the availability of equipment and Internet connectivity. According to ATD's 2015 *State of the Industry* report, a third of organizations have mobile learning programs. Keep in mind that in some regions of Africa, online training opportunities will require extra effort or may not be possible. Always assess the level of technology and Internet capabilities.

Assess Management's Attitude Toward Training

The way management feels about training affects the training approach. They may be on board and engaged, or they may be skeptical of a suggested training solution. Get to know everything about an organization's status and training needs. The good news is that 62 percent of companies in the Middle East and Africa will focus on training delivery for the coming year (ATD 2015b). Most Nigerian clients prefer classroom training. Cost is a major consideration, making a blended approach involving face-to-face delivery and technology-based delivery a win-win. Be prepared to negotiate with clients on how you plan to deliver the training event before coming up with a preferred method.

Assess Audiences' Attitudes Toward Training

Your training strategy should include an audience assessment well before moving into the design phase. Understand your audience's backgrounds, skill levels, technical abilities, and learning styles. A short, well-crafted assessment is a good way to measure attitudes toward training. I use assessments for most courses in Nigeria, and this helps uncover needs and additional work and planning requirements, such as pre-work or research, before the course. Engage an organization's leadership and, where possible, speak with some of the learners scheduled for the course. Ask questions about the learning environment as well as the technology available. Request student profiles to gain information about the audience.

Though Nigerians spend far less time in formal training than the world average of 33.5 learning hours per employee (ATD 2016), employees actively spend their money and out-of-office hours improving their skills by studying for professional certifications and higher degrees, which shows a positive attitude toward learning.

Itineraries: Plan the Learning Journey

Following is a set of best practices that have worked for me when training in Nigeria and other African countries.

Selecting Delivery Methods and Media

The most popular delivery mechanism for training in Nigeria is facilitator-led classroom training. More than 90 percent of the courses I have offered in Nigeria are face-to-face. The courses mainly address knowledge and skills, which can also be taught well using online delivery methods. However, client preferences and technology considerations have led to limited acceptance of online learning.

These preferences may change soon, though, due to improved Internet connectivity and the presence of the mobile-friendly Millennial generation in the workforce. I believe that Africa will embrace technology-based media to traverse the huge knowledge gap on the continent. Platforms like www.khanacademy.com (a free online educational website) are driving this revolution in training delivery. It is our job as trainers to design courses that harness this media.

For example, during a recent client engagement, I used Google+, Google's social network platform, as a collaborative tool for the class to get to know one another prior to the learning event. We also used the platform to discuss and reinforce foundational knowledge in our learning objectives.

Using video and audio as much as possible was helpful because the majority of learners do not like to read in English. Even though English is spoken widely, it is usually learners' second language, making text-based, self-directed activities unpopular. We then conducted a live face-to-face class and determined we could hit the ground running, having built that initial familiarity and trust online. We maintained the social media platform to reinforce learning after the classroom sessions. This blended methodology works well in most African countries.

To select the most appropriate learning methods, be sure to:

- Write clear and actionable learning objectives.
- Choose your media wisely for learning objectives. I find that social media works best for Nigerian audiences, while pre-class reading is the least effective.
- Match learning methods to the learners' unique circumstances, such as language limits, preferences, background, and experiences. I find that accelerated learning techniques work very well in Africa.
- Review functional requirements and limitations, like cost and timing constraints. Plan for last-minute changes.

Post-Work and Social Learning Plans

A sound training plan for an African audience involves an experience that goes beyond the classroom. Post-work engages these learners well after the class is over. It includes not only individual follow-up with students, but also a period of social learning that employs technology to observe and instruct, often remotely. This technique helps guide African learners' attitudes, behaviors, and values.

Measuring Effectiveness

Upon completing training in Africa, there are a variety of ways to assess the success of methods, delivery, and overall knowledge transfer. Measuring training effectiveness is an important post-class activity that allows trainers to learn from experiences and continually improve training skills. Whether it is a written or verbal evaluation, the results are often invaluable.

Packing Lists: Logistics, Technology, and Resources

With training plans in place, there are still some logistical factors to consider before scheduling. Understand the target region of Africa and what resources are available—or not available—within the local surroundings. Allow plenty of time to work through the following challenges.

Trainer Resources

One of the biggest resource challenges in delivering virtual training to African countries is bandwidth limitations. Once I was running a virtual training course, and both my main and backup Wi-Fi connections stopped working. My producer was working from another location, so he continued the session while I sorted it out. Apparently, I had purchased two Wi-Fi dongles that used the same network provider, which had a brief network failure—lesson learned. Fortunately, my producer and I had planned for a possible network outage, so the participants hardly noticed the disruption. This preparation was well worth the time; it's important to plan for the worst-case scenario.

Varying types of learner devices and Internet browsers can also be an obstacle. In many cases, the trainer cannot mandate what devices to use, so you must anticipate variation. For example, many of my courses require Microsoft Office applications, but participants often have different versions of Excel, which can mean adjusting directions on the fly. It is often necessary to adapt training style and content. I always test all exercise files for version compatibility; when I must use a new version of a software program (maybe to showcase a new feature), I make it clear in the instruction and any printed material that it's not compatible with previous versions.

To add a bit of fun in the class, right off the bat, I identify the software versions used by each participant in class, and we create a friendly "old school" or "new school" group to identify them. So I might say, "Here is how it works for the old school" and "if you're new school, do this." This requires me to prepare in advance, but the appreciation I get from participants and clients is well worth the effort. Our sessions usually prompt management to upgrade company software, or at least have a uniform version across departments, an added return on investment from your training efforts.

Trainer Backup Plans

When systems are down or unavailable within certain African countries, consider other ways to present. It is possible that alternative resources may be available, but incorporate backup plans into the overall strategy. In fact, have a backup for the backup.

For example, in Nigeria, electricity is a luxury; most organizations have a generator, and some even have a backup generator. Once, in northern Nigeria, I was in the middle of a training session when all three power sources failed. I immediately cracked a local joke related to the predicament to ease the tension. I then activated my backup plan, "natural light": I opened the windows and doors. Because this was unfortunately a common occurrence, participants weren't startled. Luckily, the batteries on each participant's laptop gave us power until the end of the day. Consider paper copies.

Learner Resources

Don't assume facilities will have what is required, even with an email confirming that everything is ready. Insist on a conference call or other means to ensure that the resources the learners need are available. Arrive at the training venue early. Check for needed equipment, writing materials, and transportation. Ask if participants have physical impairments. Also take culture into account in your selection of props. For example, I like to use local music in my sessions, especially during group activities, varying the beat to match my expectations (visit www.acceleratedlearning.com to learn more about this and other accelerated learning techniques).

Lake Victoria

Customs: Body Language Dos and Don'ts

There is much cultural diversity within Nigeria and indeed most of Africa. Understanding body language dos and don'ts is essential for creating a positive atmosphere in which people can feel comfortable and learn well. Often there are workarounds for body language differences, but it is important to do and say the right things to gain learners' trust.

Here are some suggestions facilitators can keep in mind:

- A handshake is acceptable in West Africa, but don't initiate a handshake if greeting someone older. The handshake may be unacceptable depending on the religion or customs of the recipient.
- Use hand gestures with caution, and avoid pointing fingers. However, remove hands from pockets when speaking.
- If in the presence of any traditional leader, you will be expected to bow; don't try to shake their hand unless they initiate it.
- Offer an object, like a business card, with your right hand, not your left. This exchange is important, so review the card when you receive it.
- Respecting age is important. Elders are typically addressed first and are often the decision makers.
- Follow training agendas, because time is respected.
- Wear a traditional outfit on one day of the course; it will make a lasting impression. Find local dressmakers or visit the open markets for clothing.
- Groups that often sit on the floor (mostly northern Nigeria, Mali, Chad, and Niger) never let their foot point toward another person; they also do not show the soles of their shoes. Instead, they sit cross-legged, with their feet pointed left and right.

Climate: Create a Warm Learning Environment

Few countries in Africa share the same characteristics. Using a global mindset and taking a neutral, unbiased approach will allow facilitators to experience the culture and to learn along with the students. While being warm and friendly, show complete respect for political, religious, and economic surroundings. That said, be in charge, aware of the time, and committed to the general agenda.

Consider the Environment

Explore the environment, whether live or online, based on the region. Read the news, follow a few popular Twitter handles, and get a sense of what is happening in the area. This knowledge of the environment will filter through your verbal and nonverbal communication with students as they work together in groups.

Encourage Learner Interaction

Learner interaction can be a wonderful method for creating a warm learning environment. Students often respond well to shared activities, which gives them confidence in their work. It is a good idea to plan the makeup of each of the groups. In a large class, limit the group sizes to five people and include a good mix of experiences and competencies, keeping the training environment informal but fun and respectful.

Things to Consider: Handle Classroom Challenges

Get to know students well before class begins. Consider using social media, like the Google+ example shared earlier. Learn about the students' backgrounds, cultural beliefs, and learning styles, as well as any disabilities, so proper accommodations can be made. Expect students to have various skills levels, but treat each student equally. When a challenge arises, never embarrass or harass a student, especially in front of the class.

Deliver lessons with patience, speak clearly and slowly, and give each student the attention they require to keep up. An intimidated student will not likely ask a question, so it is up to the trainer to ask if they are following along. African students in particular may remain quiet in front of others for fear of holding back the class.

To counter this, incorporate regular exercises throughout the course as an on-the-spot gauge of assimilation and understanding. I recommend TurningPoint, which helps you create polls within a PowerPoint presentation. Participants use a small responder device to answer quizzes incorporated into the PowerPoint. The system displays instant performance feedback onscreen, which helps the trainer identify and address unmet learning objectives.

Allow time during breaks or before or after class for students to speak with you and receive individual attention. This is particularly essential when there are no electronic means of gauging learner understanding available.

You will face challenges as a trainer. Be professional, downplay a challenge, and take care of it outside the classroom if possible. The following are types of challenges trainers may face.

Nonparticipation

When a student refuses to participate, I find that it is usually a result of poor planning on my part as the facilitator. You could gently call on them directly to respond to a question or problem. Speak with them after class or during a break, and try to reach them and find out more. Be sensitive to their situation. It may be possible that they are shy or suffer from some personal or family issues.

In Nigeria, while there are always exceptions, I find that female participants from the north of the country tend to be more reserved, which gets misinterpreted as nonparticipation. It is safe to say that the farther north you go in Africa, the more you can expect participants to be reserved, especially female participants.

A method I use to ensure participation in my technical courses is the round-robin review. When checking a topic or task that has many steps, I ask each learner to describe one step in the task, and then immediately pass an imaginary baton to the next person to describe the next step. The key is to do this quickly to ensure that everyone is alert. A quiet participant can anticipate their turn and prepare an answer. If all else fails, give nonparticipants a special assignment to learn more about the issue.

I've learned over the years that thorough preparation before delivery always pays off. And nonparticipation is a direct reflection of the time (or lack thereof) spent preparing for the course.

I recently started delivering virtual classes, and this new medium takes no prisoners; to be a good virtual trainer, you must engage your audience in an activity every three to five minutes. This training format has significantly improved my face-to-face delivery. Nonparticipation is a universal phenomenon and a sign that participants are bored. Arm yourself with innovative techniques to stop it before it starts.

Difficult Participants

When dealing with a disruptive participant, it is important to show respect. In general, Africans are very respectful, and participants will manage most challenges in the class. Most corporate courses include a client representative, HR staff member, or learning and development professional to act as a supervisor for the course. Discuss any disruptive behavior with them as needed. Never engage in a verbal argument with a learner.

Many participants disrupt class because they need more challenging content. These participants are often identified in the needs assessment and design phase of the training initiative, and can be assigned to a higher-level course. Alternatively, they can receive a more-complex project during class, so they remain occupied and content.

Preplanning is key, so that you can handle any potential disruption in advance. For example, in a course I delivered in southern Nigeria, a participant was disruptive because he was taking half the time to do the exercises and wanted to prove he knew more than the instructor. Luckily, I had a plan; I always build in challenging activities that are above the level of competence expected for the course. While the rest of the class was busy with an activity, I asked him to open one of my challenge exercises. He was happily occupied until the end of the session and became an active participant. This technique can also be used to gamify the learning experience through intermittent timed group challenges to earn group points.

Repeatedly Tardy Participants or No-Shows

If a learner is repeatedly tardy or does not show up for the course, take them aside privately and discuss the issues. Find out the specific reasons for tardiness or absence, and whether they are legitimate. Have a good rapport with the people responsible for managing the course, as well as with supervisors and HR representatives. Share any learner challenges and ask them for a sit-down discussion to identify the issue.

I once facilitated a five-day course, and one participant was constantly late and unresponsive; she even missed a day of training. By day four, I sat down with her privately to discuss the issue, and learned that her daughter had an operation the day before the training program began. Personal issues are often the cause of bad behavior, so compassion is the best course of action.

Tips and Warnings: Advice for Nonnative Trainers

There's plenty of advice for nonnative trainers training an African audience for the first time. Consider this list of dos and don'ts (also see the section "Customs: Body Language Dos and Don'ts").

Accept the African Way of Welcoming People

A trainer once came from the United States to offer training for orphanage directors in Tanzania. When her team entered the room, all the participants stood to sing an African welcome song for their friends who had traveled so far to partner with them. The team of trainers could not hold back their tears. Accept the warm welcome, dry the tears, and get ready to engage learners.

Connect Learners With Their Peers

The opportunity to work with a peer—sharing experiences, leaning on each other, and collaborating—can enhance the learning experience and encourage confidence among African students. Make these activities part of the training strategy, and encourage participants to share experiences and stories for the benefit of others.

Have a Plan, but Be Flexible

In Africa, people like to follow a schedule and know what they will be doing on a regular basis. Plan it that way and know the material, but be flexible regarding situations or challenges that may arise. Include multiple backup plans, and stay calm when things do not go as designed. Your audiences are eager to learn, and they see you as the expert who can do no wrong. Relax, and have alternative routes planned and ready to deploy.

Don't Lose Control of the Session

Find the poise for a smooth delivery, a professional attitude, and maintaining order. Africa has the youngest population in the world—it's sometimes called the teen continent, and has a median age of 21 compared with 40 for Europe and North America (CIA 2016). Earning respect after losing control with Millennials can be tough. Dignity is a key word, and the level of respect between a trainer and a learner in Africa keeps the learning field even.

Don't Assume Technology Will Work

Plan ahead. Know the environment, the technology, and learners' styles. It will be different in every country in Africa. Bring a Wi-Fi dongle just in case. Africa is diverse in technological advancement, and there will be times and places where bandwidth becomes an issue. Should this happen, relax and use your backup plan.

Bon Voyage

Training an African audience, whether online or face-to-face, is an incredibly rewarding experience. Enjoy this ancient and diverse continent, full of artful, lively, and talented people. One last piece of advice: Plan to stay an extra day or two—when else will you have a chance to take in such diversity? And send me postcards!

***

About the Author

David Brown has worked as a trainer and financial consultant for more than 16 years. He is the founder and principal consultant at dbrownconsulting, a consulting, training, and payroll firm in Lagos, Nigeria.

David is an ATD Master Trainer, ATD Master Instructional Designer, and a chartered accountant and investment adviser. He designs and trains on technical courses in financial modeling, business intelligence and analytics, Microsoft Excel, accounting, and financial analysis. He is also a financial analyst and financial adviser to corporations and individuals. Additionally, he advises the World Bank on oil revenue modeling.

David delivers technical courses using a blended learning methodology to maximize impact, retention, and return on investment for his clients and participants. He is a regular speaker at training events, including ATD's International Conference & Exposition.

References

ATD (Association for Talent Development). 2015a. *State of the Industry.* Alexandria, VA: ATD Press.

——. 2015b. *Global Trends in Talent Development.* Alexandria, VA: ATD Press.

——. 2016. *State of the Industry.* Alexandria, VA: ATD Press.

CIA. 2016. "The World Factbook—Nigeria." CIA. www.cia.gov/library/publications/the-world-factbook/geos/ni.html.

The Economist. 2015. "The Pioneering Continent." *The Economist,* April 25. www.economist.com/news/middle-east-and-africa/21649516-innovation-increasingly-local-pioneering-continent.

Franklin, M. 2006. "Performance Gap Analysis." *Infoline.* Alexandria, VA: ASTD Press.

Mugane, J.M. 2017. "Greetings From the Director." The African Language Program at Harvard. https://alp.fas.harvard.edu/greetings-director.

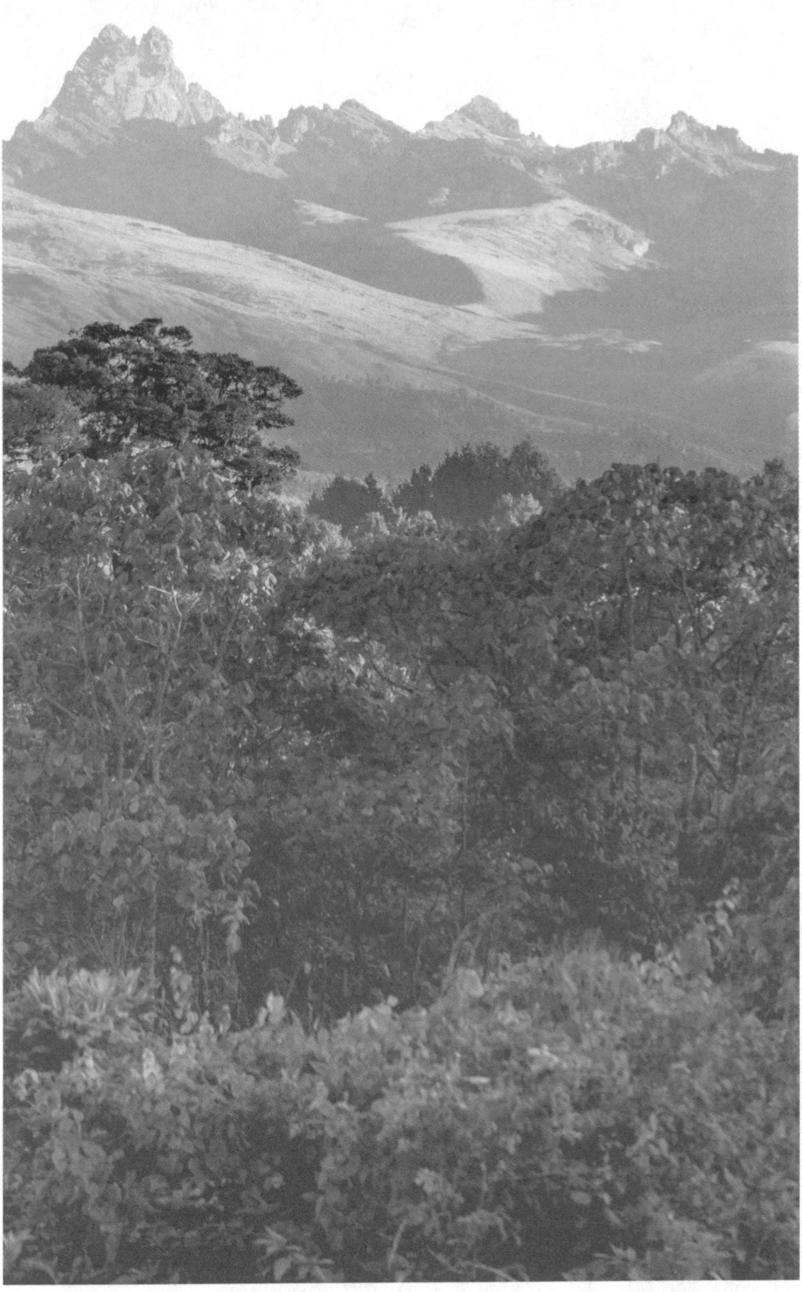

A rain forest with Mount Kenya in the background

3

Brazil

Alfredo Castro

I'll always remember facilitating a specific method to consultative selling, where the participants—sales consultants and managers—had to learn a new approach to use on a day-to-day basis. The facilitator guide suggested we create an icebreaker connected to the local culture. For Brazil, that meant it had to be samba related!

The samba is considered a dance of celebration and joy. In the consultative selling workshop, participants used the principles of a samba school to creatively introduce their teams. Introductions were about community, competitive advantage, and choreography (partnering), much like the consultative selling approach.

As executive director, partner, and founder of MOT Training and Development, a consulting company based in Miami and São Paulo, I have delivered training in more than 30 countries for more than 120 different companies, but Brazil is home. It is a paradise worth visiting for a multitude of reasons: the sun, the beaches, the music, the dancing, the football.

The Brazilian culture is one of the world's most varied and diverse, because it's a melting pot of nationalities. Centuries of European domination brought African migrants across Brazil's borders, who in turn influenced the local cultures with their customs and ideas. The European settlers also brought innovations and belief systems with them, significantly shaping local societies.

Brazil is a country made up of 208 million people who are eager for development and interaction, and who will require specific attention when delivering a talent development program. As someone who has traveled the world spearheading leadership models and learning solutions in business environments—mainly in the areas of leadership, storytelling, change management, corporate governance, and consultative sales—I invite you to join me throughout this chapter as we explore essential elements of Brazil's unique culture.

People and Culture: Get to Know Your Audience

In many of the larger cities in Brazil, English is the language of business. The local language has morphed into so-called Brazilian Portuguese. Less common languages include Spanish, German, Italian, Japanese, and many minor Amerindian languages.

When it comes to punctuality, Brazilians are notoriously laid-back. Have a deadline at work? No worries. Two hours late to dinner? No problem. Brazilians approach this with a philosophy they call *jogo de cintura,* meaning "Everything will be OK in the end!" This attitude reflects all life in Brazil. Brazilians naturally take everything easy and go at a different rate. It may seem strange at first. Remember: There are many ways to traverse the learning journey.

Octávio Frias de Oliveira Bridge in São Paulo

Keep this in mind when planning training. The schedule will be difficult to design, but realize that sometimes it is better to discuss a subject with passion and engagement than to cut short a rich discussion because of the planned agenda.

Brazilians have a looser sense of personal space than people from the United States and Canada, and are not bothered being packed together in crowded public places. They're physically expressive and convey emotional information through touch. While in some societies touching has sexual overtones, Brazilians equate it with friendship and a show of concern. Women tend to touch more than men and greet others with kisses on both cheeks, but men also welcome each other with hearty pats on the back and bear hugs. Such informality extends to conversation. Brazilians usually address teachers, doctors, and other professionals using their title followed by their first name—Professor João, Doutora Maxine, or Presidente Henrique (Adventure World 2017).

Getting Started: Conduct a Needs Assessment

Brazil has a well-established talent development association: the Brazilian Training Association, or ABTD, which is connected with the Association for Talent Development and other professional organizations around the globe. ABTD organizes a large annual conference with the latest industry trends. It's on the cutting edge of leadership development, gamification, e-learning, technology, and other talent development trends.

Due to current economic conditions in Brazil, training investments have won special attention. The training and development profession will continue to grow as companies try to close the vast talent gap in the country.

Starting in 2005, I took responsibility for organizing and interpreting the annual talent development research from MOT Training and Development and ABTD (2013). All the following facts and data are from this robust research.

Leadership development is a key focus within Brazil, with the implementation of leadership programs considered the top learning and development priority. One in five Brazilian organizations now runs a corporate university, and one in 10 businesses in Brazil offers MBA programs.

Although there are some gaps in leadership development, management in Brazil is well educated. As a result, Brazilians value training highly. The value placed on higher education by particular segments of Brazilian society, balanced with the number of training programs delivered in the local language, may explain why it receives such a large share of revenue. Economic success in Brazil is said to come more from who you know than what you know, and where you're educated influences who you know. Aside from training students in a profession, university education also confers social status that, in turn, provides the personal connections that can influence future success.

When thinking about local needs, don't create a strategy for Brazil based on what is happening in the U.S. or European markets. That is always going to fail. Again, according to MOT and ABTD research, Brazilian employees receive, on average, up to three or four times the amount of annual training than their European and U.S. counterparts—an average of 45 hours of training per year. European employees receive an average of nine hours, and U.S. employees an average of 12 hours (ATD 2016). A potential explanation: The Brazilian economy is growing at a higher rate than the U.S. and European economies, and the shorter, technology-based training modules that are popular in Europe and the United States are not as popular in Brazil.

Therefore, it is important to conduct strategic needs assessment conversations with managers of Brazilian companies. Brazilian culture requires global trainers to make first contact with local directors so that the program can be customized correctly. Prepare a questionnaire for them to answer, and combine the survey with an interview to cover some key points:

- What is the real need for training?
- What is the educational level of the majority of the participants?
- How are they connected with the global culture of that company?
- How would the managers support the training?

Rather than delivering an off-the-shelf training course, it's important to localize the program. For example, Brazilians enjoy accelerated learning programs and activities that involve the entire body and mind, including the use of all their senses. Facilitators will need to incorporate local music for this reason. Brazilians are a hands-on people who learn best by doing. They enjoy collaboration in the classroom, which enables social connection. They also know that positive emotions improve learning, so provide lots of opportunities to express feelings and opinions.

Keep in mind that asking participants to complete pre-work will not be effective. They would rather start the learning process in the program and will participate intensively.

Itineraries: Plan the Learning Journey

The majority of Brazilians would prefer to attend a program in Brazilian Portuguese. The Brazilian audience loves to take notes, and the written materials should reflect this cultural aspect. If using printed materials, consider how they sound when read out loud by asking yourself the following questions:

- Does the writer try to bring the reader into the discussion?
- Do you feel an emotional response?
- Is the material relevant to the learners?

Materials need to be concise and clear. If the participant handouts seem like the author wrote them to impress someone with a vast vocabulary, rather than to share information with the reader, the audience will not appreciate them. Look for a good translator who understands the importance of a quality Portuguese translation. Additionally, Brazilians will not like materials translated into the Portuguese language from Portugal.

In Brazil, we often use the term *training event,* which can mean a variety of activities connected with a talent development framework. The event can be a training session, workshop, microlearning approach, focus group, feedback or coaching session, or e-learning experience. Brazilian companies, in general, will choose solutions that include blended learning, especially if the classroom activities are synchronized with tech apps and incorporate smartphone use. Brazilians would love to attend a program designed with at least 70 percent of the day dedicated to completing hands-on tasks. Tying the activities to the workplace would be greatly valued by the participants. On the other hand, they would not appreciate a conceptual training program very much.

The use of blended learning is on the rise, as long as it is not at the expense of human touch. Emerging learning tools are continuing to grow in popularity globally, but as a means of enhancing traditional classroom-based tools rather than replacing them. In Brazil, for example, MOT and ABTD research found that 42 percent receive their training solely through the classroom, with the remaining 58 percent receiving training through a variety of different channels—predominantly through blended learning.

Social media can be an essential tool to encourage interaction, sharing, and microlearning, and to create a warm atmosphere for learning in Brazil. Brazil is responsible for 10 percent of total time spent on social media globally, which puts it in second place, just behind the United States. Those who do have access to the Internet in Brazil use social media constantly; the average time per visit to social media sites is longer than the average in Europe, Latin America, North America, and Asia-Pacific (Banks and Yuki 2014). Thus, there is great potential to use social media when designing the learning journey.

Packing Lists: Logistics, Technology, and Resources

Brazil is a large country—just slightly bigger than the continental United States. North to south, Brazil is approximately 4,345 kilometers (2,700 miles) and at its widest about 4,330 kilometers (2,690 miles). Brazil's 26 states are widespread, so make travel plans accordingly. Rail travel is all but nonexistent in Brazil, so plan to rely on either air transportation or intercity buses.

Don't get confused by the seasons in Brazil. They are the opposite of the Northern Hemisphere: Summer is December through

March, and winter is June through September. High season is one week before Christmas until Carnival. February and early March are the most popular times for Brazilians to travel for vacation, and may not be good for business or training sessions. Hotels and meeting spaces are expensive, and availability is quite limited during high season. There are beautiful venues to hold training sessions, such as corporate university spaces or hotels. But ultimately, the training space will depend on the value each company places on people development.

Surfers on Ipanema Beach in Rio de Janeiro. Summer in Brazil is December through March.

The Internet is open in all states of Brazil, but check the local facilities because some of them will require passwords and a fee. Many electrical outlets in hotels and newer buildings in Brazil will accept the standard, two-flat-prong plug used in the United States. In older buildings, however, expect to encounter some electrical outlets that only take a Brazilian two-round-prong plug.

Lastly, do not think that food is merely sustenance. Brazilians enjoy eating and like doing it a lot. It is very common to have one or two hours for lunchtime. If you are serving food at a training event, the best option is to hire a catering company. In Brazil, many catering companies work mostly with weddings and family celebrations, so make sure to contract one that does corporate events. Depending on the venue, reserving an additional room where learners can sit down and eat properly may be necessary.

Keep in mind that the Brazilian cuisine is very diversified, so it is important to have three options for the main course: red meat, white meat, and pasta in case there are vegetarians in the audience. As for beverages, offer both juice and soda. Most conferences held in Brazil have lunch and coffee breaks. At most business events, this time is used not only to eat, but to chat, share, learn, and feel like a team.

Customs: Body Language Dos and Don'ts

Once in Brasilia, the capital of Brazil, I got to understand Brazilian body language from a Canadian colleague's perspective. We were going to meet the director of our training program for what Brazilians call *cafezinho,* which means drinking coffee in the afternoon while having a professional conversation. The meeting was important because we would be delivering a program the next day.

It was the director's first time in Brazil, and she was a bit leery of taking taxis. She had seen a cab driver making a gesture that she could not understand and thought it might mean something bad. It turned out that the driver had been putting his fingers together and then opening and closing them. If a taxi driver makes this gesture, it means that they're carrying passengers, nothing else. It is nothing bad at all, just unfamiliar.

When facilitating with Brazilian groups, pay careful attention to body language:

- Brazilians usually greet each other with long handshakes and noticeable eye contact; close friends will often embrace. Participants expect eye contact and to hold a glance for at least three seconds.
- During a conversation, touching of the arms and back is normal. Participants speak in very close proximity, with

lots of physical contact. Back-slapping is very common among men in Brazil.

- A person clapping the back of one hand against the palm of the other hand is showing that they don't care or aren't interested.
- A thumbs-up means OK, positive, good luck, or thanks, like in the United States. However, do not make the U.S. OK gesture. It approximates an incredibly rude Brazilian gesture.
- To say thank you, give the thumbs-up sign and say "*valeu*." Brazilians do not usually say "thanks"; they prefer something like *valeu* or *meu irmão*.
- It is imperative to know how to greet people. The air kiss is stereotypical: one in some contexts, two in others. It is more of a cheek bounce than anything. Word of warning: Paulistanos, those from São Paulo, kiss-greet only on the right cheek. Cariocas, those from Rio de Janeiro, do their greeting with two kisses (*beijos*)—one on each cheek, starting with the right. When you don't know how many kisses to give, pause after the first. The other person then will or will not initiate the second.
- Get the dress right. In Rio, seeing both men and women donning fabulous colors is commonplace. In the south and the interior of the country, people tend to be a bit more conservative. In business settings, men wear full suits; for women, skirts are acceptable. Expect to see professional business attire even if it is 43 degrees Celsius (110 degrees Fahrenheit). The extreme heat and humidity can tire a person very quickly. Adjusting to the weather is vital for thriving in Brazil.

Climate: Create a Warm Learning Environment

It is imperative for facilitators to create an active and engaging classroom atmosphere. Participants will learn better and engage more in this kind of environment, which means that it is one of the most powerful tools facilitators have to encourage adult learning.

Many factors contribute to a positive classroom atmosphere; one important element is how facilitators respond to a participant's behavior in Brazil. If a trainer responds to the attendee's conduct correctly, this will help to set the tone of the program. Follow this advice and you'll be on your way to creating a warm learning environment:

- A warm, friendly approach will receive a much better response than strictly professional interactions. When building in-person relationships, try to schedule meetings to run into meal times, as sharing a meal aids in establishing connections (Weaver 2016).
- Animated and sometimes boisterous conversations—including interruptions—are the norm. Proximity and touching of the hands or arms are also common, so be prepared and try not to respond stiffly. Emotions are also involved in problem solving, so be careful not to quell participants' emotions during training.
- Brazilians conduct business mainly through personal connections, and will value training environments in which they can share and chat. There must also be an understanding that the business relationship will be long term. Brazilians often value the personal relationships within a company more than the company itself. When possible, maintain the same point of contact or trainer to retain rapport. I can recall a Brazilian client who had worked in six countries in Europe with various training providers. When I reconnected with him after many years to deliver a proposal, he remembered my performance from long ago, and we won the contract despite being up against much larger competitors. Being loyal to previous connections is important in Brazil.
- When telling a story or communicating something, show respect and knowledge of Brazil and its neighboring

countries to the south. Avoid ethnic jokes as well. For instance, locals may try to tell jokes about Argentinians; do not condone this situation. Also avoid discussions of politics, religion, and other controversial subjects. Welcoming topics include soccer, local cuisine, and Brazilian music. They also love to discuss their social activities and their children. Just remember, Brazilians are loyal to their family and may not be comfortable sharing any negative stories about them with acquaintances.

In addition to these points, you must plan to address different generations in the classroom. Around 85 percent of the country is under the age of 55, and 40 percent is under the age of 25. To put things in perspective, only 33 percent of the United States' population, 32 percent of China's population, and 30 percent of the United Kingdom's population are under the age of 25 (CIA 2013).

Millennials in Brazil are very active and talkative in a learning environment. Brazilian Millennials are eager for interaction and acknowledgment. Recognize their progress; this will show them that they are attending a relevant session for them.

It is important to consider the current economic conditions in Brazil to understand the Millennial generation. For most of their lives, there was good economic news in Brazil. However, the economy shifted in 2010 and has continued to decline over the past few years. For that reason, Millennials think they are in a stronger, deeper economic crisis than populations of other countries. The demands of the younger generations are adamant in Brazil (Flamingo São Paulo 2016). They are already knee-deep in a paradigm change. They were born into frameworks created by analog-minded generations, and they will grow old in the new, digitally conscious systems they spearhead.

Consider including topics like different generations, crises (or how to avoid getting stuck on them), and multigenerational awareness. These themes will enhance the impact of training on Brazilian audiences. As in other countries, a trainer in Brazil will notice differences between generations in the same training group. Yet in Brazil, it might be difficult to create a quick sense of teamwork during small-group activities. For example, when forming a group with three Millennials and one individual from an older generation, there will be a hidden fight for leadership, with the older-generation individual thinking they should lead, based on age and years of experience. Consider all these elements to create a positive learning environment.

Things to Consider: Handle Classroom Challenges

A major challenge in delivering a training program in Brazil is punctuality. While there are exceptions to every cultural trait, flexible punctuality is characteristic of Brazilian business culture. Accept that waiting for Brazilian counterparts will be part of doing business here.

Here are some tips for handling other classroom challenges:

- Do not judge a participant or make comments for coming back two minutes after the break. Instead, make a positive comment to learners who return on time.
- Be aware that Brazilians do not perceive themselves as Hispanic, and will take offense if addressed in Spanish. As in many South and Latin American countries, Brazilians also consider themselves Americans. Consequently, don't use the phrase "in America" or "American" when referring to the United States.
- Brazilians tend to enjoy a robust debate; expect conversations to be fast-paced and animated. Once, while facilitating the same activity in the United States and Brazil, I realized that it took the Brazilian group almost twice as long. Be aware of their fantastic ability to express themselves, talk, and participate, and how this will affect your time management.
- Consider including e-learning in the class. It is better to ask participants to use the Internet to further familiarize

themselves with the training topic than to have them switch off their smartphones and computers.

Tips and Warnings: Advice for Nonnative Trainers

Add a few additional days on to your itinerary to explore this beautiful country if you are lucky enough to come here for work. To connect with your audiences in Brazil, keep these tips in mind:

- Look for information and establish a Brazilian context: a geographical, historical, political, or economic overview of Brazil.
- Interview someone well versed in Brazilian culture and society about religion, language, diversity, family roles, and customs, and how they influence business culture.
- Identify elements of Brazilian corporate culture and business etiquette: hierarchy, egalitarianism, perspectives of time, and relationships. Also, facilitate a good needs assessment, so the links between content and participants' professional reality are easy for them to see.
- Understand the potential obstacles that may arise in the Brazilian training environment, and solutions to these challenges. Time management is a big one. Be prepared to adjust the timing of activities, which might stimulate participants to tell stories and share real experiences.
- Another obstacle is the aversion to pre-work. A good tip is checking who did the pre-work at the very beginning of the training session, and giving some time to those who did not complete the work to do so. However, don't stress this point—Brazilians will be very good participants regardless. They have a tendency not to value pre-work, but love an interactive session.
- Be aware that U.S., Canadian, and Australian citizens require a visa to enter Brazil. UK and South African nationals do not need a visa to visit Brazil.

- Learn how to greet people properly. It is the absolute first thing to do when walking into any training room, so it is important to have something to say! Locals will be very appreciative if you make an effort from the start. Here are some common greetings: *olá/oi* (hello), *bom dia* (good morning), *muito obrigado/a* (thank you very much), and *Eu sou o facilitador* (I am the facilitator).

Bon Voyage

Be prepared to learn about a unique culture and have fun. Each culture has its set of dominant values and beliefs, so have a clear understanding of the key drivers and motivators of Brazilian business culture. It is natural to make comparisons and judge people based on differences. Instead, use a global mindset, learn about others, and respect people for who they are. *Obrigado!*

***

About the Author

Alfredo Castro is the executive director and founder of MOT Training and Development, a consulting company in Miami and São Paulo. He is recognized by the international talent development community as one of the top professionals in the industry, and is a leader in pioneering models of learning, performance, and people development, improving business results in companies worldwide. He has traveled extensively in his 35 years of professional experience, and has designed and implemented blended learning programs for more than 120 companies across more than 25 countries.

Alfredo was the chairman of ATD's 2010 Program Advisory Committee. He has spoken to audiences around the world, including a keynote in front of 5,000 people on the state of the talent development industry and future trends. He also contributed chapters to *The Art of Modern Sales Management* and *The ASTD Management Development Handbook.*

References

Adventure World. 2017. "Brazil: Need to Know—Customs." www.adventureworld.co.nz/brazil/need-to-know.

ATD (Association for Talent Development). 2016. *State of the Industry.* Alexandria, VA: ATD Press.

Banks, A., and T. Yuki. 2014. "The State of Social Media in Brazil and the Metrics That Really Matter." comScore Insights, September 16. www.comscore.com/Insights/Presentations-and-Whitepapers/2014/The-State-of-Social-Media-in-Brazil-and-the-Metrics-that-Really-Matter.

CIA. 2013. *The World Factbook 2013-14.* Washington, D.C.: Central Intelligence Agency.

Flamingo São Paulo. 2016. *Trans / Crisis.* São Paulo, Brazil: Flamingo.

MOT Training and Development and ABTD (Associao Brasileira de Treinamento e Desenvolvimento). 2013. "Retrato do Treinamento no Brasil." *T&D Inteligencia Corporativa* October, 34-43. https://bc-v2.pressmatrix.com/pt-BR/profiles/93eb6586267e/editions/plVBqGDYkXF8EFap9bmX/pages/page/1.

Weaver, J. 2016. "Localization: Training & Development in Brazil." Carmazzi Global Solutions blog, July 22. www.carmazzi.com/localizationtraining-development-brazil.

4

Canada

Dan DeRoche

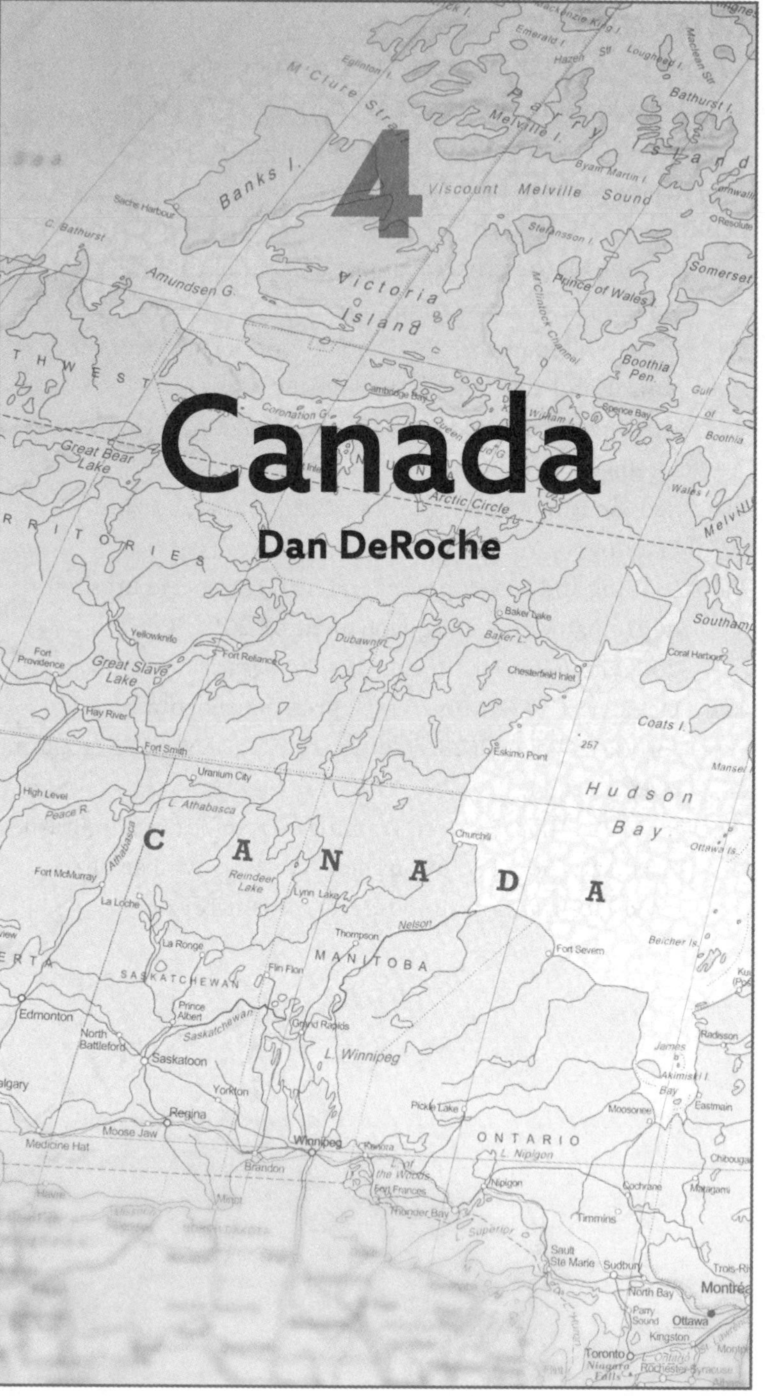

I'm an introvert and not the most comfortable with starting a conversation, so training was not something I dreamed of doing when beginning my career journey. I grew up in the western province of Alberta, the heart of Canada's energy sector, where there were many opportunities for an illustrious career as a tradesperson. Working many years as a pipefitter opened my eyes to a different path. It was a road that not only transitioned into a new career, but also gave me the satisfaction of helping people carry out their work safely: I became a safety professional.

The day I was asked to deliver training to a group of employees, requiring me to share information on how to perform their work, I was stunned. Fear of public speaking consumed me. Fifteen years later, having had roles as a corporate health and safety manager, training manager, and workforce development manager, I have had the privilege of working with and teaching thousands of people, from new workers to senior executives.

I have provided training in the United States, China, and here at home in Canada. At first, delivering health and safety courses seemed routine: Learn the material, provide it to students by reading the slides, and give them a little quiz to challenge their understanding. Simple, right? What I did not realize was that training is only as good as the person delivering it. Anyone can teach, but not everyone can teach effectively. This is particularly true when teaching abroad.

This chapter is about getting to know the people of Canada and using this knowledge to most effectively train in the country. Over the years, I have delivered a variety of courses in many locations that didn't seem conducive to learning. Having delivered sessions in the cab of a truck, the middle of an open field, and even on the shore of a lake, I know location can influence the quality of training. However, with planning and forethought, you can still be just as effective as delivering in a comfortable facility.

People and Culture: Get to Know Your Audience

Canadians can be summed up in one word: proud. The quality of detail and abilities they display in their roles define the strong work ethic that many Canadians exhibit. In any field, there is a high expectation of information and knowledge gain. One consistency is that opinions are respected. People are quick to point out any errors or discrepancies in the accuracy of material, which leads to another characteristic: We value feedback. It's requested and encouraged at the end of any training program. Canadians take pride in the output of their performance.

Canada is known for its multicultural diversity and acceptance of all nationalities. Each year, Canada accepts around 235,000 immigrants (Statistics Canada 2016). Across its 10 provinces and three territories, more than 200 languages are spoken, including Canada's two official languages, English and French, as well as indigenous and immigrant languages. Most people speak English; however, the province of Quebec is predominantly French-speaking. When planning training for Canadian audiences, this needs to be considered, as language barriers can be a concern. Groups may consist of many nationalities with varying degrees of English-language proficiency.

The Château Frontenac Hotel in Quebec, a predominantly French-speaking province in Canada

Here are a few areas to consider when you're delivering to Canadian audiences.

Arrive Prepared

Time is valuable for Canadians. With the strong work ethic that many have, it is critical for the trainer to plan ahead to ensure the training course begins on time. I recall attending a training course that a client was providing. Students had arrived early and were waiting for it to begin. Thirty minutes after the proposed start time, the trainer walked in and scrambled to set up the required media aids and training materials. It was too late. He had already lost the respect of the audience.

Have an Agenda

Canadian audiences like to know the layout of the training course they are attending. Aside from the objectives and content, give them an estimated timeline for the training session. If there are scheduled breaks or meals, let them know when. How long is the course supposed to last? If it's to end by 4 p.m., finish by 4 p.m. Do not go over the set time; this does not leave a good impression, especially if the trainer is handing out course evaluations at the end. Be punctual.

Encourage Questions From the Audience

Kindly interrupting the trainer to ask questions or for clarification is accepted and promoted in Canada. An engaged audience also helps the trainer with the content flow by sharing examples or stories, gaining different perspectives, and demonstrating an interest for further discussion of the topic. Ask questions of the group, and avoid singling anyone out individually.

With Canada's many languages and nationalities, you'll find that a mix of learning styles and communication methods is required. The three dominant audience types are:

- **Self-engaged.** These individuals have no fear of speaking out and saying what is on their minds. They'll help the trainer with direct participation by making comments, asking questions, and giving their opinions.

- **Thought engaged.** Many would refer to these individuals as the "quiet" type. Generally, they absorb the information given and do not speak out much, or do so only when they have valued feedback or specific questions.
- **Progressive.** This group is a combination of both. A trainer generally would not hear much from them at the beginning. However, as the training course goes on, they become comfortable with the audience and content, and share their thoughts for discussion.

Getting Started: Conduct a Needs Assessment

Because training is costly and time-consuming, you need to identify the benefits to the organization and to the individual for training to be considered effective in Canada. There is a new generation entering the workforce that may alter historical methods of training. Companies are building strong mentorship and training programs to help shape this new generation and groom them to become the leaders of tomorrow.

With a growing population of more than 35 million people in Canada, more than 20 percent of Canada's population will be retirement aged over the next 10 years. By 2030, Millennials will comprise 75 percent of the workforce (Dhillon 2016). Consider Millennials when determining what training needs are and who the audience is. The following are some areas to consider when conducting training needs assessments.

Identify the Gap

Before providing training to any organization, understand the specific requirements of respective clients. Canadians are very direct in sharing what is required, and will respond well to direct questions. Depending on the training requester, assessments may involve human resources associates, department managers, or administrative support to answer any questions. Conversations should be very open and casual while still maintaining a focus on the organizational objectives. Avoid any personal or probing questions when requesting information. Keep the focus on performance expectations for participants and the potential success of training.

Some questions to consider asking are:

- What type of training is currently being provided by the organization?
- Does the organization have a training department or existing curriculum?
- Is there specific training targeting various departments or groups?
- What type of impact does training have on productivity?
- Are there preferred delivery methods of training, such as classroom, online, on-site, or e-learning modules?
- What are the long-term goals for organizational needs?

Know the Audience

Many facilitators have attended training sessions and thought they could do a better job than the person facilitating. Not understanding the content or how it relates to the audience is often the culprit. It is a good idea to develop an online survey or questionnaire to measure learning styles. When possible, interview employees or stakeholders. This can be an efficient, flexible, and rewarding way of gathering information on each member organization.

Whether training takes place in eastern Canada, western Canada, or the northern territories, there are no specific differences in audiences to expect. However, there can be variances in learning preferences between training a group of oil and gas tradespeople or an office of corporate employees in the financial sector. Tradespeople are typically more technical and understand more of a hands-on approach. Audiences who spend a majority of time in offices can be more process oriented, which may change the dynamics of training delivery.

Have Clear Expectations

The training plan needs to reflect the intended outcomes without false promises. In Canada, expectations are high for the end result desired after any investment in training needs. This includes budgetary restrictions, knowledge transfer, and job applications after training. Summarize these expectations with the client to ensure understanding of the desired results. It is advisable to identify the following:

- What is the organizational challenge that needs addressing?
- Assess the employee knowledge base.
- Assess the job requirements compared with what needs to be learned.
- Is there any on-the-job training currently being provided? If so, have the process explained.
- What is the desired outcome for the participants and the organization?
- How will the knowledge level be achieved after the training program?
- Is there any support required after the training program to ensure knowledge transfer or retention?

Itineraries: Plan the Learning Journey

Many trainers spend countless hours in airports. It is easy to understand how important an itinerary is in order to have ample time to make a connecting flight or avoid rush hour traffic. The same goes for a journey to learning excellence.

When I began training technical courses in construction safety, I did not have the knowledge base to understand that we all learn in different ways. Many have heard the phrase "death by PowerPoint" and know how ineffective PowerPoint presentations can be.

In Canada, it's no different. Our culture appreciates ingenuity and charisma to create an energizing and productive learning session.

When planning the learning journey, be mindful of how you are engaging the audience. It is easy to lose an audience quickly. A great mentor once said to treat each learning experience as a workshop, not a lecture. Create the expectation by asking questions from the start. Use simple icebreakers to generate discussion or laughter.

You can also plan activities. Canadians are very active and enjoy the satisfaction of completing activities and staying engaged in learning environments. For example, I was teaching a session on learning styles to a group of supervisors and managers. I observed throughout the morning that many participants were not grasping their learning styles—the activities planned were not useful. By reverting to a backup activity involving paper airplanes and the VAK (Visual, Auditory, Kinesthetic) model, I changed the mood. The participants quickly adapted to how they understood learning methodologies and what they could absorb more easily for retention.

Face-to-face training is a standard learning delivery method in Canada and is still preferred. However, Canadian companies are seeing a huge transition to e-learning courses and web-based training, which many organizations are leaning toward for availability, productivity, affordability, efficiency, and ease of access to learning resources. Each organization differs with the type of training desired, though, so it's a good idea to conduct technology availability assessments when identifying training plans and expectations.

Packing Lists: Logistics, Technology, and Resources

When training in Canada, you'll have few issues when it comes to technology availability. Most client locations and hotels have meeting rooms that provide basic needs including tables, chairs, screens, and cords. Confirm before travel to ensure that these items will be in place and available. When possible, bring a projector. Standard voltage is 110V, so travel adapters may be required.

Most areas have adequate Wi-Fi access. However, most public networks are password protected, so you'll need permission. It is becoming more common for trainers to use YouTube and related sites to show relevant videos for learning outlets. Be mindful that bandwidth can be a concern, depending on the number of users.

It is advisable to bring prepared training materials and any other gadgets required, such as presentation pointers or adapters. Always have extra batteries on hand. I recall having to leave the hotel during one training session to run across the street to a local convenience store because my pointer's batteries had died in the middle of the presentation. Whiteboards and flipcharts are commonly used and available when requested.

Always have business cards ready to hand out to members of management or client organizers. It is advisable to have them available for participants as well to encourage any feedback or questions that may arise after training has taken place.

Customs: Body Language Dos and Don'ts

Many countries have customs that do not work in other nations. People from many different countries live in Canada, so trainers in Canada need to be sensitive to various customs and be prepared to respond respectfully. Here are some suggestions to consider when training in Canada:

- It is critical to create a relationship with the audience and take the time to get to know them on a personal level. Give participants a chance to introduce themselves to the group. Depending on the course content, it is beneficial to ask the participants specific questions as part of their introduction. When I present courses relating to safety in the workplace, I try to include an open question such as, "Why do you work safely?" or "Why is it important to identify hazards in the workplace?"

- When meeting people or participants, a simple handshake is a common way to greet people. Shake the person's hand firmly and quickly while maintaining eye contact.
- Canadians respect humility and vulnerability. While you should show confidence, overconfidence can come off as arrogant, conceited, or egocentric. An influential colleague once said, "No matter how many times you instruct a course and know the content, it is charming to be a little nervous. Nervousness shows we are all human and have imperfections."
- Canadians expect eye contact to show focus on their reactions. Similar to U.S. audiences, it is appropriate to hold contact for three seconds. Any longer can make some participants uneasy, because not everyone is eager to speak up. Focus on those who are speaking by turning to face them directly. Showing facial expressions and nodding your head are nonverbal ways to show engagement with no distractions.
- Try not to stand in one spot for too long or behind participants, because it can be uncomfortable for some. Early in my career this was a challenge for me. A colleague noticed this behavior during a training session and blocked the pathways, which helped to move me out into the audience.
- Speaking tone is almost as important as body language. Be loud enough so the person in the back of the room can still hear, yet mild enough so it does not sound like shouting. Vary your voice to show passion and conviction. Speak clearly and slowly, because Canada is very multicultural and has a wide range of languages. This helps with understanding and transfer of knowledge.
- Keep hands free from distractions, like jingling coins in a pocket. Gestures allow expression and amplification of

energy. Practice gestures in front of a mirror. In my early training days in Canada, I was instructing a technical course to a group of construction workers and did not realize I was shuffling my keys in my pocket, which disrupted a few individuals. I was kindly interrupted and informed of the distraction.

- Canadians are empathetic and enjoy sharing experiences. Tell a personal story that connects with the audience and content.
- Show a genuine smile and laugh. Humor and good-hearted jokes will be received well. Avoid jokes about religion and politics, or ethnic-related comments.

Climate: Create a Warm Learning Environment

Training involves more than just showing up and presenting a course to participants. It is important to understand Canadian culture to create a warm learning environment. Canada's current population growth is due in large part to immigration, with only a tenth of Canada's population increase due to natural population growth. In Canada, there is no core identity; however, there are shared values, including openness, respect, compassion, and a willingness to work hard, be there for each other, and search for equality and justice.

The word *Canada* means village, and it is important to build relationships and create a "village" in the classroom. Here are some ways to do so:

- Provide name tags or table cards for the participants. Canadians are very personable and appreciate being called by name.
- Canadians do have a good sense of humor, and enjoy irony, satire, and self-effacing jokes.
- Some training budgets are getting cut in Canada, and often snacks and treats are the first items to go. It can be cold for many months of the year in Canada. Nothing

starts the day out better than having a warm drink to help those chilled bones! Do what can be done to serve coffee and tea, which Canadians enjoy. That gesture will go a long way in building relationships and energizing participants.

- "Fidgets" help hold attention spans when in a training session. Provide pipe cleaners or small crafts that don't generate noise. I was once facilitating a course on learning styles for a group of executives, and I noticed some of the course material was becoming dry and not easy for everyone to focus on. So, on day two, I decided to mix it up and bring in a container filled with fidgets (stress balls, action figures, colored Popsicle sticks, and other random craft items). At first, I thought it would be more of a distraction, but it went off very well and created more conversation and engagement surrounding the course material. Many participants thought that this was a big help in remaining focused and kept the day moving at a good pace. There were even some great creations made by the group with some of the fidgets, making for a good laugh and a happy ending to the course!
- Have training materials neatly packaged for the participants and placed on each table, ready for when they arrive. Canadian audiences are curious and enjoy skimming through the material beforehand to catch a glimpse of what they will be learning throughout the training session.

Things to Consider: Handle Classroom Challenges

Canadians have their thoughts, personalities, and differences in opinions. Many participants will enjoy a good discussion with opposing viewpoints to see all sides of a particular topic. However, as time is valuable, the flow of training needs to progress to stay on point. It is important to identify clear objectives and participant expectations at the start.

Canadians are typically quite respectful of trainers, whether local or foreign. However, if a participant does become argumentative, show interest in understanding their viewpoint. Give them the opportunity to speak their mind as long as it remains respectful and nonjudgmental of others. If a participant refuses to listen, you need to take control of the situation. Politely ask the individual to leave the room if the behavior persists and contact a company representative.

I recall a training session where an individual became very argumentative on a certain topic and would not listen to the opinions of others. Constant interruptions and cutting in on other responses created tension in the room, leaving many learners seeming angry or frustrated. I respectfully intervened with the argumentative individual and asked if we could speak privately to conclude the topic at the next break. After a lengthy discussion, the individual realized their behavior was not appropriate and took it upon themselves to apologize to the class when the course resumed, following the break. Many situations can be resolved with a professional and respectful discussion without needing to involve a company representative.

Canadians can get frustrated if they do not understand the trainer. Because English is the most common language for a majority of Canadians, a nonnative trainer needs to speak clearly and pronounce their words as clearly as possible.

Don't make participants feel rushed. Plan the agenda to ensure adequate time is given to allow discussion or activities. Once I delivered a course to supervisors on leadership development, and the discussions, feedback, and stories shared among the group were creating an engaged atmosphere. However, when I realized that time was running short, instead of continuing at the same pace, I began racing through the remaining content without allowing the expected discussions. Class energy changed, and the course feedback reflected participant dissatisfaction. A valuable lesson learned.

Tips and Warnings: Advice for Nonnative Trainers

Even though Canadians are welcoming of non-Canadians, it can still be daunting for nonnative trainers to blend in and build relationships with participants. Here are some things to consider that I have noticed in travels across Canada:

- Be sensitive to attention spans. If time permits, let the participants decide on the frequency of breaks. Try to base it on the length of the training session. For an all-day session, allow for two 15-minute breaks (morning and afternoon) and a lunch break, or more as needed. After lunch, fatigue can set in, so give them a brain break.
- Be available after the training session. Some people are not always comfortable speaking in front of a group, so they may want to talk one-on-one after the session to clarify any comments or request additional feedback in a particular area. Some may find it disrespectful for the trainer to leave before the participants do.
- Ask questions about the local culture, things to see, or places to eat, which will show commitment and genuine interest about the participants and their way of life. Many Canadians love hockey, and someone is always willing to engage in a conversation when it comes to this sport.
- Some areas in Canada have long winters. Typically, traveling between October and March can be frigid and snowy in many regions. Plan to pack warm clothes, coats, and gloves, and even shoes or boots with good soles to avoid slipping. Always check the long-range forecast because weather changes frequently.
- Not all training sessions require formal dress. Communicate with the organizer before travel to confirm the suitable dress attire.

Horseshoe Falls in winter. Traveling in Canada between October and March can mean frigid, snowy weather.

Bon Voyage

I was mentored for many years by an incredible individual who was very passionate and empowering to everyone he taught. His mentoring expanded my training delivery depth, and I was better able to focus on the people in class rather than the content itself. The result is not just about getting a certificate or checking the box for attendance; it is more about what people take away from each training session. At the end of my career, I want to look back and say I helped make a difference in people's lives by extending knowledge and experiences to provide a powerful message to others.

I hope you're able to take the advice about training in Canada presented in this chapter and apply it to your next—or first—trip to this beautiful country. Whichever province or territory you visit, there is always something to discover. Enjoy our diversity in Canada. All are welcome.

About the Author

Dan DeRoche is a multiticketed construction trades professional, with more than 17 years' experience as a health and safety professional and training and development leader. He is currently the corporate health, safety, and environment manager for a leading contractor in Alberta, Canada. His communication skills have allowed him to create an influential difference when leading organizational teams in numerous areas of growth. His passion is exemplified by empowering and motivating others to succeed. He has directed and guided the development of principal training initiatives to ensure consistent training across organizational departments, with emphasis on the safety and leadership of employees. Dan is recognized as a Master Trainer, Certified Training Professional, and National Construction Gold Seal Safety professional, as well as a certified Myers-Briggs Type Indicator practitioner.

References

Dhillon, P. 2016. "The Millennial Leader: How the Next Generation Is Managing Up." *Huffington Post* (Canada), December 9. www.huffingtonpost.ca/punit-dhillon/the-millennial-leader-how_b_13510826.html.

Statistics Canada. 2016. "150 Years of Immigration in Canada." Statistics Canada, June 29. www.statcan.gc.ca/pub/11-630-x/11-630-x2016006-eng.htm.

5

China

David Xue

My morning alarm woke me as usual. My first thought was, "Where am I? Shanghai, Xian, or somewhere else?" I reached for my cell phone with that question still on my mind, as "One new message" appeared on the screen. "This is your flight summary for the year" it read: 97 flights taken; 186,400 kilometers covered; 21 cities visited. You might think that I am a pilot or a flight attendant, but no! I am a talent development consultant in China.

When I started my career as a college professor in China, I had no idea I would move into corporate life as a trainer in a sales department and work my way up to a learning and organization development director for major manufacturing and computer companies. Now, as a freelance learning consultant, my career focuses on leadership and talent development as well as sales growth programs. The unique experience of teaching in school and training in enterprises equipped me with a thorough understanding of the differences between pedagogy and andragogy.

With the rapid growth of technology and change in China in the past decades, the training industry has grown and changed as well. I have been lucky enough to witness the changing classroom delivery methods and behavior of participants during that period.

In the past, a typical Chinese training room view would be of a trainer standing beside a blackboard or whiteboard with chalk or marker in hand, lecturing to a group of participants. Participants would not ask questions; almost all would accept whatever the trainer—the expert—said because challenging a teacher was not encouraged in traditional Chinese culture.

Today's participants, especially the younger ones, demonstrate independent thinking. They ask questions, and they participate in classroom activities enthusiastically. They still respect trainers and are eager to learn, but they share different views without much hesitation. Lecturing is no longer the only major training method used. Trainers now use action learning facilitation techniques, such as coaching, visual facilitation, and even WeChat for follow-ups.

I am passionate about people development, and especially classroom facilitation. I currently facilitate more than 120 days per year to private, state-owned, and multinational companies in China. In more than 20 years of corporate experience, the scope of my responsibilities has expanded from China to Greater China to Asia Pacific to worldwide, which provided me the privilege of understanding the differences among countries and cultures in the classroom.

People and Culture: Get to Know Your Audience

China has the largest population in the world: 1.38 billion as of 2016. More than 90 percent are Han people, although there are 55 minority groups. Mandarin—standard Chinese—is the official language, but there are 129 dialects. English is increasingly popular in China, especially among young people. For English-speaking international trainers, there is no need to worry about language if delivering training in big cities like Beijing, Shanghai, Guangzhou, or Shenzhen, or for multinational companies.

The one-child policy, a part of the country's family planning program, was introduced in 1979 and began to be formally phased out in 2015. As a result of the policy, most of the workforce grew up as only children. Be aware of the typical traits of these learners. One of their most common characteristics is that they can be somewhat self-centered. Getting each individual's participation may take more of an effort here than elsewhere. Trainers need to factor this into training room activities, interactions, and discussion.

China is a typical high-context culture. In a high-context culture, many things are left unsaid, and you must read between the lines. Word choice becomes crucial—a few words communicated to a group in a high-context culture deliver a complex message very effectively. Communication is less efficient once outside that group. For example, humor is a characteristic of many effective trainers; however, a high-context joke might not translate well to someone unfamiliar with the culture. Be sure to have someone familiar with Chinese culture review any jokes beforehand to avoid creating an embarrassing situation.

Shanghai skyline

Participants in China are a little more conservative in classroom activities and interactions than participants from some other cultures. Trainers might face a terrible silence when asking a question. It does not mean students are not thinking. Chinese people simply shy away from opinion sharing. Starting with easy questions or a group activity can help to break the ice and create the interactive atmosphere trainers desire. Once they become acclimated, Chinese people are like other audiences.

Getting Started: Conduct a Needs Assessment

Growing rapidly alongside the economy, the training industry in China has a huge demand for qualified talent development professionals. Entrepreneurship is growing here, especially for medium and small consulting companies.

For needs assessment, interviews are effective when they are conducted correctly and when you have support from managers. The tradition of "face-saving" could make it difficult to uncover training needs that may embarrass an organization or manager. Use a more general questioning approach such as, "If we wanted to improve team building here, what ideas might you have?" Because it can help preserve confidentiality, use of technology is becoming more popular for both needs assessment and evaluations. Keep in mind that feedback is often still not given freely, for fear that the trainer may lose face.

WeChat is the most popular social app in China, and lots of people leverage that for needs assessment before the training program without even being on-site. For example, you can design a needs assessment survey on a website and create a QR code. The participants can then form a WeChat group, and once you share the QR code, everyone can access the website to fill out the survey. You can get instant results, and even get various charts through WeChat to make it more visual.

Here are some points to consider when conducting a needs analysis in China, focusing on past and present trends (OnDemand Consulting n.d.):

- Companies are now more focused on whether a training program improved employee performance, rather than if participants enjoyed the program.
- Priorities at enterprise universities focus on more strategic programs than general management and technology.

- Corporate universities play important roles in educating employees. We see the trend continuing and even becoming much more influential.
- Local consulting firms, especially those focusing on learning technologies, have gained more attention and popularity in the training industry.
- Almost all enterprises and learning solution providers are developing online, mobile, and other web-based learning programs to meet the mobility trend.
- Leadership and management training programs remain a focus in the training industry and come in more varieties.

Itineraries: Plan the Learning Journey

In Chinese education, teachers teach and students listen. You rarely find a situation where there is a group discussion or brainstorming. Many participants are accustomed to this method as adults and still prefer listening instead of participating. That trend is slowly changing, and trainers need to carefully balance lecturing and participating activities.

I once facilitated a leadership class where the program was designed to be 30 percent lecturing and 70 percent participant activities. At the beginning of the second day, I assigned a classroom activity, and some participants complained that they did not want to participate. Instead, they wanted to be taught and claimed that was a more valuable activity. Because the other participants were interested in the activity, we still did it, but I had a short conversation with the people who were complaining, which helped them understand the value of the activity. Trainers need to take this custom into consideration when designing their programs.

In a different situation, working on a real business issue did seem to work. I was delivering a change management training program; the training organizer shared concerns that sales leaders might not be very participative and might lose focus during the training course, due to a major project. When the organizer explained that participants were planning a process and organizational change, I realized we could use the program's activities to work on the project. We agreed that we would leverage the process, tools, and leadership behaviors in the training program to work on their business. The passion and participation the leaders demonstrated during the training program outshone all other change management sessions I have done. In the end, Chinese learners need to be able to connect with what they're learning in a very real way.

Another success story occurred at ASIMCO, a China-based auto components manufacturing company. In the ASIMCO Leadership Development Program, participants were asked to work together on a project to practice what they learned to solve real business issues. They had to find senior leaders within the company to act as coaches, and bring coaching reports to the next training session three months later. In between the sessions, there was a monthly, one-hour virtual class. One group that worked on a Lean production project during the program achieved 35 percent savings as a result. The general managers from a third of the operating companies in ASIMCO now are graduates of this program.

Of course, the learning journey does not end when the training course is over. In China, you must still evaluate the success—or failure—of your program. Most Chinese training success measurements don't reach Kirkpatrick's Level 3, but recently more organizations have been measuring training success at a higher level. Many managers ask trainers for a checklist of expected behaviors so they can leverage them as a coaching tool to ensure participants apply new behavior changes on the job. Training professionals are also under increased pressure to provide evidence of return on investment, Level 5 of the Phillips' training evaluation model.

Most people have an open mind for learning technology, and it is very popular in China. For example, one recent client program included an activity where participants pasted paper dots on a flipchart next to the objectives that interest them. Instead of using paper, I incorporated an app called UMU (meaning *you, me, us*), which is a mobile learning platform. People loved it. By leveraging UMU, participants got to vote for the objective that interested them the most. We achieved our stated activity goal and inspired a higher energy level from the very beginning. Chinese learners expect a very high level of energy in the classroom, particularly during activities.

Again, WeChat is a popular mobile app for post-training activities. Instructors and participants can use it to share work-related information, pictures, videos, and other materials.

Finally, be creative in delivering sessions. The Chinese are eager for new and inventive ways to receive knowledge and skills. I recently worked with a friend in a presentation skills training class to leverage his expertise in graphic facilitation and achieved fantastic results. At the end of each session, I called participants' attention to the visuals we used and reviewed what we'd discussed during the session. The participants were very engaged throughout and thought it was a good learning experience.

Packing Lists: Logistics, Technology, and Resources

In most situations, trainers will not face resources issues, especially in big cities like Beijing, Shanghai, Guangzhou, and Shenzhen.

However, for those trainers who prefer using flipcharts, hotels rarely provide stands, nor are all of the walls suitable for posting. So you either need to bring your own stands or find another way to present the material. You could consult the training room owner and provide a checklist of specific requests for flipcharts, stands, and wall charts.

One more thing to pay attention to is laptop connection to projectors. Most of the projectors at hotels or companies in China still use VGA cables. Be prepared; for example, if you have a Mac, bring an adapter so you can hook your computer to the projector.

The usual training start and end times are 9 a.m. and 5 p.m., with one hour for lunch. Lunch and tea breaks are provided, normally. Do not be surprised if participants take a nap at their desk after lunch, especially in Guangzhou, Shenzhen, or other cities in the southern part of China.

Customs: Body Language Dos and Don'ts

Body language in China is much more conservative compared with Western cultures, although this is changing. Here are a few points it is important to be aware of in the classroom:

- Don't stand or sit too close to participants. People prefer to sit farther from the trainer. The seats at the back of the room fill up first.
- Participants will be sensitive to you looking them in the eye.
- Avoid frequently exaggerating body language.
- In some typical state-owned Chinese companies, learners will be more comfortable if the trainer is sitting instead of standing.
- The Chinese expect professional greetings in the training room, such as a handshake. Avoid a kiss on the cheek or a hug.

Here's an example of a body language faux pas: I was training in a very large state-owned company in China. Three times during the course, the training manager came to me with a chair and said, "This is the chair for you." I didn't sit down the first two times but finally did on the third time, realizing that there must be something going on. He shared with me later that one of the senior leaders commented that my standing style made him uncomfortable.

Climate: Create Warm Learning Environment

Creating a warm learning environment is critical, because although Chinese people are warmhearted, they may appear cold at first.

Strangers in China will not normally start a conversation immediately. It is not uncommon for two participants to sit at the same table without speaking or even saying hello. This distance can negatively affect training.

Here are a few ways to create a warm learning environment:

- Let the participants choose their own seat or table at first, and then change the arrangements later if necessary.
- Encourage participants to network before class starts.
- An icebreaker at the beginning of the class can set the right tone. Even a simple one, like having participants introduce themselves by using each letter in their name to think of a word that relates to who they are, can be a fun exercise. For example: DAVID—*D* is for dancing because I like to dance. *A* is for avid reader; *V* is for very nice; *I* is for influential as a trainer; and the last *D* is for driving, because I enjoy driving.
- Design learning activities that require teamwork.
- Chinese participants enjoy going out to eat. Eating is seen as a social experience to share.

Things to Consider: Handle Classroom Challenges

Many trainers like to ask, "Any questions?" after explaining a topic. However, in China this might lead to silence. It's not that participants have no questions; rather, the question is framed poorly, so they don't know how to answer. Be prepared with several easy, specific questions to spark conversation. For instance, ask for their insights on the topic, to describe the relevance of the subject to workers in China, or how they can use what they've learned.

There may be other reasons why participants don't answer questions. They might not want to be the one who seems to be having difficulty understanding the information, and as a result look less intelligent. Intellectual appearance is critical. It could be that they have a different opinion and don't want to challenge the trainer. They also don't want to be the center of attention.

Here are a few suggestions for encouraging participation:

- At the very beginning of the program, explain to participants that questions you ask are meant to get their input or opinion. They're for making participation easier, not to test learners' intelligence.
- Start with a close-ended question to involve participants.
- Pose the question first, then pause to make brief eye contact with the participants to signal that you want an answer.
- Reward the participant who answers the question.

Many participants in China believe that learning is teachers talking and students listening without conversation. Other participants think activities and exercises are time-consuming and prevent them from getting more valuable information.

I was once facilitating a negotiation program in Chengdu, the capital city of Sichuan province (and the home of a prominent giant-panda research base). When I gave directions for a third negotiation exercise, one of the participants raised his hand and said, "Can you just tell us what points we need to pay attention to and what skills we need to use in the case? We do not need to do the exercises. We want to save time for more solid content." Looking around the room, I realized that other participants had the same concern. I had to stop to explain the value of experience, reflection, and feedback for skills learning. They seemed unconvinced, yet they completed the exercise. After the debrief, they realized how the activity could help them learn better.

In handling the need-for-more-information challenge, trainers need to understand the participants' learning preferences in advance. Describe the value of the exercise or activity in the learning process. Debrief the activity or exercise thoroughly.

A baby panda in Chengdu's giant-panda research base

Tips and Warnings: Advice for Nonnative Trainers

A fifth of the world's population lives in China. When visiting one of the world's fastest-growing economies, you will see a melding of an ancient culture and a Westernized lifestyle. The two coexist like the yin and yang forces, maintaining the balance of the universe. Keep this balance in mind when visiting China. Do not be lulled into forgetting some long-held traditions because of the modern face of China.

Here are some general tips to consider:

- Do respect elders. This tradition is still very important.
- Do speak slowly and make sure participants can follow.
- Do start with an icebreaking exercise to warm up and get the participants engaged.
- Do not delay the sessions. It is important to be punctual in closing the program.
- Do not use stories or words from Western religions, as most Chinese participants will not understand.

Also, Chinese people do not say "God bless you" after someone sneezes.

- Don't assume all Chinese people speak the same language. For example, if two people are speaking in a Shanghai dialect, I, as a Beijing local, won't understand their conversation.
- Do learn some Chinese to get close to participants: *xie xie* (thank you), *ni hao* (hello), and *wo hen gao xing lai dao zhe li* (I am happy to be here).

Bon Voyage

It has been almost 40 years since China opened up as a country to the outside world. People are getting more and more internationally minded. Trainers from all over the world are welcome in China. Bring a global mindset, and enjoy the sessions and the Chinese participants.

***

About the Author

David Xue is currently a freelance consultant, having previously been the director of learning and organization development at Microsoft, Greater China. Prior to that, he worked as the regional learning director for Asia Pacific at Ingersoll Rand and the director of talent development for the Asia-Pacific region at Dell. His specialties include talent management, leadership development, sales training and development, and facilitation.

Reference

OnDemand Consulting. n.d. "Training Business." OnDemand Consulting. www.ondemand-learning.com/index.html.

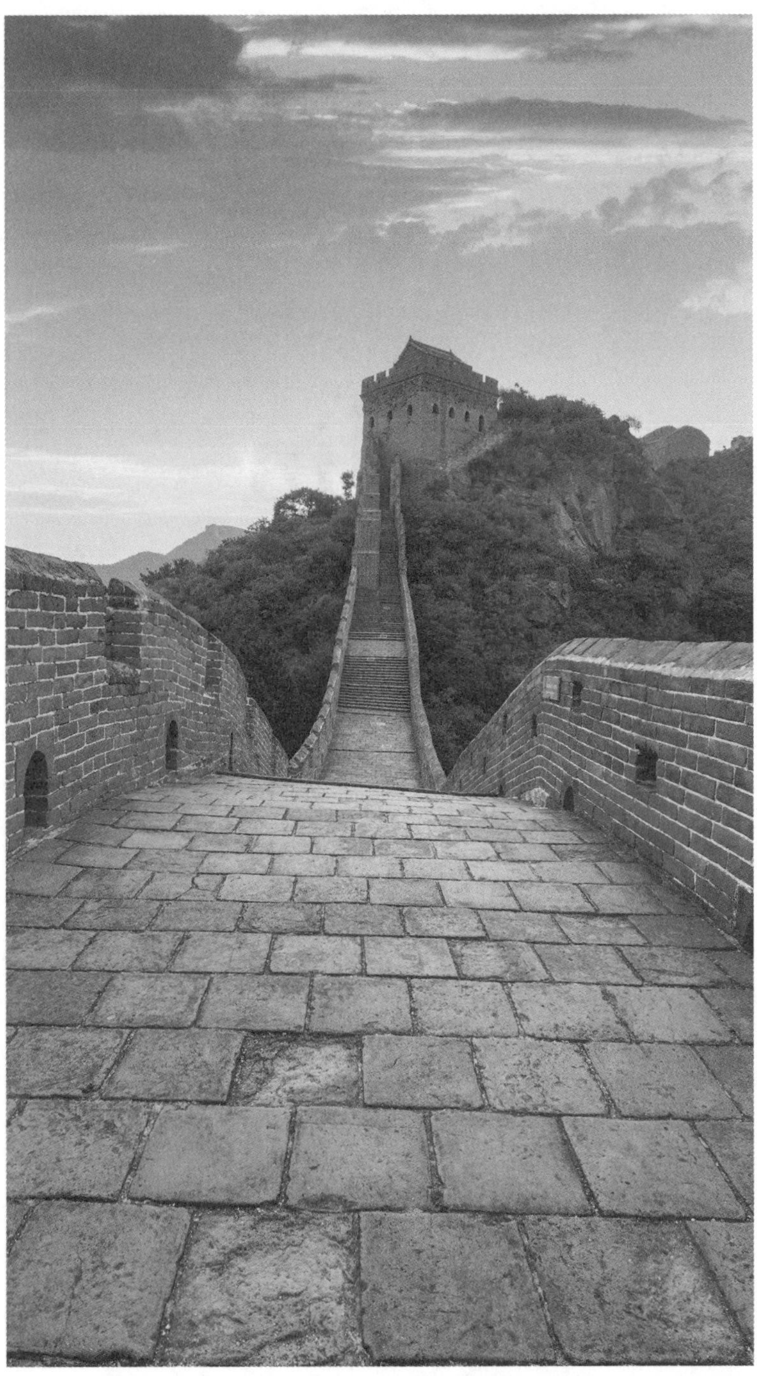

The Great Wall of China in Beijing

India

Kedar Vashi

"What's the worst that could happen?" This six-word question led to a life that has turned out to be rewarding beyond my wildest imagination. With a graduate degree in electronics and an MBA in marketing, I was already a successful sales manager with a reputable packaging company in India when my wife posed this question. We were discussing my long-cherished dream of becoming a trainer, and as usual, I was expressing all sorts of apprehensions at the idea of giving up an established career for an ambition that could well turn out to be a foolish dream.

Fifteen years, 3,100 participants, and travel across 21 Indian cities and 19 countries later, that one question has proved to be an invaluable gift. The answer led to giving up a sales career, becoming a consultant, and joining and rising to be a Master Trainer with Dale Carnegie Training, one of the world's oldest training companies. From there I went on to work with Coca-Cola and reach the head of leadership development for a group of 18 countries. Both these experiences have given me an incredibly fulfilling career.

However, all these experiences are still inadequate to providing a definitive guide to training in India, an overwhelmingly diverse country of 1.2 billion people, more than half under age 35. Among them, they speak, read, and write 22 languages, practice seven religions, and worship at least 100 gods. The people, culture, and languages are so different in various parts of the country that a person from the north of India might feel linguistically more at home in the United States or the United Kingdom than in the south of India. At the same time, Bollywood movies, the game of cricket, and a booming economy that promises a land of opportunities unite this country beyond languages and geographies.

This cultural and generational diversity creates challenges even for a native trainer who works in a different part of the country from their own. I remember an embarrassing incident when I was training in the state of Maharashtra in western India. While facilitating a session for a construction company, I was trying to throw in some local words and phrases to build rapport with the audience, rather than delivering the course completely in English. An enthusiastic participant started to converse in the local language, Marathi. I wanted to tell him, "I do not know Marathi." However, being a native speaker of another language, I ended up using the wrong word. After a slightly hostile reaction, they informed me that the verb used in my mother tongue for "to know" means "to like" in their language. So an honest confession—"I do not know your language"—came out as, "I do not like your language."

The biggest mistake you can make while preparing to train in India is to assume that India is one uniform country. There are many cultures in India, and this makes the process of training people from India both exciting and challenging.

If this sounds overwhelming, rest assured that training in India can be a fascinating experience. Indian audiences have a unique combination of intellect and hospitality, and it is a delight to conduct a session for groups who are quick to understand concepts and ask challenging questions. The sheer warmth of the people—who are known to play perfect hosts to the trainers, taking them shopping and sightseeing and inviting them to family dinners or even family weddings—is a memorable experience for many talent development professionals.

I hope that you, too, will get to experience the warmth and hospitality of the Indian audience. And when you do, the information that follows will help you navigate the Indian classroom.

People and Culture: Get to Know Your Audience

Despite the diversity, there are still many characteristics that people across India share. It will surely help a trainer unfamiliar with the country to keep some of these in mind while preparing to deliver sessions in India.

Let's start by sharing some behaviors rooted in culture that Indian audiences may exhibit in a classroom. These behaviors are relatively uniform across the country. Understanding where people are coming from will help you see things in the right context and respond appropriately.

We Expect the Trainer to Provide Answers

Most Indians grew up in an educational system that was more directive than reflective. We expect our teachers (and trainers) to know the answers and tell us, rather than leading us to discover on our own. We expect them to lead us to the light of knowledge from the darkness of ignorance. In a training context, it means that using a facilitative approach and not taking a stand about the right answer could be perceived as a lack of knowledge.

For example, a globally respected facilitator once came to our organization to conduct a series of sessions on coaching for our midlevel managers. Masterful as he was in the art of coaching, he refused to provide definitive answers to the work challenges that the audience brought, and instead kept pushing them to explore the challenge from various angles to determine the course of action. The most common complaint heard from the audience members was, "The trainer is a good person, but he does not know much. If we were to find the answers on our own, why is he here?"

A trainer can still adopt a facilitative approach. The key is to strike a balance between times to demonstrate superior knowledge and times to ask the audience to gain knowledge from their peers or experiences. The recommended ratio is approximately 50:50. Go below that regarding trainer input, and a loss of credibility may occur.

We Avoid Speaking Up

Indians have a deep-rooted cultural value of respecting elders. Unlike Western societies, disagreeing with or even questioning a senior is often seen as a mark of disrespect. This conditioning manifests in the workplace as bosses who do not like their juniors to question them. Employees tend to keep their mouths shut, although they may disagree with their senior. In many schools, it's common for students to listen to teachers deliver knowledge with an air of authority that seems to discourage questioning (although younger students are relatively less governed by these norms).

This cultural influence poses a peculiar challenge to a trainer. In class, when participants are in the same room as their boss, they are less likely to open up, share their true challenges, and say anything against workplace practices. At times, if someone decides to speak up, the boss may jump in to shut them up with a "final verdict."

For example, I once conducted a course that required the participants to open up and voice their workplace concerns and challenges candidly to resolve issues. The CEO was very keen to attend the program, but it was obvious that his presence would shut down the participants, so I insisted that he not attend. He very reluctantly agreed. However, in the introduction to the session, he sincerely urged the participants to speak up, saying that he had planted two spies in the class who would report to him if someone was nonparticipative. His message was a cleverly worded but thinly veiled threat to the participants to keep them from speaking up. As a result, I could barely get attendees to divulge any real issues. As a facilitator, avoid putting bosses and direct reports in the same class to ensure a whole-hearted participation.

Because Indian employees are conditioned not to ask too many questions of seniors, as the trainer you may also experience a lack of questions or disagreements. Encourage questions for a more participative atmosphere. Early in the program, if you establish that there are no stupid questions or answers and demonstrate acceptance to being challenged, you are more likely to have rich discussions in the class.

We Have Our Own Notion of Time

One of the first things that you'll notice while training in India is our intimate relationship with time. In most social functions, arriving within 30 minutes of the announced time may make you the only person at the venue. Lateness does not come from disrespect for others' time or disregard for their schedule. So don't take offense if people arrive late to your training course. Because people are not inconsiderate, once they understand how you view time, they will follow your schedule.

Getting Started: Conduct a Needs Assessment

A fascinating experience for anyone who visits India, especially from the West, is the way people drive on the road. Westerners have described local driving habits as ranging from disorderly to dangerous. However, there is a method to the madness, and surprisingly, India has far fewer road accidents than you would expect. This style of driving reflects the way of life for us—focus on outcomes more than the process. Reaching our destination is more important than following traffic rules. This quality makes Indian executives extremely innovative and very competitive.

This overwhelming focus on outcomes also affects the needs assessment process. The common needs analysis process comprises a gut feeling of the leaders, HR data analysis, personal interviews, focus groups, and online surveys, in that order.

When conducting an interview with a manager, it is likely that the manager will jump to offering solutions rather than describing the problems. For example, you are more likely to hear, "The team needs a one-day communication skills training program" than, "My challenge is that the team members do not communicate openly with one another" (which could very well be a trust issue rather than a communication issue).

Because people are not very comfortable speaking up, most may hold back when participating in focus groups, especially if their managers are in the room. The facilitator needs to firmly and credibly assure confidentiality. Some of the participants may still hold back due to the presence of their peers. It is for this reason that online surveys are likely to be more accurate than focus groups.

Itineraries: Plan the Learning Journey

Learning and development is still a pretty new area for a large number of Indian companies. The multinationals are ahead of the curve because they leverage their global programs and practices. Following multinational corporations are large Indian conglomerates, which are trying to strengthen their training departments to attract talent and catch up with their more evolved competitors regarding employee development. However, most small and medium-sized Indian companies are still in early stages of learning and development. Depending on the enterprise, there are different degrees of readiness at an organizational level regarding supporting training initiatives.

Delivery Methods

The most popular delivery method is classroom training. Also, Indians—being inherently social people—respond well to group activities and collaborative learning. Although not recommended, Indians also accept a monologue delivery by an instructor because that is how they grew up learning in schools and colleges.

However, the dominance of classroom training is quickly receding, and a combination of the following factors is likely to have a significant impact on online delivery:

- **Internet connections.** With 462 million Internet connections, India has the second highest Internet user base in the world (Chakraberty 2017). With the government's focus on "Digital India," this number is growing rapidly.
- **Mobile connections.** According to global mobile intelligence website GSMA (2016), India has 1 billion mobile connections, second only to China. India enjoys a whopping 76 percent market penetration. When visiting India, it is almost impossible to find a person who does not own a mobile phone. For many visitors, this contrasts

with their impression of India, with its limited resources and lack of basic amenities for many people.

- **Millennial population.** With 385 million people aged 19 to 35, India has more Millennials than any other country in the world (Peterson, McCaffrey, and Sillman n.d.). Similarly to other parts of the world, they are much more comfortable with technology than older generations.

These three factors together make India a great place to leverage technology for the entire training cycle, from needs analysis to learning reinforcement and program evaluations. These factors have also started slowly but steadily moving the needle toward virtual delivery, such as e-learning, virtual classrooms, or gamified learning. Many companies and universities are already leveraging the Internet to substitute face-to-face training with virtual synchronous or asynchronous sessions.

However, India seems to have just tapped the tip of the iceberg when it comes to leveraging technology for learning. There is great potential for training companies who are experts in this area to offer their solutions, and for trainers in other countries to expand their services to India without traveling there.

Measuring Success

When it comes to measuring success, very few organizations are making a conscious effort to do so. One of the reasons is that, outside of multinationals and some large Indian organizations, not many companies are making any significant investment in training programs. As one training manager cryptically remarked, "We do not measure the return on investment for our training programs because the cost of measurement will wipe away any returns, and we will end up with a negative ROI."

Although some companies do deploy the Kirkpatrick model to measure training effectiveness, a low percentage go beyond Level 2, assessing knowledge. Since Indians are not intuitively data or process oriented, a good way to measure training effectiveness is to collect anecdotal evidence. One of the most efficient methods

I have seen used is collecting success stories from the participants 60 days after completing the training program.

A smart way to leverage the inherent competitiveness is using social media to share the success stories. On one occasion, when a company started sharing success stories on its intranet, it saw a significant jump in people making a sincere attempt to implement what they learned in the training program.

Packing Lists: Logistics, Technology, and Resources

Like any other country, India has its set of unique logistical challenges and opportunities; ignore them at your peril. The following suggestions will be useful in ensuring a smooth execution of training programs.

Internet Connection Speeds

Although India has deep Internet connection penetration across the country, the speed continues to be a challenge in many cases. According to Akamai's Internet connectivity report, although India is second in Internet connections worldwide, it is 105th when it comes to average Internet speed (Mehta 2016).

What that means for a trainer is that, if on a company's premises—especially in larger cities—there will not be many challenges regarding good download speeds. However, if training up-country or at a hotel, then speed could be erratic. So if you are streaming videos from YouTube or any other online portal, it is best to download them onto your computer rather than trying to connect to the Internet during the session. The same goes for online simulations. I have had experiences where an online simulation could not be run effectively due to a poor Internet connection. My preference now is an offline simulation on the participants' computers, unless I'm certain of the location and Internet connectivity.

Lunch

As innocuous as it may sound, lunchtime has stumped many trainers who are not from India. Indians have almost all meals later in the day than their Western counterparts. Lunchtime is typically around 1 or 2 p.m. One of the logistical challenges faced while delivering sessions in programs designed for a global audience is that most of them had lunch planned at noon or 12:30 p.m. Often participants wanted to push back meal time, so this meant that the afternoon presentation started before lunch, required a break in the flow, and continued on the other side of the lunch hour. When designing a program for India, try to schedule the lunch break no earlier than 12:45 p.m.

Spices at an open-air market in Delhi. Indians eat most of their meals later in the day than those in the West.

A related challenge with lunch was pointed out by a colleague from the United States who was co-facilitating. When we finally took a break for lunch, she asked why she was not informed about the lavish spread for the meal. She wondered if anyone would be alert enough in her session after lunch. In India, unless the training course is happening in the office, lunch is always an extravagant affair. When in a hotel, lunch is invariably a large buffet, including regional dishes, international dishes, a choice of salads, and at least five desserts. This great meal, coupled with Indians' natural penchant for a siesta, creates a huge challenge for the trainer in the afternoon. Be ready with a handful of energizers.

Customs: Body Language Dos and Don'ts

Indian participants in training programs exhibit complex body language that can be confusing to an outsider. And while almost all Indians are proficient in English, it is not their native language. Combine that with the thick accent that varies from state to state, and trying to decipher what is said can create an interesting situation for a non-Indian trainer.

Body language and cultural nuances change when moving from one part of India to another. However, there are still some common aspects that you can keep in mind.

For example, something that can confuse and even mislead any non-Indian trainer immediately is what is commonly known as the Indian Head Shake. Indians move their heads in an incredibly flexible way to convey various messages, ranging from a simple yes or no to admiration or confusion to agreement or frustration. When it comes to communicating, our heads are like Swiss Army knives—serving multiple purposes with just a slight change in the way the tool is used. It is too complex to list all the possible variations. Be extremely open-minded and nonjudgmental when you see someone shaking their head. Just be sure to ask them what they mean and then reconfirm it.

Another general trend is that Indians are not very comfortable with physical contact. Although this is changing rapidly, especially in the corporate context, it is not very common for people of opposite gender to greet each other with a hug. In the business context, it is OK to shake hands, but accept that some of the women may not be very comfortable shaking hands with a male trainer and may offer a limp handshake or just a nod with a smile. In team-building activities, it is best to put men and women in different teams if it involves close physical contact. However, if the audience consists of younger participants (under 30), they will be much more comfortable in their body language compared with people from older generations.

Finally, it is considered rude to consume food while in class—for both participants and trainers. For example, some trainers from the United States bring breakfast into class. In India, such behavior will evoke expressions ranging from shock to disgust. In some cases, people bring tea or coffee to class, but trainers should consume any food or beverage outside the class to maintain a professional demeanor when conducting the session.

Climate: Create a Warm Learning Environment

Indians are inherently friendly people who are more than willing to share everything, from their food to their life stories, with others—even strangers. At the same time, due to a multitude of cultural factors, they also take longer to open up to foreigners. Their sensibilities, especially when it comes to humor, are different from and more conservative than Westerners'. So some techniques that help trainers create rapport with an international audience may not be very effective while training in India. Here are some suggestions for creating a warm and friendly learning environment.

Local References

Despite so many differences, there are two factors that bind Indians across the country: the movie industry (Bollywood) and their love for the game of cricket. The quickest and surest way to connect with the audience is to bring in some references to either of these. Bollywood is more popular in northern and central parts of India than in southern areas, which have their own movie industry. However, cricket is the common religion of the country. Referring to cricket legends and Bollywood movies is bound to bring down the barriers that participants may have with trainers from another country. Even if you're unable to find something that perfectly matches the training program's message, the fact that you attempted to relate it to what the country is passionate about will create an instant rapport with the audience.

Cricket is a favorite sport for many Indians across the country.

Appreciation

Indians who are otherwise warmhearted and generous are extremely reluctant to voice their appreciation to people. There is a drastic difference in the amount of encouragement a child receives while growing up in the West versus India. Traditionally, the patriarchs—be it fathers or teachers—provide more criticism than applause to a child. Many Indian managers are very uncomfortable giving praise to their employees, and it is not uncommon to come across a participant who cannot recall the last time their bosses showed appreciation. However, this cultural dimension also provides an opportunity as a facilitator. Find something to appreciate and acknowledge the participants for in class. Doing so creates a tremendous amount of gratitude and goodwill. Because the trainer is seen as an authority figure in the classroom, it will be greatly valued.

Humor

Although it has started changing, Indians do not laugh at themselves easily; self-deprecating jokes and roasts are still rare. Although in India there are stereotypes of almost every linguistic segment, they do not take kindly to humor that makes fun of them. As a trainer, use humor but avoid cracking jokes on Indian idiosyncrasies, even if you find the participant initiating the discussion.

Also, because of cultural differences, Indians may not get the jokes that a Westerner tells. One time during a train-the-trainer session, a new trainer went to the master trainer, who was from the United States, asking for suggestions on how to close the day. "Just tell them to get the hell out of here!" was what the master trainer casually suggested. The candidate confidently walked to the front of the room, and with a very professional tone and genuine expression, announced, "It is the end of the day. Now get the hell out of here." The master trainer could not understand how an otherwise sharp trainer did not get the joke. That said, a younger audience will be more open to the Western brand of humor than their older colleagues.

Things to Consider: Handle Classroom Challenges

Most of the Indian trainees will try hard to establish a relationship and seek the trainer's attention. If you find a few trainees who are hesitant to establish eye contact or form a bond with the trainer, realize it may be due to their inherent fear of making a mistake, not being understood, or not understanding due to language limitations or accent issues.

A trainer from the West needs to be cognizant of this fact. Try to identify such trainees and establish trust and a relationship with them privately. Keep in mind these two other issues:

Time

A trainer who is unfamiliar with India can work around time challenges. Factor in Indian stretch time when planning sessions. Do not over-interpret lateness as a rude or disrespectful behavior, but more as a cultural norm. Announce the starting time for the session, and after the break, invite participants to use the times on their phones versus their watches, which may all be set to different times. Also, since the stretched definition of time applies even to closing time, you can extend the end of the day without any major complaints from the audience.

Competitiveness

Indian audiences are very competitive. In almost any exercise or activity, they want to get ahead of others and win. This desire to win, combined with their focus on the outcome rather than the process, may lead them to find shortcuts in the classroom exercises. This competitiveness is a double-edged sword that can either be leveraged by a trainer or wreak havoc in a session.

Use this competitiveness as an advantage. For example, an incredibly effective trick is giving points to teams for various positive contributions during the day and deducting points for any fault, like coming back late from breaks. Although the points don't have real value, the sheer competitiveness of an average Indian makes them attach tremendous value to them. The first time I announced that five points would be deducted for each person coming late to the class or from the break, I was surprised to see people running to reach the class. Another example is giving a quiz every day to teams about what they learned the previous day. When I used this trick, the participants' desire to win led them to get together every evening to study the content of the day, and it worked great for learning retention. However, after a couple of days, they worked out an agreement among themselves: Instead of everyone studying all the content every day, they divided each day among the team. Then only one person studied the topics each day to be able to answer on the team's behalf. Of course, the rules have to be modified to keep up with the changing competitive nature of the teams.

Tips and Warnings: Advice for Nonnative Trainers

Here are a few things to keep in mind when working in the Indian culture.

Food

Indians are passionate about the mind-boggling range of cuisines available in India. Not all Indian food is spicy, so it is possible to choose dishes that are not heavy on spices, especially if you're training in a good hotel. Sharing food and food habits and being daring during lunch and coffee breaks (or tea breaks, to be precise) will immediately make you accepted.

English

Although Indians are fluent in English, they are not native speakers of that language. Most of the education in urban areas is in English. At the same time, most Indians study either Hindi or another native language in school. Many times, an Indian will think in their mother tongue and translate it into English while speaking. The translating makes it slightly difficult for trainers to understand participants, and for them to understand the trainers.

Names

Although younger generations and people working in multinationals are accustomed to calling one another by first names, many Indians are not comfortable calling their seniors by the first name. As a trainer, expect many people to refer to you as *sir* or *ma'am*, which is also how they addressed their schoolteachers while growing up. So *sir* or *ma'am* means not only respect, but specifically a respected teacher. Most participants will be OK with being called by their first names. In fact, I trained for a company where everyone addressed one another by their surname, but after I started to address them by their first names, participants listed it as one of the best parts of the course. Some Indian names are very long and complicated, especially in the south. However, most of them will either use a short name, such as *Ramki* for *Ramakrishna,* or initials, such as *VS* for *Venkatesh Somayajulu.*

Language

Learn a few words of Hindi to create instant goodwill. *Namaste* is a universal greeting. *Shukriya* is thank you. Moreover, if either of these greetings are used with folded hands, which is a sign of respect and not surrender, the effect is multiplied.

Bon Voyage

Hopefully this chapter has provided some enlightenment for training Indian audiences. Despite the country's challenges and peculiarities, be assured that the experience will be extremely enriching, both personally and professionally. Enjoy the magic of Indian hospitality and intellect during training days. If there is any way I can be of help, reach out to me at kedarvashi@gmail.com.

***

About the Author

Kedar Vashi is the director for learning and development for Coca-Cola's Bottling Investment Group (BIG), where he oversees leadership development of more than 40,000 employees spread across 17 countries. His areas of expertise include leadership development, talent management, knowledge management, coaching and mentoring, and behavioral competency training. He is also a Global Master Facilitator for some of Coca-Cola's topmost leadership development programs.

Prior to joining Coca-Cola, Kedar served as vice president for trainer development and delivery for Dale Carnegie Training's Indian operations. He was also a Master Trainer and part of Dale

Carnegie's Global Delivery Team, and has trained participants from across the globe on some of the Dale Carnegie Leadership Modules.

Kedar is a very active member of the L&D community in India, passionately partnering with various forums for supporting its growth. In recognition of his long-standing contribution, he was named one of the Top Training & Development Professionals in India by the World HRD Congress in 2013, and received the Training Leadership Award from the Asia Pacific HRM Congress in 2015.

References

Chakraberty, S. 2017. "India Now Has 462 Million Internet Users." Tech in Asia, January 26. www.techinasia.com/india-462-million-internet-users-79-traffic-mobile.

GSMA. 2016. *The Mobile Economy India 2016.* London: GSMA. www.gsma.com/mobileeconomy/india.

Mehta, I. 2016. "India Jumps From 114 To 105 In Internet Speed Ranking, Still Lowest in Asia-Pacific." Huffington Post, December 23. www.huffingtonpost.in/2016/12/23/india-jumps-from-114-to-105-in-internet-speed-ranking-still-low_a_21640732.

Peterson, E.R., C.R. McCaffrey, and A. Sillman. n.d. "Where Are the Global Millennials?" A.T. Kearney Global Business Policy Council. www.atkearney.com/web/global-business-policy-council/article?/a/where-are-the-global-millennials-.

7

Japan

Matthew Axvig

My adventure in the Land of the Rising Sun began in 1997, after taking a teaching job in the small town of Awano, Japan. This traditional rural community, which grows the best strawberries in the world, was a perfect complement to my small-family-farm upbringing on the High Plains of North Dakota.

My teaching responsibilities included instructing first through sixth grades. Teaching was a great way to learn about the Japanese culture and education system, and I stopped using U.S. slang, idioms, and challenging vocabulary pretty fast. Such complexities and nuances are a barrier to communication when working in a foreign country.

Moving to Tokyo in 2000 opened business opportunities for me. Seventeen years later, as a manager at a corporate training firm, I have worked with hundreds of foreign and domestic companies, learning a great deal about the Japanese business and training culture in the process.

Perhaps one of the most interesting lessons I have acquired is the understanding of Japanese learning environments. When doing corporate training in Japan, you need to be flexible toward the learning environment provided. Some companies do not think cosmetic improvements to facilities are necessary. For example, one company offered a room that doubled as the smoking lounge. The once-white walls were stained brown, and it was necessary to open the window to prevent participants from getting a headache.

Another lesson is that complaining might cause you to lose the contract. The environment can significantly influence the quality of training, but complaining about how it looks is not the answer. What is necessary is a little forethought and due diligence to circumvent the more undesirable situations diplomatically. For example, visiting the client's training facility or asking for a few photos of the training room before choosing a location can help to avoid uncomfortable arrangements. Start by explaining the challenge and what help is needed. Be careful to phrase it in a way that doesn't blame anyone. Emphasize what might make the situation better, and using a teamwork approach, develop a solution. A teamwork approach is the best option for almost any talent development problem faced in Japan.

People and Culture: Get to Know Your Audience

Japan is a country dedicated to detail, tradition, and hard work. The Japanese are very respectful and polite. Even if participants see or hear a mistake, they will not point it out. That's because in Japan teachers (sensei) are expected to be all-knowing. While training, if you make a mistake, nonchalantly correct the mistake and advance to the next topic. Also, answer any challenging questions as well as possible and then check on it later. In one instance, a company had to replace a facilitator who was otherwise knowledgeable and talented. The instructor was asked in a meeting skills class how to spell a word. He did not know and replied that he was terrible at spelling. The students thought that if he could not spell this word, he was not qualified to teach this meeting skills class. Modesty is an admired quality in Japan, but be careful not to be too self-effacing.

Many Japanese people define their sense of self through the company that they work for, the position that they hold, the team that they are on, and their age. Most individuals like to work in groups and don't like to be singled out. Often, they will even fake mistakes to not outperform the senior members of their group. They are very hardworking, sometimes to the detriment of their health. Many Japanese people have a tough time saying no and setting limits. Most tend to appreciate orderliness and very clear, distinct, right and wrong ways of doing things. Harmony within training and society is a crucial concept to maintain at all costs.

In many cultures, the customer is considered to be always right. Japan takes that belief to an even higher level. In fact, even when the client is obviously wrong, they are still right. When dealing with customers, it is necessary to keep this in mind and avoid language that uses the subject *you* too often. The second person is rarely used in Japanese because it can seem too direct. For example, the sentence, "You need to send the payment by Tuesday" would be more commonly expressed as, "It would be good if the payment was made next week." Normally, native English speakers do not speak in the passive voice, but the Japanese often do.

The following tips will help you have more effective interactions with Japanese audiences:

- **Engage the group.** Participants will not interrupt when an instructor is speaking; it is considered very impolite to interrupt or to ask questions. Many who are not familiar with this communication style misinterpret it to be boredom or disinterest. As a facilitator, you should encourage participation.
- **Frame questions.** Be sure to ask questions in a way that does not require individuals to commit too strongly to an opinion. Ask a question that participants can answer with a "We Japanese do X" format.
- **Remember that Japanese culture is homogeneous and individualism is not encouraged.** There is a Japanese saying that loosely means "a nail that stands up from the floor must be hammered down." Manage the participants in a way that they do not feel forced to stand out too much. Making them stand out in front of their supervisors can make them very uncomfortable.
- **Get to know participants.** Many companies in Japan periodically have their employees take the Test of English for International Communication (TOEIC) to get a better understanding of their language needs. It would be helpful to ask for a list of the participants with their departments and TOEIC scores. However, some of these scores might be old and won't accurately reflect an individual's ability to speak English. This information is considered very sensitive and confidential. After the program is finished, copies should be shredded or deleted.

- **Be specific about time.** The Japanese are flexible in regard to doing exercises and accomplishing tasks. Be specific about how long a certain task should take. It is often better to assign a shorter timeframe and add a minute or two if needed than to give too much time and have participants struggling to do the task slowly enough to fill the time allotted.

Getting Started: Conduct a Needs Assessment

For many big Japanese corporations, the idea of providing lifelong employment to their workers remains a social obligation. There is a need to balance this commitment and respond to the competitive pressures of the global market. In other cultures, the competitive marketplace might result in a downsizing of the labor force. Instead, Japanese corporations are shifting some of the workloads from severely overworked, salaried workers to temp staff and part-time employees. Japanese companies are caught between a rock and a hard place because they cannot fire any employees due to public condemnation. But there is always market pressure to improve business, increase sales, maximize profits, and grow the company. Many companies approach this situation with a make-do attitude.

Because of the mix of lifelong salaried employees and temp workers, corporations often see mentorship as the most expedient way to train employees. Companies have been using this approach for many years and can benefit from external consulting and training.

Convincing a client of the need for a formalized training program may not be easy. But when the client is ready, always conduct a respectful, thorough needs analysis discussion. Following are some suggested behaviors and activities.

Start With the Right Attitude

Don't be rigid and fight the Japanese culture, assuming your way is the best way. Instead, be open-minded and accepting of the Japanese way. Learn from it and work with it to achieve goals.

Ask Questions, Then Listen Carefully

It is important to have a clear idea of what exactly the client wants and needs. It may be especially difficult in Japan due to the cultural tendency of answering questions vaguely and politely. It is imperative to listen closely to get to the core issue of any problem. The Japanese will try to avoid as much confrontation as possible, so phrasing questions in general terms that don't specifically single out any individual enables a deeper understanding of the main contributing factors and the client's true needs. An example of such a question might be, "What are some problems that managers face in Japan?" or "What do you think are some of the challenges that workers face in your industry?"

Gather Additional Information

If the training course is in English, the first consideration should be the audience's English skill level. Most talent managers in Japan rely heavily on TOEIC scores to reflect the participants' English-language ability. Unfortunately, TOEIC focuses mainly on reading, listening, and grammar comprehension, not speaking ability. The students' jobs and how frequently they interact in English is a much better reflection of their actual abilities. Be prepared to adjust visual aids and support materials accordingly. A short teleconference should give you a good sample of their language skills. The teleconference is also an opportunity to ask participants about workshop expectations.

Confirm Targeted Outcomes

Once you have a clear understanding of the client's needs, confirm the target outcome with the sponsor or training program organizer so that they have a clear understanding of what will be achieved in training. Confirmation is particularly important in Japan because it is often the only time when the client will offer additional information or guidance. Most Japanese clients expect the trainer to have the expertise to assess the situation, define what the program should achieve, and provide a professional solution. Many talent development managers still confuse wants with needs, so it is often helpful to clarify with them what the program will target and how that connects to the company's goals.

In Japan, a common misleading want of human resource departments is to provide English-language training so that employees will be more global, even though the company itself does not have any English-speaking business partners or overseas offices. By accepting such a want as the goal of the program, both teachers and students become demotivated. They know they are wasting time, energy, and money on skills that most likely will never be put to use.

Itineraries: Plan the Learning Journey

The most common form of instruction in Japan is a lecture format, where participants politely listen without interrupting the lecturer. If there is too much deviation from that expectation, talent managers and participants may become uncomfortable. For the most part, role plays, simulations, group discussions, and pair work are acceptable skill-building activities. Games of any sort are considered unprofessional and should be avoided. In Japan, around 60 percent of training is instructor-led, another 20 percent is in the form of asynchronous learning systems, and the remainder is mostly structured, on-the-job training. Mobile learning is slowly increasing in popularity, but human resource managers still favor small group classes because of the personalized attention they provide.

Design learning methods that focus on a collaborative effort. The Japanese are excellent at working in groups and are more comfortable with expressing what they have learned from an exercise as a group than individually. However, it is usually uncomfortable for participants to give other members constructive criticism, so pair work often results in flowery, ambiguous feedback. Group-oriented activities where participants are allowed to connect feedback to content will work better, so no feelings are hurt. Periodically ask participants what they found interesting in the lesson and how they might use the targeted skill or knowledge in their jobs. This question should be thrown out to the whole class to avoid putting any individual on the spot. Questions can be used to get more accurate examples that connect with the participants as well as to help segue to the next section.

Measure success without making participants feel uneasy. While most Japanese people are uncomfortable evaluating others, they are often overly critical of their own performance. One effective way of getting a critical evaluation is to have each participant list what they thought they did well and where they thought they could improve. Ask the most active members in the class if they would like to share their list. During this time, help participants balance their modesty with praise and temper their harsh criticism with perspective. In Japan, many human resource departments and training companies conduct Level 1 of the Kirkpatrick four levels of evaluation in the form of smile sheets. Less than 10 percent conduct Level 2 evaluations, and Levels 3 and 4 occur only in very large companies with global operations.

Follow-up training and social learning aren't common. According to Apex Research, the most popular social media app in 2015 was Line, with 50 million (40 percent of Japan's population) monthly active users. Twitter came in second with 26 million, Facebook took a close third with 22 million, and LinkedIn was a distant fourth place with only 340,000 Japanese users (Charles 2015). It is very rare for clients to request follow-up training and even more extraordinary for them to ask for training that incorporates a social media element.

Packing Lists: Logistics, Technology, and Resources

Technology limitations are rare in Japan. Most companies have projectors, screens, extension cords, tables, chairs, and whiteboards. Bring any specific adapters or connectors that might be needed. The electric outlets in Japan have the same plug-in configuration as America, but are only 100 volts.

Flipcharts are not included in most classrooms. If a flipchart is needed, give the company advance notice. Whiteboards are found in most business meeting rooms.

Ask the organizer of the event about transportation. Japan has an excellent mass transit system. Most signs are written in Japanese and English, as well as in Korean and Chinese on some of the bigger train lines. Navigating with so many people is the most challenging part of the system. Some of the more congested stations, like those of the Yamanote circle line, are almost frightening during rush hour, which is 7:30-8:30 a.m. and 5-6 p.m. Plan accordingly and allow an extra half an hour to an hour to get to your destination. Taxis are also an option, and are relatively inexpensive if the destination is not very far.

Bring many business cards. Whenever meeting someone new in Japan, especially talent development personnel or upper management, exchange business cards to learn how to address each other properly. When you present your business card, hold it out with both hands and introduce yourself. When receiving someone's business card, take it with both hands and spend just a few seconds looking over the details to show interest in who they are, their position, and their department.

Review visa requirements. Depending on your nationality, you may need a visa to enter Japan. If the stay is more than 90 days, a proper work visa is required, and the application process can take several months.

Japan is a gift-giving culture. As a gesture of appreciation, consider bringing a box of chocolates or candies from your local community for the sponsor or main organizer of the training event. The key is that it should be something they can easily share with others in their office.

A subway station in Tokyo. Most signs in subway stations are written in English and Japanese.

Customs: Body Language Dos and Don'ts

It is important to be aware of the following body language dos and don'ts.

Appearance and Gestures

Appearance is paramount. The Japanese expect facilitators to always dress as business professionals. For men, this means a suit coat, preferably black, with matching dress pants, a tie, a nice dress shirt, and dress shoes. Women have a little more flexibility with dresses and blouses, but should wear similar formal attire. Please don't take this lightly. The Japanese are very attentive to detail and are prone to making broad assumptions about professionalism based on appearances.

You also may have to exchange your shoes for slippers. It all depends on the company and facility, but don't be surprised if you're asked to put on slippers at the entrance. It might seem that the cheap plastic slippers clash with formal business attire, but for some companies, wearing slippers is still a major tradition and refusing to do so isn't good manners. A word of caution regarding stairs and bathrooms. Going up and down stairs can be dangerous in slippers. As for restrooms, most likely there will be special slippers to be worn within the confines of the bathroom. To become instantly famous, forget to take off the toilet slippers and wear them into the classroom.

Don't put your hands in your pockets or chew gum. In general, the Japanese view both of these habits as very unprofessional. In fact, a boss of mine once said that walking around with toilet paper dragging from one shoe would be more acceptable than chewing gum in class.

Be careful not to make too much eye contact. The Japanese can misinterpret this as aggression or flirtation. Likewise, when Japanese people look away when they are speaking, don't misread this as them being untruthful or aloof.

Introductions and exits are critical. The Japanese bow when they greet people and when they say goodbye to show respect. The depth of the bow represents how much respect is given to that individual. Foreigners are not expected to bow. In fact, an incorrect bow may give insult. It is advisable to stick with a handshake. However, most Japanese people do not have much experience shaking hands, so they often hold a hand too long, too hard, too softly, or just strangely. It will be up to you to shake and let go. Most physical contact beyond a handshake when making introductions or saying goodbye makes Japanese people feel quite uncomfortable.

Avoid pointing with your index finger. Usually, the whole hand is used to direct attention. When asking a Japanese person to come over to you, it is best to use the Japanese "come here" gesture, with palm and fingers down while pulling the hand toward the body a few times. The Western gesture of palm and fingers up while closing to a fist several times quickly is not used in Japan. One of the only times that Japanese people use their index fingers to point is when they are referring to themselves. When they do this, they will point to their noses, not their chest.

Space, Speech, and Phone Etiquette

Be respectful of personal space. Contrary to what it seems by looking at a packed 8 a.m. train in Tokyo, the Japanese are uncomfortable with people moving into their personal space. Of course, this can vary with individuals, but be aware of standing too close. When Japanese people start to step back, move into a more closed posture, or begin looking away, most likely they are starting to feel uncomfortable. Approximately one arm's length away is a comfortable distance when speaking to someone who is Japanese.

Be mindful of speaking too loudly when in public spaces. In the classroom, speak as loud as needed, but on a train or in a lobby, lounge, hallway, restaurant, or elevator, a lowered voice is expected so as not to disturb others.

Checking your cell phone in class is a big mistake. It is only acceptable during breaks. Viewed as terrible manners, it is unprofessional, especially of a facilitator.

If on the train, do not talk on the phone unless it is an emergency, because it is very upsetting to many Japanese people. With that said, texting, emailing, listening to music, watching videos, and playing video games with headphones on are all acceptable behaviors when on the train. The key here is not to make any loud noise that might bother others.

Social Interactions

Drinking is a part of doing business in Japan, and taking clients out for drinks or dinner is common. This custom functions as a way for Japanese to connect and communicate in a less formal environment. Eating and drinking together after a training class helps to establish goodwill, promote open communication, strengthen team spirit, and defuse any conflicts that might have occurred during the day. A few things to note:

- Let the organizer of the event tell people where to sit. Seniority determines the protocol and seating arrangement. It is best to allow the leader to sit first.

- It is bad manners to allow someone to pour their own drink, and it is especially injurious for guests and senior staff to pour their own. The host will feel obligated to keep glasses full. When someone is refilling a glass, it is customary to hold the glass up with both hands, and after they have filled the glass, say thank you (*arigato gozaimasu*) or thanks (*domo*).
- Don't start drinking until the first toast is made. After that, drink freely. Sometime during the event, it would be a very nice gesture on your part to make a short toast thanking specific hosts as well as the support staff in general. When you make a toast, stand up and give people a small head nod or bow. At the end of the toast, say "Cheers!" (*kanpai*).

Many Japanese businesses require you to trade your shoes for slippers while in the office.

Climate: Create a Warm Learning Environment

Participants are respectful of their instructors and managers. Professor Geert Hofstede's work on cultural dimensions describes the Power Distance Index, which measures the equality of workers and supervisors. Japan is a high-barrier culture: It is unacceptable to speak up or confront someone in a leadership role.

Sometimes more senior executives confuse their role and believe they are there to critique the lesson, not participate. One way to get them on board is to recognize their position and experience. Involve them by asking for their expert opinion on what they believe it is important to learn from the exercise or training course, as well as how it might relate to their jobs. Other things to do:

- **Focus on building confidence and enthusiasm.** As Emerson once said, "Nothing was ever achieved without enthusiasm." This is also true with any learning journey. Many Japanese people suppress the expression of self-confidence, seeing it as an aspect of pride or vanity. It is the instructor's responsibility to bring energy and enthusiasm into the learning environment by stating how the class is making progress and connecting the learning objectives. One way to do this is by having each participant group list what they can now do better because of the exercise. Endorsing these improvements will also set the tone for how the participants will view these accomplishments.
- **Be energetic and animated.** The Japanese like energetic, happy, and animated instructors. A good way to set the tone and start the lesson on a high note is to greet them with an energetic "Welcome!" It might be their first time meeting a foreigner, and this will help them quickly get over any shyness. It is reassuring for them to see assertiveness so they can be comfortable with you taking the lead in the interaction.
- **Pay attention to seating arrangements.** The Japanese appreciate when the host assigns seats because they will not have to figure out who should sit where according to seniority or protocol.
- **Refreshments are not required.** It is not standard practice to provide refreshments for training events.

Beyond bottled water, candies or occasionally a pot of coffee may be offered. Most participants and facilitators expect to bring their own refreshments or get them from vending machines during breaks. That is not to say that students would not appreciate such amenities; it is just a practice that has been slow to catch on.

Things to Consider: Handle Classroom Challenges

Many Japanese people do not feel comfortable standing out and expressing opinions, especially if it is on a controversial topic. To get much more honest and open responses, frame questions as hypothetical and ask for the group's opinion. For example, instead of asking individuals, "What are some problems that you have in your office?" it would be better to ask each table, "What might be some problems that Japanese people have in major foreign companies?" Here are some other classroom challenges to keep in mind:

- The Japanese are quite comfortable with silence, and this sometimes gets misinterpreted as acceptance, anger, or disinterest. To get a more dynamic two-way exchange, explain that feedback helps English speakers to know if the audience understands and whether they can move on to the next topic.
- To be inclusive of most English-proficiency levels, simplify the language on learning materials and provide Japanese-language support through translated subtitles. Simplification means avoiding slang, idioms, difficult vocabulary, and complex sentence structure. The focus should be on explaining content as simply as possible.
- Role plays are a popular training technique. Remember to make a clear distinction between participating in the role play and giving feedback in instructor mode. One way I do this is by taking off my suit jacket while role-playing and putting it back on before commenting or giving advice. When doing role plays, be careful not to

lose the natural, realistic speed and tempo of speaking. It will better prepare participants for the real world.

- It is not uncommon for managers and their direct reports to take classes together. If the manager is very supportive and open-minded, they can be very helpful by modeling good participation. However, sometimes power differences get in the way, where students with better skills tone them down to match those of the manager. One way to counteract this is to do more activities in pairs and smaller groups. Frequently changing group arrangements will help minimize that person's effects.

Tips and Warnings: Advice for Nonnative Trainers

The following is a list of important information to keep in mind:

- **Listen carefully.** Japanese training participants tend to voice complaints very subtly. Make it a goal to listen more than speak. The Japanese are very gracious audiences. It would be advisable to periodically ask if they are comfortable or if they have any questions or comments.
- **Arrive five to 10 minutes before the scheduled meeting time.** It's considered poor manners to make Japanese participants wait. Trains run like clockwork in Japan, but occasionally there might be a delay. If this happens, it is imperative to contact the manager or another person from the client's organization immediately to tell them about the delay and to adjust the meeting time.
- **Show respect to the senior members of the team or group.** It is a smart idea to recognize the experience of senior members to get their buy-in and participation in the classroom. Their level of involvement will often set the tone and level of what is acceptable participation for other colleagues in the room.

- **Be comfortable with less concrete answers.** Avoid confrontations at all costs so as not to upset others. The Japanese have mastered the art of speaking in ambiguous, noncommittal language. Sometimes foreigners find this terribly frustrating and push Japanese people to speak with less ambiguity, but for the Japanese, this can feel very harsh and too frank.
- **Be careful not to overemphasize individual achievement.** The Japanese get much more satisfaction from group accomplishments. Allow participants to think on their own first, and then share their ideas with their group. Finally, have the group report their consensus on the topic.
- **Don't rush the consensus process.** At the beginning of a project, Japanese people need time to form a consensus on how to proceed as a team. The teams will move quickly after reaching an agreement, because everyone knows their roles.

Bon Voyage

Teaching in Japan is exciting and rewarding. The Japanese culture is a vibrant mix of traditional values and modern approaches to doing business. Japanese society keeps in touch with its past, while adapting to an increasingly global community. Most Japanese workers understand that being competitive means being more global, and they are now actively exploring what that means for their company, their team, and their job. Japanese learners have a very positive attitude toward learning; they study very hard and are quite appreciative of the guidance and expertise that foreign trainers can provide. Additionally, corporate Japan has immense and varied training needs. The country holds a wealth of opportunities for those willing to navigate the cultural sensitivities and understand the way Japan does business.

About the Author

Matthew Axvig grew up on a small farm on the Great Plains of North Dakota. He attended the University of North Dakota and studied Russian at the Pushkin Institute in Moscow. After graduating with a bachelor's degree in Russian and minors in space studies and biology, he spent four years in Awano, Japan, where he worked on sister city projects and educational programs as the city's international projects coordinator. In 2000, he moved to Tokyo and began his career as a corporate trainer. A year later, he became HR administrator and was put in charge of trainer recruitment, curriculum design, teaching, and logistics. In 2005, he accepted a similar position at another Tokyo-based training firm, where he now manages more than 40 consultants and has designed, developed, and delivered training programs for hundreds of domestic and foreign companies throughout Japan. Matthew earned the Certified Professional in Learning and Performance credential in 2015 and the Master Trainer certification in 2016.

Reference

Charles, K. 2015. "5 Things U.S. Techies Need to Know About Japan's Social Media System." VentureBeat, November 28. https://venturebeat.com/2015/11/28/5-things-us-techies-need-to-know-about-japans-social-media-ecosystem.

8

South Korea

Chan Lee

During the Asian financial crisis in the late 1990s, I was assigned to the HR department of a major toy manufacturer in Korea. My first assignment was not the development of human resources, but instead, laying people off through performance assessment. I had to dismiss several people who had worked, ate, and drank with me just a couple of days earlier. Neither their performance nor their competencies defined them as underperformers. Still, assessments were made to identify personnel with comparably less performance outcome.

The layoffs were inevitable, because the crisis forced Korean corporations to go through restructuring and reduce the size of their workforce. It was a brutal and unforgettable experience. But it sparked my genuine interest in developing and managing human resources, and I decided to pursue an academic career as an HRD professional.

Today, I work as a scholar, consultant, and professor of HRD in Korea. Through 12 years of experience in the field and with the accomplishments of my research team, I have followed Korea's trends in and its forward-looking vision of human resource management and development based on the deeper understanding of Korean people and workplace culture.

Korea is famous for its cultural and technological advances. South Korea's rapid economic development—from a war-torn wasteland to the world's 11th-largest economy (Rauhala 2012)—has been heralded around the world as one of the primary examples of developing countries. Also, Korean culture has seen a recent surge in popularity, led by generations that are deeply connected with online media. *Hallyu,* or Korean Wave, is now on trend, along with Korean pop music (K-pop), cinema, and drama.

Korea's cultural popularity has resulted in various projects on official development assistance and on benchmarking of foreign companies, especially in the field of HRD. Developing countries in Southeast Asia are adopting the HRD systems and structures of the

Korean government, and various foreign companies are trying to benchmark the best cases of HRD in Korean companies.

Still, we have a long way to go; Koreans have struggled to keep up with global HRD trends and incorporate them into their HR structure. Traditionally, Korean corporate culture is strictly hierarchical. From time to time, this creates tension as Korean companies strive to innovate into more globalized companies and set a new tone for the internal culture, allowing junior staff to speak and act freely.

Throughout my journey to innovate Korean HRD, I have observed many different responses among Korean HRD professionals and others. Some people were reluctant to adopt new methodologies, casting doubt on their effectiveness; others were eager to try new, innovative solutions. These days in Korea, a plethora of businesses are attempting to change their culture, people, and management practices to keep up with the ever-shifting global environment. Thus, it is truly important to understand the country to follow its fast-paced HRD trend. I hope this chapter will be a useful guide to grasping Korean audiences and their culture.

People and Culture: Get to Know Your Audience

The population of South Korea is just over 50 million. Despite the influx of foreign workers, the population is relatively homogeneous; approximately 96 percent is native Korean, with people from China, the United States, Vietnam, and Thailand mostly comprising the remainder.

One remarkable thing about the Korean population is its unprecedented pace of aging. As of 2015, around 13.1 percent is elderly, which will soar to 40.1 percent in 2060, according to Statistics Korea (2015).

A residential area in Seoul. The population of South Korea is just over 50 million.

This rapid pace has two negative implications. First, it means the decline of economically active people. The shrinking labor force will likely have an adverse impact on the overall economy, including the deterioration of potential growth rate, decreased investment and expenditure, and a limited social insurance budget. An aging society may also lead to an imbalance between younger and older generations in the workplace. In response to this, organizations have been trying to bridge the gap between Millennials and older generations by raising awareness of each generation's unique traits.

Ironically, Korean society is famous for its vitality. According to the Better Life Index, published by OECD (2016), South Korea ranked third in average annual hours worked, approaching 2,124 hours annually, which is 354 hours more than the average among OECD-member countries. The long hours signify not only that Koreans are some of the most hardworking people in the world, but also that the imperative to work hard and play hard imbues Korean society. Similar to what Johan Huizinga (2014) described in *Homo Ludens*, a book about the play element of culture, Koreans value the meaning of their professions and pursue playfulness in their lives. In this sense, Korean audiences could be summed up with three keywords: fast-paced, adaptable, and playful.

Getting Started: Conduct a Needs Assessment

A needs assessment is crucial in designing training programs in Korea. Current HRD goals are to maximize the effectiveness of training solutions while minimizing travel and time out of the office. Corporations want training programs to deal with the constantly changing skill levels and tastes of Korean audiences.

Korea has the highest smartphone penetration in the world—nearly 90 percent of the population is using smartphones, according to the Pew Research Center (Poushter 2016). It is important to consider technology use when assessing needs. Mobile learning can be a great way to engage a large number of audiences with little effort. In particular, surveying people with a mobile messenger app would facilitate the process of accumulating data. HR analytics using big data have enabled Korean HRD professionals to assess their target audiences' individualized interests and motivations for learning.

Here are some recommended steps for conducting an effective needs assessment:

- **Define the trainer and trainee.** Before initiating a training session, carefully consider who the trainer and learners are and from which generation they come. For example, someone from an older generation may not be accustomed to using technology adeptly, or they might be unable to read small text written on a screen. It is a good idea to survey trainers and learners for technology proficiency if you are considering using any e-learning.
- **Make it concise and simple.** Korea has a *pali-pali* culture, which means "hurry up" or "faster" in the Korean language, and demonstrates their fast-paced, hardworking character. Korea's *pali-pali* culture is one of the driving forces behind the accelerated pace of development in every aspect of society. Given this trait, Koreans are accustomed to managing tasks and

working in a very fast and efficient manner. Try to make the assessment questions concise and straightforward. Otherwise, results might be vague.

- **Inform both participants and managers of how important training is.** We erroneously consider our customer in learning to be the audience (or participants). However, the managers (or departments) who are sending participants in the hope of performance development must also be considered customers. Unfortunately, some managers think it's inappropriate for direct reports to be doing something else during the working hours (even training), which may make the result of needs assessment invalid. Therefore, it is important to stress the importance of training to both the participants and management.
- **Get honest feedback in a needs assessment.** The concept of "face" (*kibun*), found in many Asian societies, also exists in Korea. Koreans strive for harmony in business relationships, avoiding confrontations and sometimes responding to needs assessment surveys with what the assessor wants to hear rather than identifying issues head-on. Westerners often find this approach confusing. Rephrasing needs assessment questions to a more indirect approach may be necessary: "If there were a typical obstacle a worker in that occupation faced, what might it be?" Koreans are very protective of personal dignity, so be very careful in business discussions about performance gaps and always be respectful and mindful of *kibun*.

Itineraries: Plan the Learning Journey

In the past, Korean companies were notorious for a strict corporate culture and centralized decision making. Many workers were required to show excessive employee loyalty and productivity, which would force them to work until late at night, skip holidays, or follow whatever their employers' orders might be.

However, as the Millennial generation begins making up more of the workforce, Korean companies are transforming. Millennials are not willing to sacrifice their private lives for their work and expect their workplace to be more democratic and free. Companies must transform their corporate culture and try something new and innovative—particularly in HRD—in response to their fresh and energetic audiences. Moreover, these audiences expect their learning to be engaging and fun.

Here are some practical strategies that could improve the learning experience.

It's Show Time!

Whenever I deliver sessions on HRD issues and trends, I use a multitude of visual examples that relate to the audience. People want to see how different HRD practices can be implemented in a real setting. Words are not enough. It is best to engage audiences by using all kinds of examples. Recently, I adopted a short clip from a television drama to show how communication between a boss and employee could get worse with poor coaching skills, which prompted a deep discussion.

Bridge the Generation Gap

Although the younger generation is more willing to share opinions about a freer corporate culture and work practices, a generation gap still exists. Existing hierarchical structures make the situation worse: In most cases, the older generation is working as executives or decision makers, while the younger generation is staff. Thus, their differences create a sense of disharmony that is often perceived as a conflict between employee and boss. A challenge, then, is to find ways to bridge the generation gap, breaking boundaries by creating a harmonized atmosphere, which provides a free flow of communication. A well-facilitated classroom discussion can open up the lines of communication.

Quench Workers' Technological Thirst

As some of the most connected workers in the world, Koreans show little reluctance to incorporating technology into their learning experience. Moreover, because Korean people show high adaptability to different technologies, HRD professionals should proactively integrate technological elements to improve workers' learning experiences. For instance, people can learn by using their smartphones. Learning takes place wherever or whenever the they want; they can select content based on their personal interest and motivation, creating authentic, self-directed learning.

Use Structured On-the-Job Training (S-OJT)

The changing generational composition of the Korean workplace provides a rationale for trainers to facilitate more practical and immediate learning, as companies strive to keep new talent from leaving. In a recent survey in Korea, 92.3 percent of team leaders who have hired new personnel responded that S-OJT was helpful, while 46.2 percent of new employees replied that S-OJT has significantly reduced their time to competency. Managers saw how it was useful for new workers to get training with content similar to actual work tasks. New employees thought it was easier to learn useful content necessary for the job compared with other training methods, and was more helpful with adjusting to a new workplace environment (Lee 2013).

Packing Lists: Logistics, Technology, and Resources

Most companies in Korea are up-to-date on the use of technologies. It is likely that companies will have projectors, screens, extension cords, tables, chairs, whiteboards, and e-stations. However, some companies may not have the latest versions of programs, such as Microsoft Office or the Windows operating system, which may cause compatibility issues. Always bring a laptop in case such matters occur. Also, if using any devices other than a PC or laptop with a Windows operating system, bring a connector for RGB cables, because many companies do not have cables compatible with Apple products. The electric outlets are 220 volts, unlike the ones used in America, so purchase a multiadapter. Here are a few more pieces of information to keep in mind:

- **Ask for a flipchart.** Although flipcharts are commonly used, some companies may not have them on-site, so do not forget to ask for one before your course.
- **You may have to ask for Wi-Fi access.** Wi-Fi access is limited. Although many businesses have Wi-Fi that is accessible for nonpersonnel, it may be necessary to ask for Wi-Fi access, because the primary Wi-Fi routers are password protected. Some companies may provide an extra computer that has access to the Internet when outside computers are prevented from connecting.
- **Ask the organizer of the event about transportation.** Most companies will provide transportation for your convenience, but if not, it is easy to use public transportation. Korea has a great mass transit system, and it is not exaggerating to say that getting anywhere in Seoul or a nearby city is easy with public transportation. Just purchase a rechargeable transportation card from the nearest convenience store or subway station and use it for any public transportation. These locations also have machines to reload transportation cards. Buses, subways, and even taxis accept the transportation card.
- **Bring business cards.** Exchanging business cards is East Asian etiquette. After shaking hands, immediately share a business card. This practice shows respect and properly introduces people. Some companies use e-business cards with phone applications, but most upper management still use the traditional business cards.
- **Check the visa status for your country.** Although South Korea shares a loosened visa system with many neighboring countries, it has strict visa requirements

for several nations. Don't forget to double check the visa status for your country.

Customs: Body Language Dos and Don'ts

Here are a few behaviors to keep in mind while training in Korea:

- **Appearance greatly affects impressions.** Koreans are very sensitive about appearances. They expect professionals to look like professionals, which means a man should dress in a formal suit and tie and a woman should wear business attire or a loose-fitting dress.
- **Bow slightly while shaking hands.** Bowing is important for cultures in East Asian countries, but Koreans do not expect full 90-degree bows from foreigners. A slight bow with a handshake may be the best way to show respect.
- **Receive with two hands.** There will be lots of giving and receiving during your stay in Korea. Using both hands is regarded as polite in Korean culture, including receiving gifts or even a handshake.
- **Keep eye contact.** Don't use too much direct eye contact, but show that you are paying attention. Too much looking away or looking at your phone may seem impolite and unfocused. To show respect, some Koreans may not make eye contact when in the presence of a perceived authority figure, such as an instructor. However, this is changing, so make and expect direct eye contact as an indication of honesty and interest.
- **Try not to have too much direct physical contact with someone who seems older.** This is seen as disrespectful, particularly touching on the head or shoulders, because many elders do such actions to children or people younger than them. Stay friendly, but try not to be too friendly before getting to know people.
- **Don't forget to share.** Sharing is something that is found commonly in Korean daily lives. It could start with just

sharing a piece of gum or utensils for writing. People will return things that are yours after they finish using them. Keep valuable belongings with you, but most things will stay where they were left.

- **If possible, don't cross your legs when sitting down.** This may be seen as disrespectful to others. Try keeping both legs on the ground, with the bottom of your shoes facing down.
- **Going out for food and drink is part of business in Korea.** Similar to other East Asian countries, Koreans expect to enjoy food and drinks after the official schedule to show gratitude and share welcoming remarks. Some even suggest going for a second round or more, which means to move to another place for additional drinks. It is OK to refuse politely.

Bulgogi, a classic Korean dish. Koreans enjoy going out for food and drinks at the end of a training program.

There are eating and drinking etiquette guidelines in Korean business culture; here are some to keep in mind:

- Usually, the oldest or highest-ranked person picks up chopsticks to eat, and the rest follow. If you're the highest-ranking person, they'll invite you to begin eating.
- The person in charge will most likely create the seating arrangements. Someone will invite people to sit in a designated seat, so wait for instructions.
- When drinking Korean alcohol such as *soju,* it is traditional to have someone pour a drink for you. Hold the glass with two hands, and wait for the cheers (cheers in Korean is *gun-bae*). When drinking, try to look away from the table or colleagues to show a gesture of respect.
- Try not to refuse drinks too strongly. If you cannot or do not drink, tell the host ahead of time so that they will not offer drinks in the first place.

Most important, Koreans in business will know you are from a foreign culture, and they will respect cultural differences. Many Korean businesspeople have a global mindset and know various customs and cultures from around the world, so they will do their best to make you feel comfortable. Do not take these recommendations too strictly; rather, they're to help you prepare for Korean culture. Demonstrating these behaviors gives the impression of a knowledgeable professional.

Climate: Create a Warm Learning Environment

In Korean culture, acknowledging age or rank difference is crucial to showing respect. The way to speak and react is different for people who are older or higher up than you, for people who are the same level, and for people who are younger or junior.

Therefore, in training sessions that consist of employees holding different positions, you're likely to see less input from participants in higher ranks. Create an environment that will encourage their full participation with these tactics:

- **For group activities, group people with similar positions or ranks.** When grouping individuals with diverse positions, it is common to see people in lower ranks doing most of the work. If you create groups of people with similar positions, you are nudging them to participate as equals within the team. They will be more open to share ideas and respect one another's ideas.

- **Try to form groups with men and women.** A group with both women and men is more likely to form more diverse ideas.
- **Avoid criticizing in public.** All criticism of participants should be conducted in private to reduce or prevent loss of face. It is also advisable to avoid opposing a participant in public as this, too, can mean a loss of face. Express opinion or concerns privately in a one-on-one situation.
- **Give participants time to consume snacks.** It is common to see refreshments and snacks provided for workshops and meetings. However, most of the time, they are located at the end of the room or outside. Give the participants plenty of time to eat, and let them bring snacks into the classroom to create a more relaxed environment.
- **Use humor.** Koreans love little puns and jokes within a session, but may show discomfort if you expect an active response from them. Watch their reactions to humor and decide if it is being well received.
- **Be humble.** In Korean culture, modesty and humility are important. Therefore, it is best to avoid overselling your credentials when beginning your session. Keep humility in mind also when meeting participants and assessing their skills. Participants might understate their abilities and knowledge in a topic to appear humble.

Things to Consider: Handle Classroom Challenges

The lecture format is the most common training method used for orientations or instruction. However, many group activities are also facilitated in Korean companies. Participants have experienced various group activities and lectures, so it should not be difficult to incorporate activities used in your culture. But because it's not as common a form of training, it is important to clarify what kinds of activities participants will perform, along with their outcomes. Clearly written explanations and examples will encourage active participation.

Here are some other situations to be aware of:

- Koreans are known for not speaking out loud or asking questions in front of people during a lecture. Instead, they will ask questions or express their ideas after the lecture is over by approaching you personally or contacting you through email. Be available to talk with participants during breaks and lunch, and be sure everyone has your email address.
- There may be significant differences between participants from different generations. Try not to make it visible, but help them help one another. It is also important to help them understand one another and embrace their ideas, because it may be hard to close the generation gap. If it seems like a group consisting of various generations will not work well together, create groups with members of the same generation. Once a group is working together well, do not change the team too soon. It may seem as if someone is being pulled away from the group.
- Never act as if your viewpoint or perspective is the right one. There are diverse views, and it is important to realize that as a foreigner. Sometimes, although you may be right, the participants may feel uncomfortable if pushed too hard to change their viewpoints. If it seems that the participants are having a hard time with your ideas, let it slide or try to find a more subtle way to influence them. Remember never to discriminate or put

down a participant's ideas or viewpoints, because it will bring conflict to the session.

- Sometimes it is hard for participants to find consensus. If so, don't force it; instead, remind people to embrace the opinions shared. In other words, facilitate consensus, but don't put down one opinion for another. Otherwise, the participation from those opposed will be lost.

Tips and Warnings: Advice for Nonnative Trainers

Here are a few final suggestions for working with Korean audiences:

- **Arrive at least 10 minutes before the scheduled meeting time.** It is considered bad manners to show up late, and most participants will be early. Use the time for personal introductions and getting to know people before the session begins. If you think you will be late, call someone in advance to let them know, and they will understand.
- **Let the senior members realize that you appreciate their participation because of how busy they may be.** Do not show less respect for the others, but it is crucial to acknowledge senior members' contributions.
- **When receiving input or answers that are not as clear or concrete as you'd like, work to get a clearer answer.** Usually, participants either believe that the question demanded such answers, or they feel uncomfortable giving out answers in long sentences. Koreans tend to shorten their answers to summarize all their ideas.

Bon Voyage

Nothing is more special than greeting Korean audiences in their language and thanking them in Korean. It is also a sign of respect. Consider using *Ahn-nyeong-ha-seh-yo* (hello), *Gam-sah-hap-ni-da* (thank you), or *An-yŏng-hi ju-mu-shŏ-ssŏ-yo* (good morning) in your introductions.

Remember that a pillar of Korea's Confucianist traditions is to demonstrate respect. Value the individual who has given their work time or personal time to come to the training session. When you start with respect, participants will return respect wholeheartedly.

* * *

About the Author

Chan Lee is a professor at Seoul National University in Korea, focused on vocational education and workforce development. Prior to his career in academia, Chan worked at LG Electronics as an HRD team leader. He holds a PhD and a master's degree in HRD from Ohio State University. Chan has been a speaker at ATD's International Conference & Exposition since 2006, and was a member of the conference's Program Advisory Committee in 2010 and 2011. He was a keynote speaker and one of the organizers for the ATD 2017 Korea Summit. He was also a speaker at ATD 2011 Singapore, ATD 2014 Taiwan, and the ATD 2015 Japan Summit. He contributed to the book *Implementing On-the-Job Learning,* part of the ASTD in Action series. Chan holds lectures and conducts research on strategic HRD, social learning, smart learning, performance management, coaching and leadership, theories and applications of job analysis, and structured on-the-job training in many countries.

References

Huizinga, J. 2014. *Homo Ludens: A Study of the Play Element in Culture.* Eastford, CT: Martino Fine Books.

Lee, C. 2013. "Analysis on Issues of Global HRD Trends in ASTD 2013 ICE & ISPI." *HRD Monthly* 274.

OECD (Organisation for Economic Co-operation and Development). 2016. *OECD Economic Survey of Korea 2016.* Paris: OECD Publishing. www.oecd.org/eco/economic-survey-korea.htm.

Poushter, J. 2016. *Smartphone Ownership and Internet Usage Continues to Climb in Emerging Economies.* Washington, D.C.: Pew Research Center.

Rauhala, E. 2012. "South Korea: One of the World's Great Success Stories Heads to the Polls." *Time,* December 6. http://world.time.com/2012/12/06/is-south-korea-the-greatest-success-story-of-the-last-century.

Statistics Korea. 2015. "Population Trends and Projections of the World and Korea." Statistics Korea, July 8. http://kostat.go.kr/portal/eng/pressReleases/8/8/index.

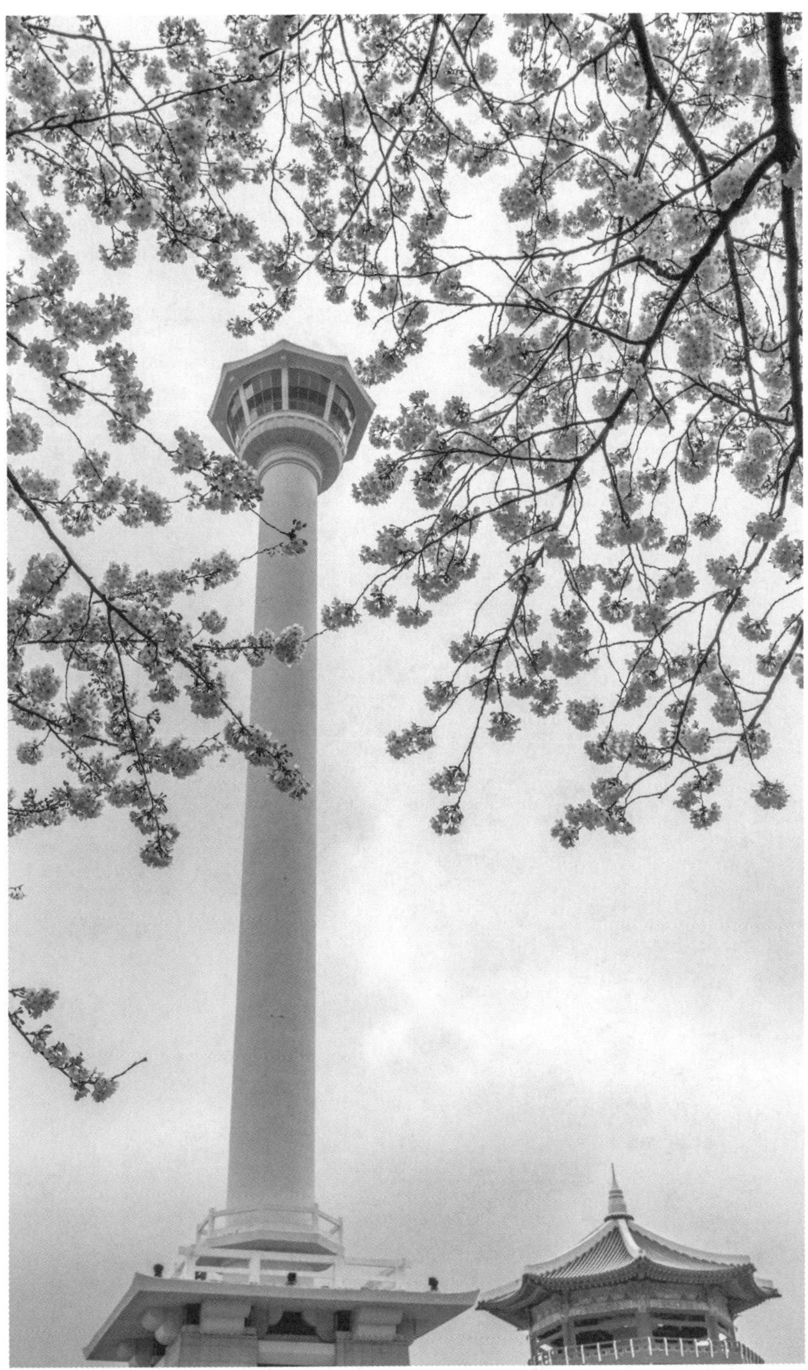

Busan Tower in Busan, South Korea

9

Latin America

Claudia Salazar

Being the daughter of a school teacher and a university professor, teaching runs in my blood. However, I was not fully aware of that interest until volunteering to work with marginalized Colombians. That's when I realized my deep passion for helping and teaching others.

A few years into my career, I was asked to design a training program for a Colombian company that represented two global, well-known, premium German brands. While attending a train-the-trainer program in Germany, I became hooked on this profession. Learning organization skills, punctuality, and how to strictly follow a content plan made sense to me. Other training programs in the United States taught me to be more creative, take more risks, and explore new training methodologies and tools. The big challenge was applying all this knowledge in a Latin environment, where there is so much improvisation, movement, and color. I began to fuse German, U.S., and Latin styles together to create viable and attractive training courses based on adult learning principles.

Becoming a freelance trainer and consultant finally gave me the opportunity to discover Latin America, as I had hoped it would. I have trained in eight countries and worked with participants from Mexico to Argentina. Every day brings new experiences with using technical jargon and relevant evidence while interacting with various audiences from the operational level to the CEO. Even though I speak the same Spanish as the participants, occasionally I feel tongue-tied and sense the need to adapt behaviors and adjust idioms to match the country and skill level of participants.

Training is about passionately developing others. Trainers must be like chameleons, with the ability to adapt to new situations and participants, always keeping in mind that what is important in a classroom are the trainees and not the trainer. This chapter is about how to adapt to all the vibrant colors and experiences of Latin American classes.

People and Culture: Get to Know Your Audience

Latin America, so-named for the speaking of languages derived from Latin, comprises a variety of countries and territories across the Americas and the Caribbean. The countries and territories primarily speak Spanish. Brazil is the only country where Portuguese is the official language.

Latinos are recognized, for the most part, by their openness, happiness, colorful personality, and hospitality. Visitors and tourists are welcomed warmly and made to feel at home. Expect a smile and a kiss on the cheek, and hugs are customary even among strangers. Contrary to customs in Saudi Arabia—where it is common for men to kiss each other on the cheek as a greeting—many Latin American men do not kiss each other, but Argentinians do. Women usually greet with a kiss, and it is customary for a man and a woman to greet with a kiss on the cheek.

Even though Spanish-speaking countries share the same language, each one has its own expressions, grammar, pronunciations, and even swear words! It is not always easy to understand the different Spanish dialects, so it might be better to facilitate the program in English. However, note that Latin American people can be quite literal when not familiar with another country's expressions. For example, in English, "piece of cake" is a way to say that something is easy to do. However, if they do not know the meaning of this English expression, trainees will be confused if you talk about cake in the middle of training. Before using an expression, be sure they know it or explain it.

Each Latin American country has diverse temperatures, altitudes, and climates. Meridian countries like Colombia, Ecuador, Panama, and Nicaragua have warm seasons. The Southern Cone countries of Argentina, Brazil, Chile, Paraguay, and Uruguay have four seasons. Remember: When it is summer in the United States or Mexico, it will be winter in Argentina or Chile.

Consider altitude; there are low-elevation cities like San Jose and San Salvador and high-elevation cities like Bogotá, La Paz, and Quito. The higher the altitude, the more time needed to adjust. Expect to feel altitude sickness, like a headache and dizziness. Donna Steffey, the editor of this book, learned the hard way when she came to Quito, Ecuador, to facilitate a train-the-trainer class. Fortunately, she arrived early and did not schedule a training session for the next day. She said, "It felt a little like jet lag, but more light-headedness." One of the remedies is to drink lots of water and eat light meals with carbohydrates.

Basílica del Voto Nacional in downtown Quito. Drink lots of water and eat light, high-carb meals to prevent altitude sickness in cities like Quito.

When we talk about Latin America, many people think we share one culture. The reality is that many distinct cultures and subcultures exist. Here are a few of the cultural differences to be aware of:

- Different countries handle scheduling workshops differently because not all countries work the same hours. For example, training in Argentina and Mexico usually begins at 9:30 a.m., with lunch at 2:30 p.m., and ends at 6 p.m. However, in Colombia and El Salvador, training begins at 8 a.m., with lunch at 1 p.m., and ends at 5 p.m. In smaller cities, 90 minutes for lunch is common, because people usually go home for lunch and then return to work.

- Participants' formality level will differ in the way they dress and talk to one another. Argentinian, Uruguayan, Colombian, and Chilean people tend to be more formal than people from Central American countries like Panama, Guatemala, and Costa Rica. Inside each country, there are subcultures to take into account. For example, in Argentina, people in Mendoza are more informal than people in Buenos Aires.
- Audience style will vary with the weather. In warm cities, dress in linen and wear light colors. In colder cities, use dark colors and warmer material like wool. For company managers, suits are expected for men, and women wear formal dresses and pants. For factory workers, attire is usually pants and comfortable shoes.

Getting Started: Conduct a Needs Assessment

Many Latin countries now value training as a means to increase productivity, and have allocated budgets accordingly. Keep in mind, however, that external political, economic, or social situations can affect the company. In that case, the first budget protection mechanism is to avoid hiring external facilitators.

Before delivering training, it is important to understand the organization's needs, while respecting company privacy restrictions. Note that the training needs assessment discussion requires assertiveness. The more assertive the talent development professional is, the more the information will be useful, and the better the connections are with the client. Here are some additional tips for conducting a needs assessment:

- **Don't assume anything.** Listen carefully to what the client says. Be careful to clarify ideas because words have multiple meanings. When I interviewed the operational area head of one of the biggest airlines in Latin America, he said he needed a train-the-trainer course for the professional level. When I asked, "What does professional level mean?" he answered, "Basic level." In some companies, a professional is the basic level, while in others it refers to middle management or even senior executives.

- **Talk to everyone.** Interviewing direct supervisors is most helpful. Conducting a focus group with future trainees, using work observations, or administering a pre-test will help determine the business reality. However, Latin countries are not completely open to external consulting companies, because they are uncomfortable with outsiders telling them what to do. They would prefer to assess the organizational climate themselves through surveys or through performance evaluation using 360-degree tools.
- **Customize solutions.** Latin American companies prefer to see a formal proposal that resolves fundamental questions. Consider including in the plan:
    - a course overview, business drivers, and objectives
    - content and activities, including a brief description of outcomes from activities
    - what they'll be able to do at the end of the session
    - what material and handouts trainees will keep
    - time, budget, and payment terms.

Clients can then ask questions. Prepare to defend the proposal and explain how training will be customized to their needs.

Itineraries: Plan the Learning Journey

Latin Americans have a tremendous capacity to improvise when things go wrong. If there is an obstacle, they usually can figure out suitable solutions. However, a good plan for learning is still essential because Latin American companies, influenced by multinational corporations and the need to be globally competitive, are becoming more organized and professional in the talent development field. Following are best practices for a successful learning experience:

- More and more Latin Americans are well informed and prepared. Companies have done a great job exposing staff to a variety of training topics, and for that reason, participants will seldom be at level zero. Do not start from the basics; give a little context and continue with relevant and useful information for attendees.
- Asynchronous learning is not well accepted yet across the region, even if it's a good way to lower costs. Latin people prefer physical contact to virtual platforms. If you design a blended learning approach and include an online component, give participants alternatives to reach the goal without the use of asynchronous online tools.
- Prepare activities, examples, and supporting evidence relatable to the trainees' industry and daily reality. Latin American participants do not like to do homework. Favorite activities are case studies, business simulations of realistic situations versus theoretical ones, or participating in a game with an in-depth debrief.
- After each activity, debrief using the heart, mind, in situ process. The process begins by asking questions that address attendees' feelings (heart): How did you feel doing the exercise? Continue by asking questions about the information they received (mind): What did you learn about this content? Finally, ask a question to close the gap between the classroom and real life (in situ): How will you apply this information in your role or workplace?
- In general, Latin American people are expressive, using body language including touch. Take advantage of kinesthetic elements to help participants cement the memory long term.
- When preparing trainees' print materials, consider a combination of 60 percent text (information, examples,

appendices), 30 percent images, and 10 percent white space (to write content notes, resolve exercises, and highlight key information).

- Format handouts so that people can use them back on the job. For example, during a project management program in Argentina, Chile, Peru, Colombia, and Mexico, trainers gave out a pocket-sized, laminated job aid that highlighted the key points of the training course. Design job aids and summary tools that give participants easy access to information.

Packing List: Logistics, Technology, and Resources

In Latin American countries, projectors are called video beams. Screens, tables, chairs, markers, masking tape, colored paper, whiteboards, and flipcharts are easy to find.

- **Flipcharts.** Like many things in Latin America, flipcharts come in different sizes and styles, and trainers need to be aware of the differences. For example, some do not have a place to put the markers. If more than three flipcharts are needed, for economic reasons, there might be some difficulties in getting them, especially in Chile, Colombia, Peru, and Ecuador. The on-site logistics team might not always speak English and will not understand what you mean by flipchart. It is best to bring a picture of what is needed, because there are many different Spanish names for flipcharts. For example, they're called foam boards in Mexico, *papelógrafo* in Argentina and Colombia, and *pizarra acrílico* in Uruguay and Paraguay.
- **Extension cords.** In Latin American countries, computers, laptops, and projectors use the U.S. plug, but cell phones and tablets use the two-hole connection. Three years ago, while setting up a classroom for training in Chile, I noticed the plug connection was far away from where the projector needed to be. When I asked for an

extension cord, the logistics team said that all the room supplies in the hotel were in use due to a significant event in the main room. The only available extension cord had two holes, not three (U.S. format). This problem could have resulted in no projection, but fortunately, the manager found someone in an office who brought an extension cord. Lesson: Always carry a five-meter (16.5-foot) U.S.-format extension cord.

- **Tables.** Different styles of tables are in use in various facilities, so take that into consideration when preparing activities. While training in Mexico a few years ago, the tables were attached to the floor. The topic was assertive communication, and the training plan included rearranging the seating three times in eight hours. After discovering that the tables did not move, it was important to remain calm and utilize my Latin capacity to improvise when things go wrong. Hanging a few posters around the room with labels like *hallway, lunchroom,* and *coffee station* allowed participants to gather in those areas for role-playing conversations rather than remaining seated.

Customs: Body Language Dos and Don'ts

Body language for Latin America is crucial. The next few tips will help non-Latino trainers fit better with the culture.

- **Move around.** Latin American people like passionate, engaging people. Use your hands to express an idea, and move your body to represent something you want others to feel or imagine. Walk to invigorate speech, and use facial expressions to demonstrate amazement, happiness, or sadness. The challenge is to find the correct blend of expressiveness and not overdo it.
- **Be careful with pointing.** Instructors often say, "Do this, don't do that, you should, you must." A bad habit is to use your forefinger to emphasize that point. In Latin

America, it is considered extremely ill-mannered to point your index finger directly at people.

- **Make eye contact.** Maintain steady eye contact with people during a conversation. However, steady does not mean staring. Staring in Latin cultures may indicate that you are trying to challenge or intimidate someone.
- **Don't think that warm means closer.** Although Latin Americans are a friendly people, it is still important when first meeting someone to respect their personal space. Remaining at about arm's length is important. That is why we handshake when we introduce ourselves instead of kissing or hugging. After a period of interactions, if others hug, respond by being friendly. At the end of the training session, it would not be unusual for participants who feel close to the instructor to say goodbye with a kiss and hug.

Climate: Create a Warm Learning Environment

The Latin Americans' collective spirit shows up in different ways. One way is the importance of personal relationships. They expect to be treated with courtesy and kindness while they work. Constant jokes are not well accepted. People connect through sensations and genuine communication, and prefer to share knowledge rather than keep it for themselves.

Latin Americans like to have fun in class. Here's some advice to engage learners and receive comments on evaluations like, "We learned so much from you!" or "We want more time with you!"

Plan Ahead

Demonstrate management of the classroom by arriving at least 45 minutes early and using a checklist. Remember to prepare contingency plans in case something fails. Consider additional time for security measures or checking in at the reception desk, and for locating the room. Identify the nearest bathroom, coffee table, and trash can. At the beginning of the course, give participants a heads-up regarding break times. By knowing when they will have a break, they will be able to focus on the lesson.

When I delivered a training course for a well-known soft drink company, I arrived 40 minutes before the start time to set up the classroom. But it took me around 10 minutes to reach the receptionist and be allowed to go upstairs. I then had to rush to organize the materials. What's more, I needed two flipcharts, but only one was in the room and it was broken. The logistics staff was doing their best to set up the computer with the video beam, but it wasn't working. When I finally had a few minutes to prepare myself before beginning the course, the bathroom was in another section. What a morning! From that moment on, I decided to get to my classroom 40 minutes early, not the lobby.

Have Fun

Fun is not the enemy. Latin people adore collaborative activities and find more value when these activities connect to theory. Lecturing about theory and having participants stay seated for a long time is likely to cause disengagement. Use simple games like picking a colored ball from a bag to mix up participants for each activity—each group is one color. Alternatively, use a deck of cards, with each card from one suit belonging to the same group. Adding color and a kinesthetic element increases the fun. Instead of handing out the instructions to activities on a piece of paper, tape it under their chairs or tables before they enter the class; when it is time for the activity, let them know where they can find the directions. Play music before class. Some good choices include bachata, reggae, chillout, lounge, and bossa nova. Avoid rap and heavy metal so as not to agitate learners.

Learn Names

The star of the session is the participant, not the trainer. When welcoming learners into class, ask for their name and greet everyone by name. Latin people usually have two names. Always ask which name they want to use. For example, someone named Carlos Antonio may prefer to be called Antonio. Correct their name tag to show respect.

Allow Learners to Share Experiences

If necessary, ask for elaboration to get a better idea of their proficiency level. Participants are not typically shy, but they may not know how much information they should share. Later, when talking about topics, weave in the learner's experiences.

Listen

When trainees raise their hand to ask a question or share an objection, facilitators need to be aware of their body language. Do not be too rigid. Walk to a position in the room where you can see who is speaking, as well as watch the other participants to gauge reactions. Listen until the end of their statement without interrupting. Good listening behaviors give the participants confidence to continue engaging in the class. Acknowledge comments with a simple thank you. If ever sharing a story that an attendee told you privately, be sure to ask permission before sharing and let the group know permission was given to share so as not to break any trust.

Things to Consider: Handle Classroom Challenges

Latin Americans are respectful and like to learn. Ask hypothetical questions or ask about real-life situations and you will likely get a variety of opinions. Opinions can cause disagreements, so prepare them to accept opposite points of view. Here are some other possible challenges.

Leaving the Classroom Completely

Once in a while, a trainee might exit the classroom during or after an activity. Talking about this with my Latin American colleagues, we concluded that in most cases, this has little to do with the activity. There is usually a bigger reason for the exit. Have a private conversation with the participant to find out what happened. Use reflexive questions like: What happened? Why did you react like this? Is there something that is going on at work? Can I help in some way? Ask these questions in a gentle and kind manner, taking care to use body language to show a real interest in understanding and helping. In many cases, trainees return to the classroom and actively participate.

Going In and Out of the Room

Last year, while training the commercial heads of a leading Latin American company, I noticed several of the attendees started going in and out of class and talking among themselves. Suddenly, it was almost chaos. Being direct, I asked them what was happening. It turned out it was the end of the month, and they were distracted because they had to get the end-of-month reports done. We agreed to shorten the session by two hours. In exchange, they committed to 100 percent concentration on the key points during the remainder of the session. With Latin audiences, flexibility is key.

Training Materials Missing

A colleague, Manuel, was scheduled to deliver five days of training in Chile. The first day included four icebreaker activities in the morning. The afternoon was supposed to focus on the training schedule, objectives, and introduction of each participant.

Manuel arrived in Santiago de Chile the day before the training course, but the luggage with his training materials was missing. The airport authorities told him they would do their best to deliver the luggage to the training site after lunch the following day. Manuel had prepared a plan B that consisted of flip-flopping the training plan on the first day. He moved the morning activities to the afternoon and started the training with the material he had planned for later that day. Fortunately, the luggage arrived that afternoon.

Facilitators can have baggage delays anywhere in the world. The lesson is: Learners don't know your high-level design. Use your experience to find a good solution; if you handle it in a professional way, learners won't notice.

One Word, Different Meanings

Delivering training in Spanish requires remembering that every Latin American country has its own idioms and expressions. A word may have a positive meaning in one country but may have a different meaning in other areas. My colleague Alberto was in Mexico delivering a leadership training course to participants from various Latin American countries. One team member shared his opinion about an issue using a common word in his country, but to the others, this word had a bad connotation. Participants began to laugh and make fun of the participant. Alberto managed this situation by organizing an activity to value cultural differences, which prevented future bullying and allowed the training program to be a success.

Trainers should protect themselves by saying at the beginning of the course, "Even though all of us speak the same language, it doesn't mean we'll understand everything due to our many idioms." Let learners know you'll use appropriate words for your home country. Apologize for any language gaffes that might occur.

Tips and Warnings: Advice for Nonnative Trainers

Here is some friendly advice if you are lucky enough to be invited to train in Latin America:

- **Always find something positive about each participant.** Even if they share an experience that is irrelevant, thank them for their contribution and find a way to connect their statement with the topic.
- **Use creativity and high energy.** Do not be afraid to try new things. Latin American people want to feel they are in specialized training, not in an ordinary class. They love training that offers color, activities, mixing of participants for groups, and hands-on activities.

- **Try not to plan training for a weekend.** The majority of Latin American countries are Catholic or Christian. Sunday is our official holiday. On Saturdays, few companies may work, so if asked to deliver training that day, prepare a plausible justification for it.
- **Use some Spanish words and refer to famous cities, countries, streets, places, or food names familiar to the trainees.** Learning these words will make them very proud and demonstrates interest in their culture. Here are some basics: *hola* (hello), *buenos dias* (good morning), *buenas tardes* (good afternoon), *muchas gracias* (thank you so much), and *¿cómo estás?* (how are you?).
- **Unless you know the audience well, avoid starting the training course with a compliment.** Trainees will take it as insincere or flattery just to get approval from the group. By the middle or end of the training course, after you have gotten to know the group, it is fine to share a sincere, specific compliment.
- **After breaks, especially after lunch, do an activity with body movement.** This will help wake up participants, and leave them at the right energy level to continue learning.
- **Don't talk about religion, politics, or soccer, and—even worse—don't say anything negative about the trainees' city, country, or culture.** Avoid using absolute terms like *never, always,* and *all.* It is better to say *some* or *few.* It is hard for us to accept people who use absolutes.
- **Avoid using American measurements like inches, miles, or Fahrenheit.** The participants will stop listening because they will be busy converting Fahrenheit to Celsius, inches to centimeters or meters, or miles to kilometers.

Bon Voyage

When traveling to Latin America, be prepared to experience passion, joyfulness, and kindness. Be willing to change your mind, and especially your heart. *¡Bienvenidos!* You are welcome!

***

About the Author

Claudia Salazar is an ATD Master Trainer and Master Instructional Designer. She has more than 14 years of experience as a consultant and classroom facilitator delivering training related to train-the-trainer, high-impact presentations, assertive communication, team building, interpersonal relations, people management, and retail sales processes.

Claudia fuses the content and high-level design of a German program and U.S. training methodologies with Latin American dynamism and improvisation. As a result, her learners receive a combination of styles that generate high retention rates. She is able to adapt to different styles of learners and industries, helping people apply what they learn on the job.

10

The Middle East

Bahaa Hussein

What a journey my career has been, from accidental trainer in a multinational company subsidiary in Egypt to head of the learning and development department for a Middle East–Africa region sales and distribution firm. Early on as a sales manager, I was eager to spend hours coaching the team and had a passion for helping others succeed, so it seemed like a natural career progression for me to move into training.

A mentor taught me solid foundations of training, such as how to break complex tasks into small chunks of teachable parts. After I learned the basics, an opportunity came to deliver a sales training workshop. With natural talent, intuition, and communication skills as a good salesman, I figured the engagement would be easy.

My mentor cautioned me to be aware of the cultural differences among Egyptian audiences. The differences are a result of varied educational and social backgrounds, as well as the different dialects of 60 million people at the time (today's population is about 96 million). It did not take long for one of the participants to make a joke about Upper Egyptians (Egyptians living in the south of Egypt). For the rest of the program, one table was totally shut down by this participant's "humorous intervention." Although I should have noticed the dialect sooner, it took a while to realize that the group at this table was from Upper Egypt. They never objected to the participant making fun of them. In their culture, there is "a boss," or *al kabeer* in Egyptian dialect, who should have stopped this ridiculing right away. What I did not realize was that, because I was the trainer, they looked to me to be the *al kabeer.* It was my responsibility to create a safe learning environment, but I did not.

The basics are not enough for someone who wants a training career in the Middle East. I had to learn more structured concepts, theories, and models. In this chapter, I will share some best practices and cultural understanding for designing and delivering training in the Middle East.

People and Culture: Get to Know Your Audience

Looking at Egypt and the Arabian Peninsula gives a good representation of Arab culture to examine similarities and differences.

Most of the Arab world consists mainly of desert land, except in some areas with sizable rivers, such as the Nile River. The Nile, which is the longest river in the world, molds life and culture in Egypt.

It's important to recognize the unforgiving nature of this part of the world. Although the oil boom of the 1970s brought about a modern living style, people need to be tough to survive and adapt to severe conditions. It's accurate to say that the Islamic religion in its true form, not in its misinterpreted one, made life more tolerable.

The Nile River in Egypt. The Nile is the longest river in the world.

The following values have contributed to shaping Arab culture. I learned about them from my readings of history, particularly from the prize-winning work *The Sealed Nectar* by Safiur-Rahman al-Mubarakpuri (2002). I can confirm that these values still exist today, so understanding some of them will likely make it easier to understand a little about Arab culture.

- Hospitality is proudly praised in both old Arabic poetry and contemporary stories. When Arabs receive a house guest, they are expected to present a wide variety of food and insist that guests eat some of everything, if not all of it. The simplest form of showing hospitality is to warmly welcome participants as soon as they walk in, and connect with them during a brief chat, showing genuine interest in getting to know them.

- A sense of honor and reputation is also found through Arabic culture and literature. In a workshop, someone may always take the lead in answering questions (even though they might not have exactly the right answer), especially if it takes some time for others to volunteer. Recognize this courage positively and avoid exposing their mistake or in any way causing humiliation to not lose participant focus.
- The nature of truthfulness derives from the simple Bedouin life. Bedouin life manifests itself in participants attending classes in their simple national dress of white *thobs* for men and black *abayas* for women. Hence, they avoid newly adopted urban and modern appearances.

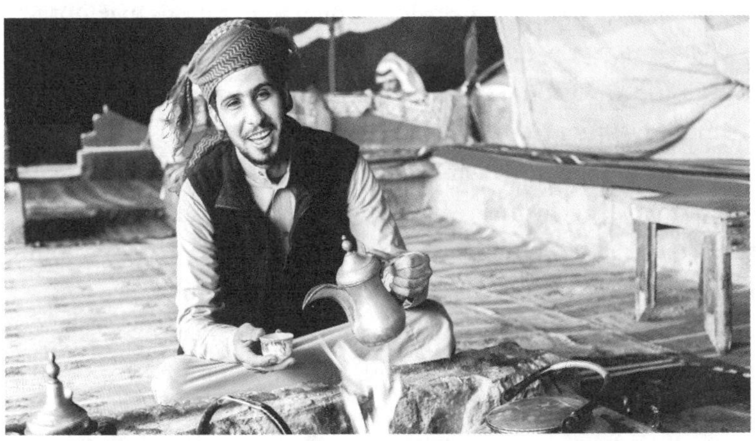
A Bedouin man serving coffee in Jordan. Hospitality is an important part of Arabic culture.

Some of these profoundly ingrained ideas reveal themselves in the behaviors and beliefs of Arabs today. Even Arabs who are familiar with other cultures through extensive traveling or living abroad will be bound, in most cases, to these principles.

Another important and sensitive topic to understand about the region is relationships between men and women. Despite what many believe, since the beginning of Islam, women have acquired a prominent and respectable status. For example, in true Islam, many women have the final say in delicate family matters. This principle has become deeply rooted in Arab culture as well. Some extreme practices may lean toward overprotecting women, but I think this is more of a cultural practice than an Islamic religious requirement.

One of the simplest ways to treat women with respect in a mixed-gender training classroom is to honor their choice to sit at a separate table from men. Throughout this chapter, I will share more gender customs.

Getting Started: Conduct a Needs Assessment

Market dynamics have changed tremendously in the region since 2011 as a result of the Arab Spring. Military operations in countries such as Iraq, Syria, and Yemen affect training because they cause a drain on the economy across the region. Uncertain economic turmoil resulting from regional political instability is expected to continue into the foreseeable future. The result is higher pressure on companies regarding recruitment, training plans, and budgets. Many enterprises in the private sector have either frozen recruitment or started layoffs and restructuring activities.

For the first time in years, training budgets are experiencing cuts. Moreover, there is a greater necessity for well-considered needs assessment exercises. Previously, management would send training requests to the training department, which would be automatically fulfilled, either internally or externally through routine use of third-party providers. Even now, only a minority of organizations go through a proper training needs assessment process.

A common practice is to let employees decide which training course they want to attend. Often a favored employee will be sent to an advantageous training course regardless of suitability, especially if the course was being hosted in an appealing destination. This often makes other employees resentful. However, this practice is becoming less prevalent with tightening budgets and better needs assessments.

One challenge is the willingness of clients to admit that they might not have all the answers about teams' needs or may be wrong about them. In most cases, after initiating assessment interviews based on client assumptions, trainers end up with an entirely different outcome.

The principal challenge for the Middle East is to delicately handle the ego and dignity of the manager requesting training. You can overcome the pride challenge through probing deeply, asking valid questions, and trusting the manager's judgment until opinions can be validated with surveys or additional evidence. When reaching a conclusion, it is important to give the manager full credit for the right outcome due to their understanding of their people, situation, and needs.

To conclude, economic pressure and shrinking recruitment budgets demand trainers concentrate on developing existing talent. A proper needs assessment process is necessary to ensure training budgets are well spent, rather than being spent frivolously.

Itineraries: Plan the Learning Journey

A few years ago, a career change allowed me to lead the learning and development department of a major regional sales and distribution firm based in Cairo and covering the Middle East. It was here where I realized the importance of the entire learning journey, rather than just the event itself. Within the first few days, an incident happened by chance when a facilitator was late due to an unexpected situation. I entered the classroom to have an informal chat with the participants who were waiting for the facilitator to arrive. After asking a few random questions, I learned that most of the participants did not know the training subject, the objectives, or the reason they were invited to attend. Some participants were even called that morning and told to show up to training. The waste of time and resources was shocking, the training session was canceled, and everyone went back to work.

Another incident happened when I was looking at the execution standards of one of the core programs for our sales organization. An external provider was running the program with an entirely different set of standards. The class was two days instead of four. Each class had twice the ideal number of participants in attendance. A critical part of virtual sales training involved video cameras, but the trainer eliminated that element. Overall, the objective of running the course turned into a mere "ticking the box" for achieving the target number of participants rather than for giving any importance to learning transfer and workplace impact.

Don't let these things happen to you. Here are some ideas for planning a valuable learning journey.

First, start each learning journey with a pre-workshop. We call it a change contract session. Managers are asked to sit with their direct reports before they can send an employee to training. They need to discuss and document why the employee is attending a workshop, what objectives they need to achieve, and what performance improvements are expected to happen. The performance improvement must relate to specific technical key performance indicators or an observable gap versus the needed standard.

In addition to the manager–direct report change contract session, start engaging directly with the participants a week before the program on social media. This allows them to get to know one another, discuss the manager–direct report session, and agree on the main concepts.

In this region, it is important to replace the slide-lecturing approach with the more experiential approach, thereby creating a deeper learning experience. To ensure program effectiveness, have the training team assess the workshop regularly for knowledge transfer. Experiential activities must relate to learning objectives to make this a valuable learning journey.

The current economic conditions, improved Internet infrastructure, and a boost in use of mobile devices are expected to drive e-learning as an alternative delivery method to classroom training. Still, the preferred method of regional learners leans more toward classroom training, because it also has a social context.

Consider Arab culture when designing experiential action learning activities. Remember the principles of honor and pride, and avoid activities where there is a clear loser. Avoid asking women, especially conservative ones, to participate in activities that require too much body movement or action.

With a highly active activity in a mixed-gender group, give women the responsibility to observe and record observations, to point out rule violations, or to control timing. Involve the women in a nondiscriminatory way. It is customary to ask a male trainee to come forward and present his findings; however, the trainer cannot insist on calling on a female trainee to do the same. In such cases, it is typical to let her present her ideas while sitting at her table. Unintentional discrimination will result in lost engagement for the rest of the session.

Is this a general rule across all countries in the region? Absolutely not. For example, in countries like Egypt and Lebanon or even cities like Dubai—only when nonlocals are attending—it is normal to engage all participants in physical activities. When in doubt, ask about local customs and be observant of body language.

Specifically, keep in mind the Gulf Cooperation Council countries, like Saudi Arabia or the United Arab Emirates; facilitators need to be careful if there are local women. Cultural values and restrictive attire for both genders may be an issue in all of these countries with a few exceptions, like Kuwait and Bahrain.

Packing Lists: Logistics, Technology, and Resources

When it comes to logistics and technology challenges in the Middle East region, there can be countless variations related to readiness and preparation of the venues. It varies not just from one country to another but even within the same country. Five-star hotels are an excellent choice for running major training workshops. There should be few issues when it comes to logistical support because staff quality and assistance are high. Clearly state any specialized equipment, tool, or technology needs in writing. It may also be necessary to negotiate the Internet charges separately.

Show up at least 60 to 90 minutes early to avoid surprises. Trainers consistently face the issue of not having correct seating arrangements, regardless of the clarity of communication. For example, I was once scheduled to facilitate two sessions back to back. I instructed the hotel to set up chairs theater style for the first session, and U-shaped for the second. They reversed the setups. Arriving early allows for quick adjustments. Surprises are usually the result of misunderstanding or miscommunication, and people do act quickly to fix issues.

If you're running a class training at a client venue, it is advisable not to assume that everything will be planned perfectly as per request. Remember to communicate needs and get confirmation in writing. Communication and confirmation is frequently even more important at a client's venue than at an outside venue, because clients may have additional last-minute requests.

In the Gulf, it's better to make the training day shorter than the typical work day. Moreover, if participants are government or public sector employees, they might not even agree to stay beyond 1 or 2 p.m. Again, this will differ from one country to another. Private sector employees will agree to remain in a training session until 5 p.m., but not a minute later. As for a start time, it differs completely. In Egypt, it's OK to start at 8:30 or 9 a.m.; in the Gulf, the hot weather requires you to start as early as 7 a.m., and no later than 8 a.m.

Always plan the agenda in a way that respects prayer times. In all Muslim countries, there are five prayers a day. That usually means at least two prayer times during a workshop: around noon and later in the afternoon. Ask about the exact time of these prayers and plan breaks to coincide with the prayer schedule. Those who practice praying will appreciate the respect. Prayer should take about 10 minutes. Plan break times to be a minimum of 15 to 20 minutes to accommodate time for prayers in addition to other standard break-time practices.

One critical caution around the resources you plan to use in your training: Review videos and printed materials, including photos, carefully. In many cases, trainers have been told to amend photos on slides or not to use certain videos because they are not appropriate to show according to the Middle East region's acceptance standards (for example, is a person decently dressed?). Of course, this differs from one country to the other. Exert extra caution in Saudi Arabia.

Customs: Body Language Dos and Don'ts

One of the biggest dilemmas in the region is understanding the best way to greet one another. As a trainer, greet people warmly as they arrive at the training room. Culturally, due to gender differences, this can be challenging.

It is not easy to tell if a male or female participant is conservative, with a very solid religious discipline. If you are a female trainer, regardless of where you come from, a handshake with some very conservative men might not be accepted and, in some situations, might end up causing embarrassment to both parties. This is more likely to happen with local men from Saudi Arabia than anywhere else. Don't initiate a handshake with the opposite gender; give them the time to take the first step.

A woman's dress is not enough to judge how conservative she is, because there is no specific rule. However, it is more likely that a head-covered woman is more conservative than a noncovered woman.

Arabs dress in a very non-Western way; women often wear *abayas* and men wear *dishdashas* (or long white dresses). Locals take tremendous pride in their ethnic wear, so expect to see it in classes and do not show any surprise.

In general, women in the Gulf states tend to speak very softly. If they must speak in public, they will do so, but they will likely be too shy to use a microphone. It is always better to get women together in small groups talking to one another rather than talking to the entire group. Ask a woman politely to raise her voice if she must speak to the larger group. Of course, every rule has exceptions.

In Saudi Arabia, by law, women must be separated from men in training or meeting sessions by partitions if they are in the same learning venue. Only the presenter or facilitator may have eye contact with all audience members.

A visiting trainer in Pakistan should be extremely cautious when quoting examples of leaders from India. Instead, do research and quote a local leader to connect more directly. Read about the country, history, religion, culture, politics, and national occasions. When in doubt, ask if something is appropriate or not. Many foreign trainers feel uncomfortable asking if something is acceptable, or maybe think it might be insulting if they ask for more information. The fact is, most of the time, locals appreciate foreigners asking if they do not know. Participants will be more than happy to explain. Asking questions shows that you have a willingness to learn and demonstrates caring.

Climate: Create a Warm Learning Environment

In general, people across the region are warm and welcoming. If they seem shy or not engaged or interactive in the workshop, a language barrier might be the challenge. Participants might not want to admit a limitation and will act bashful. The best advice is to treat everyone more like a friend until proven otherwise. In most cases, even if a participant did plan to be challenging, they will likely reconsider these intentions when a trainer displays positive signs of friendship.

If you unintentionally embarrass someone, apologize immediately rather than waiting to finish the session and trying to do it in private. This move will leave a good impression.

During introductions, it is advisable not to mention all your past experiences or career achievements. Participants may consider it pompous. Better to mention your name and a very brief introduction about the reason you are there, and then let the participants discover your experience through corroborating anecdotes and explanations.

In cases where top management is present, gain their support by treating them as members of a training review board versus treating them like learners. This practice will greatly satisfy their egos. Make sure to emphasize that as the instructor, you need their support.

One of the main obstacles while training at a client's location is the training room. Even in big firms, due to a shortage of space, training rooms are arranged in classroom style or even theater style. Be clear and specify instructions ahead of time. It is also important to note that the training rooms in newer firms have many pictures and photographs that could distract trainees' attention. Make sure the room is suitable for training purposes.

In some cases, the training room temperature won't be adequate, whether too warm or too cold. Book a five-star hotel when possible or find a nearby space where trainees can perform some of their activities.

If training outside the main city in the region or in a less-than-five-star hotel, you might be faced with some unusual surprises. For example, in a few cases, I discovered that a training room turned out to be a small restaurant or café that was made into a training room. Once again, make sure to ask for photos of the room beforehand and confirm that the needed equipment will be readily available with technical assistance support.

Things to Consider: Handle Classroom Challenges

People from the Middle Eastern region give much respect to foreign trainers if they act within expected principles. It is very rare for a participant to challenge a foreign trainer just to give them a hard time. However, as part of being proud of their heritage, some local participants might challenge some of the concepts by stating that they are not necessarily applicable to their region. Accept the argument and do not challenge it. Show a sincere interest in trying to understand the reason why, then try to engage the rest of the class in the discussion to gauge if that assumption is true or not. There will always be someone to support you and to help redirect and conclude the discussion.

There will be participants who show up late to the class, and some may be considerably late. Show respect to those who arrived on time by thanking them. Tell them that it is their right to start on time because they were here on time. However, it is a good idea to let the class decide whether to start or to wait 10 to 15 minutes. Other participants may have more knowledge about the situation that is causing lateness than you do, so let them choose. If addressing lateness, do it in a casual and humorous manner, not sarcastically.

Mobile phones are a tricky matter. Many options can be used to ensure that you take control of cell phone usage. First, discuss with the participants how they plan to handle mobile phones as part of the class rules, which they need to agree on from the very start. If the rule is broken, refer to the list of standards in a humorous way—you can even post them on the wall. Alternatively, pause and remain silent with a neutral expression until the phone conversation is over. Using silence once or twice should stop the phone disruptions once and for all. A final option is to do nothing and totally ignore the mobile interruption, then state that it is a personal choice to break the rule, but it could be done without interrupting class.

In the case of two participants talking, asking them to share the discussion is the best approach, especially if done in a professional and intuitive way.

Tips and Warnings: Advice for Nonnative Trainers

In addition to the advice provided in the earlier sections, here are a few quick tips for the nonnative trainer in the Middle East:

- Allow participants to design class rules for managing the session by facilitating a discussion about ground rules. This discussion gives them some control, so whenever they break the rules they have selected, they take more responsibility.
- Smoking is a big issue because there are many smokers in the region, and they lose focus if not allowed to smoke as frequently as possible. Depending on the number of smokers in the room, design more frequent five-minute breaks rather than fewer, longer ones. They'll appreciate it a lot.
- Food is one of the few entertainments that locals enjoy in the region, and the lunch meal should be a rich one. Coordinate with a local contact to ensure that an enjoyable meal is provided. Having said that, make sure to plan for a very active energizer after lunch!
- Across the region, people are extremely patriotic. Praise the local food or the beauty of the country. Praise is a good way to get buy-in from participants, and it is easy to give because every country in the region is unique and beautiful. For example, in Pakistan, praising the beauty of northern areas would resonate with Pakistani participants.
- Do not get involved in political or religious issues, no matter how bizarre or contradictory to your ideas, and do not express opinions on these topics. Due to the sensitive nature of these topics and the unrest that has been going

on for some time, do not give examples using them. For instance, in a country like Iraq, it is very normal to find four participants from the same city sitting at the same table, each with very different ideologies despite common religious beliefs.

- Do not insist on or suggest having mixed-gender groups if participants have divided themselves by gender.
- Do not look surprised if men greet each other with a hug or one or two kisses on the cheek. As a foreigner, you are not required to greet in the same local fashion unless you know the person well. In some Gulf countries, a kiss on the tip of the nose and/or shoulder is common.

Bon Voyage

This part of the world is well known for its warm feelings. The social side of life is the most important side of life. Therefore, any foreign trainer will enjoy a welcoming atmosphere while adding substantially to their experience in the field of training worldwide.

* * *

About the Author

Bahaa Hussein is the head of learning and development at Abudawood Group, responsible for developing and delivering all training programs across six markets in the Middle East–Africa and Arabian Peninsula and Pakistan regions. He's passionate about delivering meaningful training programs that create future leaders and professional performers in his organization and across the region.

Since 1989, Bahaa has been training people across Europe, the Middle East, and Africa regions to excel in the areas of communication, selling, and coaching in the workplace, helping employees reach their maximum potential. Graduating from the American University in Cairo with a bachelor in business administration and a minor in political science, he began his career in 1986 with Procter & Gamble Egypt, working his way up to become one of the key managers for the company in the Arabian Peninsula, heading a sales operation in Saudi Arabia. Then, in 2008, discovering his real interest in genuinely and positively changing peoples' lives through improved human performance, he shifted his career to be fully focused on learning and development. In 2010, he earned ATD's Certified Professional in Learning and Performance certification, and the Master Performance Consultant credential in 2014.

Reference

Al-Mubarakpuri, S-R. 2002. *The Sealed Nectar.* Riyadh: Darussalam International Publications.

11

Southeast Asia

Marby Tabungar

fter attending nursing college, I realized it was not my dream to become a nurse. So I explored opportunities in the business process outsourcing industry in the Philippines. I might still be looking for that dream job, were it not for an opportunity to teach a program on culture and communication skills. That first step to the front of the class triggered a flood of memories. I wanted to become a teacher when I was young; I remember asking Mom to buy a blackboard and a box of colored chalk. Now, as a trainer, I stood in front of a whiteboard with a box of markers.

Ten years after that fateful class, I am an experienced learning and organization development professional who has programs and initiatives through different platforms globally. As a project manager, I have focused on everything from design to measurement and evaluation. Throughout my journey, I have met people with various personalities, learned different cultures and values, and worked with multiple local and global organizations who all want to make a difference in this world.

Being a trainer is life changing. As talent development professionals, we are not just facilitators or designers. Our primary role is that of a coach, mentor, and dream maker. When we do our job right, we inspire and encourage someone to become a better person and achieve their goals.

I usually ask participants during the icebreaker what they wanted to be when they were young. It is funny how people find it challenging to remember what their childhood dream was. At the same time, it is fascinating to see individuals who feel so accomplished because they are now living what was just an ambition earlier in their lives.

I'm delighted to take you on a training journey through the Southeast Asian region, based on my experiences preparing training resources, traveling around, and establishing relationships. Southeast Asia comprises Brunei Darussalam, Cambodia, Indonesia, Laos, Malaysia, Myanmar (also called Burma), the Philippines,

Singapore, Thailand, Vietnam, and East Timor (Timor-Leste). In this chapter, however, I will focus on some of the larger countries I'm more familiar with, such as the Philippines, Indonesia, Singapore, and Malaysia.

People and Culture: Get to Know Your Audience

Southeast Asia is home to 11 countries; the region is divided into mainland and island zones. The mainland zone (Burma, Thailand, Laos, Cambodia, and Vietnam) is an extension of the Asian continent. The island region—also called maritime—includes Malaysia, Singapore, Indonesia (with more than 17,000 islands), the Philippines, Brunei, and Timor-Leste. The largest cities are Jakarta, Bangkok, Singapore, Manila, and Ho Chi Minh City. The region has more than 570 million people, and a huge variety of languages, religions, political systems, and histories.

The Istiqlal Mosque, in Jakarta, Indonesia, is the largest mosque in Southeast Asia.

Southeast Asia has a tropical, rainy climate. The temperature is usually warm, with the exception of the highland areas. Tropical forests cover most of the region. In the Philippines, there are two climate changes in a year: the dry season, which starts in late

November and ends in May, and the wet season, which begins in June and lasts until October.

Banuae, Philippines. Wet season is from June to October.

As an international trainer, it's important to understand the differences in geographical regions, nationalities, values, and culture that could help you design and deliver training programs successfully. Here is some guiding information:

Meet the People

Southeast Asians are known to be fun-loving, compassionate, gentle, hospitable, and friendly people. In my courses, they seemed more excited about games, and were smiling a lot and warm-hearted. They have also developed a strong sense of courtesy and respect, which is evident in how people treat elders, parents, and even superiors.

Communicate Successfully and Sincerely

Southeast Asia has thousands of spoken languages. This fact alone makes the region very diverse. Tracing the history, we see that the most influences, including language, came from Chinese and Western sources.

Some of the major languages used in the region include Malay, Bahasa, Mandarin, Burmese, and Filipino. Note that English is not used as a primary language in most countries within the region, although more nations are enhancing the English-speaking capability of their people. While this could create a barrier to communication, it is the trainer's responsibility to find ways to communicate and connect with learners effectively. Sometimes that means using gestures and visuals.

Communication styles also vary. However, most Asians tend to have a high-context manner when communicating. In other words, the meaning of the message is derived not only from explicit verbal or written messages, but also from contextual factors such as the relative status of the individuals involved, nonverbal signals, and the strength of the relationship.

One good example happened while I was running a class on coaching. The discussions were so engaging that the class was 15 minutes behind our lunch schedule. Wanting to summarize the topic, I asked the class if it was OK to extend the discussion a bit more. They did not respond right away. Instead, they looked at one another and then suddenly, one by one, they said "Umm, OK. How long will it be? If it is not too much, then yeah, we can extend." Just by hearing their low-pitched voices, observing their closed body language (such as crossed arms and looking away), I knew that it was *not* OK, so I sent them to lunch.

Embrace Diversity

Southeast Asia has a rich history of varying civilizations that has resulted in a diverse society today, including differences in religion, values, and beliefs. Today, Islam is the predominant religion in most countries within Southeast Asia, such as Malaysia, Indonesia, and Brunei. Thailand, Burma, and Laos practice Buddhism. Christianity is another religion in the region, predominantly in the Philippines and Timor-Leste.

As a trainer, it is important to take note of these differences. I remember once facilitating a meeting with leaders coming from various countries in Asia. There were a few Muslims in the group, but the lunch prepared for the meeting did not have any food appropriate for them. To the leaders' disappointment, they had to step out and grab lunch. This issue could have been prevented if these details had been asked for ahead of time.

Getting Started: Conduct a Needs Assessment

Regardless of the country or region, conducting a needs assessment plays a significant role in ensuring the effectiveness of a program and improving the performance of individuals and businesses. According to the *Global Trends in Talent Development* study conducted by ATD (2015), in Asia-Pacific countries the most prominent concern is around linking learning to performance.

As trainers, we know that the alignment of training objectives to performance requirements starts at the assessment stage. Completing a thorough assessment of gaps and needs is essential before implementing any program. It is a common practice in the region to use multiple tools and approaches in assessing the training needs of individuals or an organization. More information is always better. Following are the most frequently used approaches to needs assessment.

Conversations and Focus Group Discussions

The needs assessment conversation can be very different in each country in Southeast Asia. In Indonesia, needs assessment conversations will start at the top of an organization and then move down to the manager level to discuss performance issues. Decisions will be finalized back with the head of the organization. In Malaysia, decisions are made slowly, so you need patience. Malays will probably involve you in polite conversation for a lengthy period before identifying the real training issues. In Singapore, I had to spend a significant amount of time explaining the purpose of discussions and activities, building context to answer the manager's many questions even before I explained the content. Clarity is a top priority in working efficiently with Singaporean stakeholders.

In the Philippines, conducting interviews or focus group discussions is the preferred training needs analysis method. By doing this, you can speak to your target audience, which helps to get a better picture of the current challenges or needs. When using an interview or focus group, ensure a comfortable environment for the participants to share more information. Remember that Southeast Asians highly value relationships, and this could all start in open conversations. They may be reluctant to share any negative opinions to avoid speaking badly about someone.

Thanks to technology, this method can take place online through Skype or conference calls. However, it is still a good rule of thumb to confirm with the client if they prefer to discuss in person or if an online meeting works.

Review Performance Scorecards

In the 2017 *State of the Industry* study that was conducted by the Philippine Society for Training and Development (PSTD), 28 percent of the respondents said they use performance reviews as a training needs assessment tool. It seems that organizations are embracing the importance of objective performance reviews. Leaders use scorecards to assess the performance of their team members against their metrics and targets. This type of assessment is usually done monthly and often serves as the foundation for annual reviews. These documents can provide the training leader with clues as to the training solutions needed.

Also, an external consultant can ask for copies of employees' scorecards. This medium can provide baseline data, then help measure the effectiveness of the solution after implementation.

Itineraries: Plan the Learning Journey

Planning a learning journey in Southeast Asia requires making the needs of the learner a priority. Because of the difference in culture and personalities, a cookie-cutter approach might not work for all Southeast Asians. However, the goal should always be to engage the learners and ensure their full commitment to applying what they learn back on the job.

Here are a few examples of the variety of practices you might find in different Southeast Asian countries:

- **Philippines.** In the Philippines, training plays a major role in the development of employees in an organization. Most companies have a dedicated training department but could also seek an expert consultant in providing training solutions. Moreover, since Filipinos are always excited by new opportunities, the employees appreciate and value it. The best approach to get the commitment of a Filipino is to align training objectives to career progression.
- **Vietnam.** In Vietnam, most organizations do not usually provide in-house training, and when they do, it is more on an individual basis rather than skills training for groups. Group training is typically done for safety training or other, broader purposes.
- **Brunei.** In Brunei, most organizations only provide initial onboarding. Skills development happens once they do their jobs, usually without structured development programs.
- **Singapore.** Singaporeans appear to have little tolerance for chaotic learning situations with unclear objectives and road maps. During training, clearly communicate the training objectives and purpose of activities. Building relationships with the trainees would also help a trainer to create an open environment in class that could encourage active participation.
- **Thailand.** Thais prefer to work with other people rather than individually. Their emphasis on cooperation and harmony becomes evident in any kind of business environment. For a successful training program, encourage the participants to build relationships with one another until they become comfortable and perform

collectively. It is also a common practice for superiors to mentor those who are junior to them. So, in designing a program, involve the manager as a contributor to the development of their team members through mentoring.

Utilize a Blended Approach

Because of the increasing complexity of business processes, the methodologies used to deliver training must keep up with the constant changes in the organization. According to the *Global Trends in Talent Development* research report, the Asia-Pacific region still delivers 54 percent of learning hours through instructor-led classrooms, 16 percent through technology-based methods, and 24 percent through a blended approach (ATD 2015). Mobile learning is also an emerging technology used in the region to deliver formal learning.

In the Philippines, coaching and mentoring came up as a preferred methodology according to the 2017 *State of the Industry* study conducted by PSTD. It is a part of Filipino culture to respect and look up to someone who is more senior, not just in age but also in experience. Therefore, mentoring is embedded in the DNA of learning and development practices in the Philippines. In fact, early in my career, a mentor influenced my strong foundation and values in training. She has always been a part of my career triumphs as a trainer, and even in my personal life.

Take Advantage of Technology and Social Learning

Southeast Asia is seeing a dramatic shift in the technologies used for social learning and education. Fast-growing markets, such as Indonesia and Malaysia, are embracing social media tools. Currently, Singapore is the third most connected country in the world. These markets have large Millennial populations that can leapfrog over their senior managers through learning that is more accessible and personalized. The rise in learning and gamification related to social media is changing the way learners access knowledge and interact with one another.

But there are still challenges. For example, connection speeds in areas of Southeast Asia are still too slow due to technology limitations. While Singapore has an average of 20.3 Mbps, one of the fastest in the world, most countries in Southeast Asia average between 3 and 9 Mbps (Fastmetrics 2017). This could make some learning programs that require connectivity inefficient and inconsistent.

Packing Lists: Logistics, Technology, and Resources

I once delivered a three-day customer service workshop for a client in Dumaguete, a city in the Philippines, where the client selected the venue. I arrived an hour earlier than the start of the session to set up everything. First, the room was too small for a conference room setup, but I could fix it. Next, the audio and video outputs on the projector were not working, but I was able to make adjustments as well. The client also asked to add participants to the session, so I had to print more workbooks before we started. During the session, the laptop froze, so I had to use an assistant's laptop. To make matters worse, I began to lose my voice. It was a nightmare.

Of course, I made it appear as if everything was OK. The participants deserved the best learning experience, and that is what I gave. In a crisis like this, it is vital that the trainer knows how to manage logistical and technical issues and not let them affect the program. Have a list of emergency numbers in case all your troubleshooting skills are exhausted.

The sophistication of the venue depends on the preference of the client or what the program needs. The leading cities in Southeast Asia—like Jakarta, Bangkok, Singapore, Manila, and Ho Chi Minh City—have high-end hotels, while most provinces have smaller hotels or stand-alone training facilities. It would be good to determine the requirements first before booking any venue.

If delivering training in more rural or provincial areas, it would be best to research if the materials needed will be available. In the Philippines, for example, training rooms are more sophisticated in Manila compared with those in the provinces. Logistically, transportation in Southeast Asia can be as complicated to figure out as the region itself. Commuting using public transport in the Philippines is quite complex compared with other countries. If the session is around metro Manila or major cities, car services like Uber or Grab are reliable. You must anticipate traffic—it is better to travel three hours ahead of the session, especially during rush hour.

In Singapore, the Mass Rapid Transit (MRT) system is the quickest way to get around the city. Taxi services are also available, especially if the training venue is not by an MRT station. There may be a surcharge on taxis. In Jakarta, use the Tansjakarta bus service, which offers a very efficient and reasonably priced option for commuters going into the central business district. Taxis are available in all large cities in Malaysia, and most have meters—although drivers may not use them. Bicycle rickshaws (trishaws) supplement the taxi service in George Town and Melaka, and are handy ways of getting around the older parts of town, which have winding, narrow streets. However, they may not be the best means of transportation if you need to arrive early to the training venue.

A trishaw in George Town, Penang, Malaysia. Trishaws are a good way of getting around Penang's older neighborhoods.

Customs: Body Language Dos and Don'ts

Actions speak louder than words. Hence, as trainers, we should be mindful of our body language to maintain an open and respectful learning environment. Utilizing a global mindset and remaining flexible to feedback from people you meet in Southeast Asia will help. This region is complex, so let's break down body language behaviors by country.

Behaviors in the Philippines

- ***Mano po.*** *Mano po* is a gesture of respect from the Philippines; young Filipinos usually do this to greet and show respect to elders. The elder will hold out their hand, and the younger person will raise it to their forehead, while saying "*mano po.*"
- **Animated gestures.** Because English is not a native language, Filipinos sometimes find it difficult to explain all ideas in English, so they supplement statements with actions. A trainer should be able to read and interpret these gestures. A good example is when asking a Filipino for directions; they might use their lips to point out the location without providing exact instructions. However, don't hesitate to ask further if you're lost.
- **Eye contact.** Filipinos find it impolite if a person does not look at them when speaking. It applies even in training. With a big class or audience, make sure to connect with all participants through eye contact. It is a sign of sincerity and a means of communication.
- **Energy and enthusiasm.** Trainees will get energized when they feel the high energy and enthusiasm of a trainer during facilitation. Filipinos also appreciate a presentation that is based on a story or real-life experiences. Be sure to add a human feel to the session instead of just talking about facts and technical information.

Behaviors in Singapore

- **Dress.** Singapore is one of the most religiously diverse nations, and thus, dress is very conservative, even in business.
- **Introductions.** Singaporeans shake hands when introduced. Men and women usually greet each other with a handshake. Outside that, never touch, hug, or kiss a person of the opposite sex at a business meeting. When making introductions in meetings or training courses, always use the person's title and family or personal name.
- **Respect for elders.** Singaporeans show respect for elders, similar to most Asian cultures. Establishing credibility with the audience is imperative. Have an important person (elder) from the organization introduce you and highlight relevant credentials.
- **Eye contact.** Do not get offended if a Singaporean does not look you in the eyes during training. Their eyes are cast down or away as a sign of respect and politeness.
- **Conversations.** A common greeting in class might be "Have you eaten?" or "Where are you going?" instead of "Good morning." Good conversation topics include food, scenery, the arts, and tourist attractions. Avoid subjects like religion, personal relationships, money, racism, sex, or politics.
- **Feet.** Be careful when crossing your legs. Never point toward or inadvertently show the sole of your shoe to other people. Also, do not tap your foot.

Behaviors in Malaysia

- **Greetings.** It is OK for men to shake hands at business meetings, but it is better to nod or give a slight bow when greeting a woman or an older person. Introduce higher-ranking people or older people first. Western women should greet Malay men with a nod of their head and a smile. Avoid touching anyone of the opposite sex.

- **Hands and feet.** Do not use a single finger for gesturing. Use your right hand to pass items, such as a marker. Do not point at another person with your foot.

Behaviors in Indonesia

- **Meeting and greeting.** Greet people by slowly and sincerely saying *selamat* (sell-a-mat), which means peace. Shake hands and give a slight nod when meeting for the first time. Shake an Indonesian woman's hand only if she initiates the greeting.
- **Eye contact.** It is considered rude to look someone straight in the eyes. Prolonged eye contact may be viewed as a challenge and may cause defensiveness.

Climate: Create a Warm Learning Environment

Southeast Asians like to build family-like relationships and environments—for example, Indonesians value loyalty to family and friends above all else. We involve emotions in whatever we do, and that is why we expect sensitivity among our peers. Even a simple gesture, like putting your hands on your hips when presenting, can be misinterpreted. In Singapore, that gesture can mean anger.

Here are some tips that could help build better connections with Southeast Asian learners.

Smile and Be Personal

This one is very simple. The trainer should welcome participants with a warm greeting and a smile. Before class starts, introduce yourself to each participant according to their culture. It will build rapport, which could help in maintaining a trusting relationship throughout the session.

Be Casual and Conversational

Most Southeast Asians are very conversational, and are OK with answering almost any personal question. Participants will also appreciate it if the trainer shows interest in the exciting things they do outside work. These discussions make good icebreakers. Filipinos will respond more if they are feeling comfortable. Find out what their hobbies are, what they did over the weekend, or something unique about them, and you will be surprised with how much they open up.

Know the Locale's Pride

It can be a tourist spot or a famous restaurant. People like to talk about how great their town or community is. If you're staying in the area for a while, ask participants about the best places to visit or things to do.

Inspire Participants

Especially true of Filipinos is that they are encouraged to perform when they know other people have done it. Share your own experiences, struggles, and solutions.

Insert Games Into the Program

When designing a program or facilitating a class for learners, include activities and games. This strategy fosters relationship building, creates a fun environment, and brings out participants' competitiveness, which makes training more engaging. Be aware of cultural, gender, and generational differences when dividing participants into groups.

Things to Consider: Handle Classroom Challenges

Southeast Asians are polite, so it is rare to face very difficult learners in class. However, being familiar with the culture and values would help the trainer manage the class better. Here are some common scenarios and tips on how to handle them:

Pay Attention to Time

A bad habit that most Filipinos have is tardiness. For example, if a meeting were set to start at 7 a.m., participants would probably arrive at 7:15 or even 7:30. That is why they are flexible when setting the start time of events and celebrations. In Singapore and Malaysia, the trainer is expected to be on time. Singaporeans will be on time, but in Malaysia, the participants might be slightly late.

Give Feedback

"Praise in public, criticize in private" applies to Southeast Asians. They are emotional and sensitive, and tend to take feedback and comments personally, which means that anyone who provides feedback should be conscious of the manner of communication and the words used. Saving face is one of the most important aspects of Southeast Asian culture. It is important never to cause anyone to lose face. Speak to a participant in private if there is a problem in class. The sandwich approach of beginning and ending with a compliment works best.

Do Not Assign Homework

Southeast Asians value work-life balance, and believe their time outside work should not be spent doing work chores. So, avoid giving homework to the participants that would require too much of their time after training hours. If necessary, provide the rationale for such activities. Doing pre-work during office hours before the start of training session is a common practice.

Read the Audience

In Southeast Asia, it is not common to hear "no" in response to anything. It is important to give participants a way out of any activity in class. Remember silence, a hesitation, or sometimes even a yes might actually mean no. Read the participant's body language.

Speak Slowly

Not all Southeast Asians can understand and speak English; some will even struggle to understand the accent of fluent English speakers. People may not explicitly say that they do not understand, but as a trainer, it is better to ensure this does not become a communication barrier. Encourage the participants to interrupt if they are having trouble following. Usually, establishing a hand gesture that signals when to slow down is a gentle way to give feedback to the trainer.

Encourage Participation

If the learners are not participative enough, here are some ways to encourage them:

- Have them gather their thoughts as a group and assign a representative who can share the team's response.
- Have participants write their answers on a piece of paper and share them with the class.
- Give them time to gather their thoughts and come up with a reply. The trainer can ask the question before sending them on a break, so it gives them more time to think.

Tips and Warnings: Advice for Nonnative Trainers

To ensure that Southeast Asian learners get the most from the learning experience, here are additional tips and warnings for guidance.

Allow Interactions to Take Place

I once attended a leadership training facilitated by a foreigner, hoping he researched how Filipinos behave in class. However, it became apparent that he was managing the session as he would manage it if he had participants from his country. He was too focused on the concepts and topics. He did not provide many opportunities for group interaction or activities. As a result, we felt disinterested and disengaged.

Manage Time and Conversations

Another item to handle is the time spent on class interactions and conversations. If these activities are already taking too much class time, politely insist on moving forward. The following can be used: "This is a fascinating discussion. However, we need to turn to the next section. If we have time later, we can go back to this topic and discuss further. Is everyone OK with that?"

Refocus on Results

Establishing the objective of the session is a good way to ensure that everyone is aligned with the expectations. Filipinos tend to focus on the fun and experience during the session, so it is important to refocus on the results from time to time.

Wear Appropriate Clothing

Attire can go from formal to casual depending on the topic and the audience. However, standard dress is conservative. Even if the venue or theme calls for casual clothing, the trainer still should mind their clothes, especially women. Low necklines, shorts, or sleeveless clothing might be considered revealing. Stick to polo shirts or denim when choosing casual attire.

Use the Native Language

It's a great idea to initiate a conversation using the native language. Here are a few Filipino and Malay words you can use:

- **Filipino:** *mabuhay* (welcome), *mending usage* (good morning), *maraming salamat* (thank you so much), and *paalam* (goodbye)
- **Malay:** *apa kabar* (hello), *sa-ya tee dak fa-ham* (I don't understand), *terima kasih* (thank you), and *selamat jalan* (goodbye).

Bon Voyage

Facilitating learning in Southeast Asia is an eye-opening experience. With beautiful places to visit, rich culture to experience, and lovely people to meet, Southeast Asia is a place where learning and teaching are fostered. Come and share your expertise with us. The meaningful relationships we form will help us all grow.

We are looking forward to seeing you train in our beloved region!

About the Author

Marby Tabungar is a training and quality manager for HR operations at Genpact. She has more than 10 years of experience from the IT business process management industry, with the last seven years dedicated to learning and development. She is a key contributor in the elevation of talent development practice in the Philippines as a member of the executive committee and the board of trustees for the Philippine Society for Training and Development (PSTD). She also leads the research and publication team, which captures and shares trends and best practices in learning and development in the Philippines. She has built her expertise in HR technology and managed services through multiple implementation projects and establishment of end-to-end HR processes.

References

ATD (Association for Talent Development). 2015. *Global Trends in Talent Development.* Alexandria, VA: ATD Press.

Fastmetrics. 2017. "Internet Speeds by Country (Mbps)." Fastmetrics. www.fastmetrics.com/internet-connection-speed-by-country.php.

PSTD (Philippine Society for Training and Development). 2017. *State of the Industry.* Mandaluyong City, Philippines: PSTD.

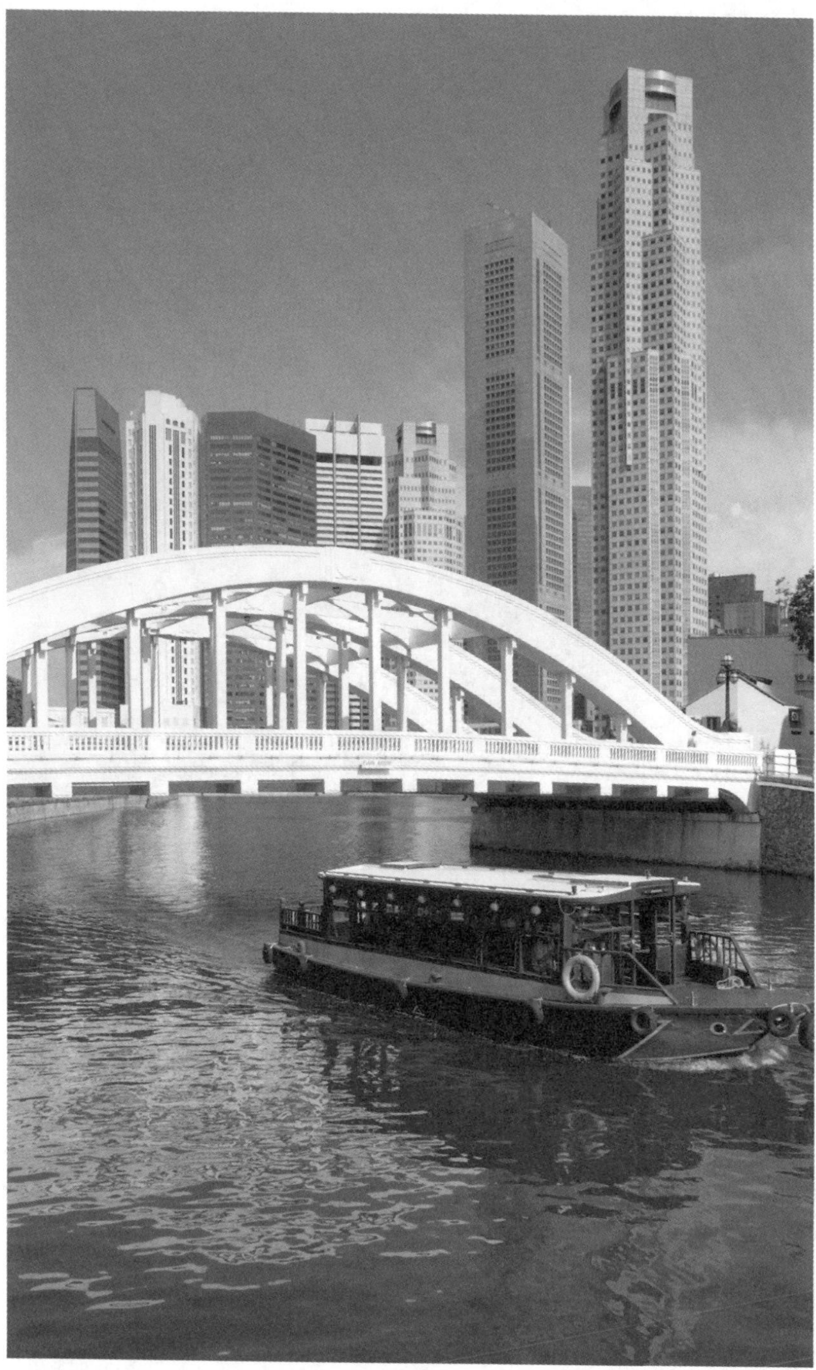

The Elgin Bridge, in the Singapore financial district

12

United Kingdom

David Smith

Many people think of the United Kingdom as a nation of tea drinkers all speaking the Queen's English. Be assured that, during the past 15 years as a talent development professional traveling extensively across the United Kingdom, I have had the absolute pleasure of working with a diverse range of learners, from individual contributors to board-level executives.

My experiences in working with British learners in both face-to-face and virtual environments have provided me with the opportunity to meet some amazing people from all corners of the British Isles. I remember quite a linguistic adventure in having British learners from a pharmaceutical company whose speech ranged from very thick dialects from Scotland (which, as a native of Aberdeen in Scotland, I was comfortable with) to heavy accents from Newcastle. The Irish lilt and the Queen's English from London and the South can be a wonderful cocktail of accents for the traveling trainer.

Being Scottish has made the job of supporting British learners less challenging for me than maybe for those of you turning to this chapter to better understand the culture of the British learner. It is important to win trust and establish credibility as a trainer when meeting the British learner. Brits like to understand the expert they are learning from in the training session. I learned this while supporting clients in developing sales specialists, managers, and other training professionals in a wide range of subjects.

Of course, every country and culture appears to have its stereotypes or misconceptions. There are nuances and best ways to approach and work with learners from the United Kingdom. In this chapter, I will share experiences as well as many tips and best practices. The British are unique and independent (especially given recent events around Brexit and the Scottish referendum), yet they share some similarities with learners from other cultures. I am eager to provide you valuable insight into the world of the British learner.

People and Culture: Get to Know Your Audience

Britons are insular in nature, part of Europe but separate from it at the same time. They are hardworking, driven by deadlines, and divided by a centuries-old class system. They like their privacy but are also obsessed with celebrity culture and gossip. They are skeptical with a strong sense of irony (Brake 2017).

Most British people are relatively well traveled, with a strong awareness of world events. They are individualistic and nationalistic and can be pioneering and entrepreneurial. At the same time, Britons are still considered very polite and formal by the rest of the world and are driven by a strong sense of fair play (Brake 2017).

British society is also highly diverse, with many second- and third-generation immigrants forming sizeable chunks of the population and ethnic minorities developing a stronger voice. Due to the globalization of the workforce around the world, the learner audience in any training event is unlikely to be 100 percent from a single culture. Britain has benefited from a migrant workforce over the years, with the open borders initiative with the European Union (EU) allowing the free movement of people within the 28 EU states. There has been a compelling influence from other cultures on the British way of life that has made British trainees very multicultural in their experiences.

British English is a minefield of nuance and understatement for anybody not familiar with the culture. Indirect, ambiguous language (and humor) are often used to mask the speaker's real feelings and intentions. The British prefer to avoid argument and confrontation, as this is often felt to be embarrassing. Politeness is paramount to the British, who use a lot of "please" and "thank you" in their language and will often apologize for disturbing someone before asking them a question. Humor (especially irony) is an acceptable way of defusing tension, building rapport, and expressing criticism. Inside jokes may be used to build group solidarity.

A street sign in Kent, England. British language (and humor) is often nuanced and understated.

Rather than say no directly to a request, they may become vague and suggest the possibility of acceptance, even if they have no intention of doing so (this is done so as not to cause insult). In a dialogue, people will wait for their turn to speak because it is not considered polite to interrupt. Too much silence will feel uncomfortable for most, as will excessive verbal expression or gesturing.

Britons have a healthy respect for deadlines. Once committed to one, most professionals would view a deadline as a promise to deliver and feel morally obliged to do so. Arriving on time for meetings will often depend on the attendees expected. If higher-ranking management is present, then timekeeping will be stricter. Project meetings without management present may start 10 to 20 minutes late, depending on the company culture. It is acceptable to use this time for refreshments and social chit-chat until most people have turned up.

Getting Started: Conduct a Needs Assessment

In the UK market, like many other markets, there's pressure on organizations to align learning to business goals and requirements. There is a great emphasis on making learning support business growth, and as such, there is more scrutiny from senior stakeholders on ensuring that training creates return on investment for the company, rather than just providing training for training's sake.

Here is some guidance on how to conduct a proper needs assessment in the United Kingdom:

- **Discovery phase.** Learning professionals need excellent investigative skills and persistence to work with client organizations. In many instances, training needs analysis is completed by the L&D contact within the customer's organization, or they have a strong view that a specific training need exists and want to move quickly to the development of the training content or program. Remember, Brits do not like to be challenged. Proceed with caution.
- **Stakeholder interviews and observing.** Common methods of establishing training needs are based around exploration with various groups within the organization—these may be stakeholders within the business, focus groups, or learner groups. These groups tend to provide concrete examples of training needs and gaps upon which the learning architect can create the optimal learning journey.
- **Assessment and evaluation.** Many employees prefer to see concrete evidence as to where the skills gap is so that they can visualize what knowledge, skills, and competencies need to be developed. Profile tools like Myers-Briggs, StrengthsFinder, DiSC, and Firo-B are used in corporate Britain, where an output of current state is provided and gives insight into how the learner is doing as well as showing what changes may need to take place. The British learner enjoys and takes pride in having a good sense of where they are in their careers and learning.

The Chartered Institute of Personnel Development (CIPD), the recognized professional body for HR and people development in the United Kingdom, found the following key trends in its 2015 survey of learning and development. By heeding these trends when you're conducting your needs assessment, you'll be better equipped to deliver effective training.

First, in-house methods are most common. On-the-job training, in-house development programs, and coaching by line managers or peers remain the most popular development methods, in line with findings from previous years. In particular, three-quarters of organizations currently offer coaching or mentoring, and an additional 13 percent plan to offer it in the next year. Most expect to increase their use of coaching and other in-house methods.

Learning technologies are more common in larger organizations. They are more likely than smaller organizations to include e-learning courses and blended learning among their most common L&D practices and to anticipate growth in the use of various learning technologies.

Most L&D content is developed from scratch. There is considerable variation across organizations, but on average, about half of L&D content is developed by internal or external L&D practitioners, two-fifths through adapting or curating existing internal or external materials, and a tenth through user-generated content.

Itineraries: Plan the Learning Journey

Learning journeys in Britain are expected to be a lot more than a traditional "e-learning sandwich" (adding e-learning on either side of the learning event). The use of technology in learning is not new to the British learner. In fact, according to research conducted by Bersin by Deloitte (2016), the learning journey should consist of many different moving parts.

L&D professionals looking to provide a training solution in the United Kingdom must leverage more than traditional face-to-face training. It has become increasingly apparent in recent years that

L&D practitioners are seeking equilibrium in training, attempting to reach employees in diverse, complementary ways.

While instructor-led training is still the primary L&D delivery method (32 percent of training hours), it has declined 45 percentage points since 2009, when it accounted for 77 percent. Online training accounts for just over a quarter of L&D delivery methods. And informal, continuous learning—especially experiential learning, on-the-job training, collaboration, and feedback—are becoming increasingly prevalent (Bersin by Deloitte 2016).

Research from Towards Maturity (2014) also indicates that half the L&D professionals it surveyed are using 16 different technology options to support learning, including e-learning, live online learning, learning management systems, and online assessments. This extends beyond face-to-face training, which accounts for around 56 percent of the learning journey, and into digital and virtual learning, with blended programs being offered more and more to the British learner (Towards Maturity 2016).

Best-Practice Techniques

All that said, education in the United Kingdom still affects what training techniques are acceptable as best classroom practices. Consider these best practices from my experience:

- The British learner tends to favor more conventional teaching methods. They are naturally somewhat reserved in their view of more unconventional methods that trainers bring to add creativity and innovation to training. A good example would be that a British learner audience may not be too keen on stepping into creative sessions using paper clips, pipe cleaners, and rubber bands, because they may see the utilization of these items as being trivial or unimportant to training. There are always exceptions to the rule, but in the main, Britons expect their learning to be served up in conventional ways.
- The British learner is educated in the very traditional way, where an educator is leading the session with

learners learning from and with the educator. Expect to be challenged by British learners—they are very comfortable with doing this. Learners do not mean to insult the educator's expertise, but are simply trying to get a better understanding of the topic.
- It is good practice to support the line managers of the learner group in being able to hold a conversation and inquiry with the learners as they go through the learning journey. Provide managers checklists and tools that support the learner group in applying what they learn.

Measuring Success

Most organizations conduct some form of evaluation or measurement of their L&D initiatives. Many organizations will use learner and customer satisfaction surveys. Few organizations that I have worked with have taken evaluation or measurement beyond Kirkpatrick Level 1 smile sheets.

That might be changing, however. Research from CIPD (2015) shows that "20% (of organizations) assess the behavior change of participants by evaluating the transfer of learning into the workplace. Evaluations are considerably more widespread and more in depth in organizations where L&D is aligned with business strategy and where the development of L&D capability is encouraged and enabled."

Packing Lists: Logistics, Technology, and Resources

Few challenges will face the global trainer coming to the United Kingdom to deliver training. There are many airports, both international and national. The road links and public transport infrastructure provide excellent access between the main cities, with car rentals widely available. One word of caution, however, is to leave plenty of time for journeying around. Distances between cities may look relatively short, but the United Kingdom is a small island that is well populated. And remember, driving is on the left side!

Technology-wise, the United Kingdom is well served, with high-speed Internet access in most major cities and 3G or 4G cellular networks supporting roaming mobile phone service. The technology devices available to the traveling trainer vary from one facility to another—most hotels, conference rooms, and training venues will supply regular computer projectors or TVs to hook your laptop up to, either using the conventional multipin VGA or HDMI adapters.

Power sockets in the United Kingdom use a three-pin configuration, so bring a travel adapter, widely available at the airport and major shops. Some training venues can provide adapters if they support a diverse international traveler community.

British learners will expect the trainer to be fully prepared for the day, to be first in the room, and the last to leave. In preparing to train in the United Kingdom, here are a few more elements I suggest you consider:

- **Itinerary.** Lay out the itinerary and plan the time that it will take to travel between the airport and training venue. As stated earlier, the United Kingdom is very densely populated, and many cities have multiple suburbs to navigate before reaching city centers. Likewise, the training venue may be in a rural area (a trend in the United Kingdom is to have hotels and training venues placed in the countryside, which may limit travel options).
- **Resource requests.** Check ahead with the training venue to determine any special needs. The usual trainer toolkit of computer projector and TV, flipcharts, and refreshments are commonplace, but if there are specific requirements, do not assume that because it is usually available in your country it will also be available in the United Kingdom.
- **Materials.** It's best to have all materials shipped to the training venue, or source a local printer early in the planning and have them shipped locally.

Largs, meaning "the slopes" in Scottish Gaelic, is a resort town in Scotland. Many UK training programs are hosted outside big cities.

Customs: Body Language Dos and Don'ts

Brits are unique in their body language. Here are some general tips:

- British learners are not tactile. They often display discomfort with perceivably intimate physical contact, such as hugging or back-slapping, in a formal situation. Unlike other European countries, there is no kissing on the cheeks to welcome people; a firm handshake will suffice.
- Personal space is also important; set up training rooms so that every learner has adequate room. Britons are very territorial about their personal space, whether it is their desk, their car, or their seat on the London Underground. Don't stand too close to a British person when addressing them or put your hand on their arm to make a point, as they may shrink away feeling uncomfortable.
- Use gestures sparingly, and keep emotions in check. Observe British learners for a short while to see how much they do or do not emote before deciding whether it is just the culture that appears to be showing a lack of emotion, or whether they are not connecting with the training topic. If training British learners in a virtual

environment, where personal space will be invisible, still be cognizant of potentially limited emotion.

- Putting your hands in your pocket while speaking is considered too laid back, and is regarded as rude.

Climate: Create a Warm Learning Environment

The British learner is typically very receptive to training and will engage very well with fellow learners and the trainer alike as they come together in a training event. They are naturally curious, and appreciate strong signposting of agendas and receiving a clear understanding of what they will be doing during the training.

While the language in the United Kingdom is English, like many countries, various regional accents and dialects may cause the traveling trainer to be somewhat challenged. However, as a nation, Britons are used to others asking them to repeat themselves several times because of not being understood at the first attempt. In the United Kingdom, there is much fun poked at individuals with different accents, and in general, it is taken well.

If a group of learners is coming together for the first time, there will be a natural curiosity among them of who else is in the program. Participants enjoy good introductory activities at the start of a session, such as interview and introduce your neighbor, or network and establish common interests or themes. However, if the group of learners knows one another, trainers can jump straight into the training without having to do detailed introductions.

Of course, part of the reason for doing introductions is for trainers to know more about their audience. To avoid the perception of an unnecessary introduction, be creative in establishing why the group should do them. For example, using a topic-opener activity, which includes a brief introduction, will work. My favorite is to use topic continuum knowledge lines: Draw a long line on a whiteboard. At one end of the continuum, write "little awareness of the subject." At the other end, write "expert on the subject." Have participants line up according to their understanding of the subject. Then ask them to introduce themselves and to explain their position or experience level. This exercise also identifies who may need more help and which participants may be able to assist others. Another quick idea is to use a pre-event questionnaire or survey.

Things to Consider: Handle Classroom Challenges

British learners won't intentionally bring any unique challenges to the traveling trainer. However, common challenges may come from:

- **Reluctant learners.** These learners attend training because they are told to or because it is part of the standard development. I have found that this type of learner responds well to being asked to consider how they can use the information, rather than feeling they have no choice but to attend.
- **Interruptive managers and colleagues.** In today's time-pressured business world, managers or colleagues of the learner often interrupt the learning event itself. It is not something, in my experience, that tends to be intentional or deliberate—more just the pace of business life and the demands on our time.
- **Time.** Be very clear in the time commitment involved in the training session. Provide clarity around stop and start times, breaks, and when learners can step away from training if needed.
- **Technology in the classroom.** This is more of a business challenge of the ever-connected learner, but be wary of learners using tablets or smartphones in the classroom unless they're meant to as part of the course. Our ever-connected world means there are potentials for distraction and interruptions all through the day. British businesspeople are likely to have multiple devices, with phones provided by the company as well as their personal phone. Audiences are accustomed to being asked to switch devices off, but that may cause challenges with

Millennial learners using digital note-taking—many use smartphone cameras to capture slides. Be clear on what is and is not acceptable.

Tips and Warnings: Advice for Nonnative Trainers

In having trained thousands of British learners over the last 15 years, here are some guidelines for the traveling trainer:

- There will be expressions in your vocabulary that may not translate well with the British learner. Trainers from the United States often use sports phrases about baseball, like "hit a home run" or "knock it out of the park!" Baseball isn't a mainstream sport in the United Kingdom, so the analogy likely will be lost in translation.
- British learners aren't keen on trainers who spend large amounts of time sharing how successful they have been, war stories, or anecdotes that do not relate to the learning event. Modesty is an inherent trait in the British character. Be measured in the amount of time devoted to establishing credibility, and remember that the training course is about the content and what they can do with it.
- British learners make good volunteers—be comfortable with eliciting help from learners in setting up activities or annotating flipcharts while debriefing activities.
- British learners tend to emphasize style over substance. Generally, they favor a less enthusiastic and flamboyant style than some trainers use while presenting.

Bon Voyage

The British learner has many differences and similarities compared with other nationalities, but the key to collaborating, communicating, and connecting with any learner audience, as we know, is to get to understand them better. Half the challenge trainers have is creating an environment in which learners trust, respect, and are comfortable working and learning with us. We owe it to them to ensure an environment that can help them to learn, work with others, and see how they can apply what they learn. I wish you much success working with fellow Brits!

***

About the Author

David Smith is co-founder of Virtual Gurus, a global consulting firm supporting organizations in leveraging the potential of web-conferencing technologies to be more effective in meeting, presenting, marketing, and training virtually.

David is a globally recognized thought leader, a published author, and a keynote speaker on the opportunities and challenges that digital technologies like Adobe Connect, WebEx, and Skype for Business can bring virtual colleagues and clients. He is a passionate speaker who brings high levels of energy, practical tips, and advice to his audiences, allowing attendees to take actionable ideas and best practices back to the workplace.

References

Bersin by Deloitte. 2016. *UK Corporate Learning Factbook 2016: Benchmarks, Trends, and Analysis of the UK Training Market.* Oakland, CA: Bersin by Deloitte.

Brake, T. 2017. "Infographic: Top 10 Insights to Understanding British Business Etiquette." *Country Navigator,* June 1. https://countrynavigator.com/blog/infographics/infographic-understanding-british-business-etiquette.

CIPD (Chartered Institute of Personnel Development). 2015. *Annual Survey Report: Learning and Development 2015.* London: CIPD.

Towards Maturity. 2014. *Modernising Learning: Delivering Results.* London: Towards Maturity.

——. 2016. *Unlocking Potential: Releasing the Potential of the Business and Its People Through Learning.* London: Towards Maturity.

13

United States

Donna Steffey

Delaware was the last of the 50 states I checked off my list of places to train in the United States. From classrooms, I have watched the sun set over the Statue of Liberty in New York, experienced the miller moth invasion in Colorado, and heard the jubilant sound effects of slot machines in Las Vegas.

Beyond the United States, I have facilitated learning programs in 25 different countries in the past 20 years. Travel has shaped me as a trainer, helped me develop a global mindset, and given me a beautiful collection of both stamps in my passport and Starbucks mugs from around the world. Understanding talent development in the United States seemed easy compared with the complexities that I experienced abroad.

However, while working as a lead designer on a global leadership program, I learned a valuable lesson. We had designed a multiday leadership program that would be rolled out across Asia, Europe, and the United States. We were careful to ask design partners in Europe and Asia to provide region-specific case studies for us to use with topics like coaching, conflict management, and managerial courage. We thought that by putting region-specific examples in the back of the participant materials, facilitators could select the appropriate case study for their audience, and we could use one workbook for all regions.

Participants from around the globe attended the pilot programs. The U.S. participants came from the Northwest, the Mid-Atlantic region, and New York. The feedback we received suggested that none of our well-written, one-size-fits-all case studies for the United States fit all. For some of the conflict management examples, pilot participants from the Northwest could not picture such a conflict situation occurring. Attendees from the Mid-Atlantic region suggested that employees would not discuss the situation but would instead probably "bury" the conflict. New Yorkers thought that the situation did not even describe a conflict;

it was just a regular discussion. We realized we could not serve the U.S. learners with one case. What was interesting was that our global partners had provided us with multiple cases for their large regions. We needed to go back and do a more thorough audience needs analysis to design local case studies for U.S. participants.

Our U.S. design team was not alone in making this generalization that all U.S. audiences were alike. It is a common misconception. This chapter will help other talent development professionals tailor their design and delivery for diverse U.S. audiences.

People and Culture: Get to Know Your Audience

"How are you guys doing?" seemed like an innocent enough question, but it quickly became apparent to learners that I was not from their area, where "y'all" is a more common expression. They responded to the question with a grin, making it evident that I had chosen the wrong greeting due to the various English dialects spoken throughout the United States.

There are 315 million people and many ethnic groups in the United States, due in large part to its immigrant population. The country can be divided into five regions grouped by history, traditions, economy, culture, characteristics, and geography: Northeast, Southeast, Midwest and Plains States, Southwest, and the Pacific Northwest.

Jersey City, New Jersey, is one of the most culturally diverse U.S. cities (Bernardo 2017). There are more than 300 million people and many ethnic groups in the United States, due in large part to its immigrant population.

You might understand the importance of adjusting your content and style for delivering learning when you travel internationally. However, many trainers fail to go through the same preparation to figure out how to adjust their style or content for regional differences within the United States. That strategic oversight could hijack training efforts. Here are three must-dos.

Appreciate Differences

The United States is a melting pot of cultures. It is one of the most culturally diverse countries in the world. However, some well-meaning articles on cultural differences have a potential to do harm with their generalizations and stereotypical information. A more thorough approach is to use cultural intelligence and to be open-minded about ethnic themes and receptive to interpersonal feedback when interacting with people from different U.S. cultures. Use good observation skills and ask questions to learn more about people. Incorporate icebreakers and inclusion activities in class to learn about participants and to help attendees get to know one another. A favorite icebreaker of mine is to ask people to share something they have done that they believe no one else in the class has done. We learn about their uniqueness with that simple request.

Sharing meals with participants can also be an appealing idea. I was invited to facilitate a team-building class for financial experts who were not communicating. The course included communication styles, team exercises, and discussions. However, the real change in the team's dynamics happened when we shared lunch together. Someone asked why a team member was not eating. That question sparked a conversation about religious customs, and the floodgates of cultural diversity opened. In the United States, participants are generally a little nervous about discussing religious or ethnic differences. Creating a safe environment where people feel comfortable can open the lines of communication, so people understand and relate to one another rather than avoiding the differences.

Talk to People

The best way to understand more about the region of the United States where the facilitation is taking place is to ask lots of questions:

- **Discuss regional quirks.** The United States has many unofficial holidays. Ask how locals respond to holidays like Halloween or St. Patrick's Day. Do they dress up and expect a little celebration, or ignore the holiday?
- **Probe for even the slightest cultural differences within the organization from region to region.** Recently, I trained in the Pacific Northwest, where people are more environmentally conscious than the average American. Someone suggested that I should "cut fresh sprouts growing over by the window in the cafeteria to put on your sandwich." The look on my face revealed my lack of understanding of their commitment to a sustainable environment.
- **Ask how people dress.** I had an embarrassing experience once while teaching in a southern state. On my way out to lunch, someone looked at me and asked what was on my legs. After a brief scare, I noted she was referring to my pantyhose. Her reply was, "It's too hot here. We don't wear hose." Another client in the Midwest said that the dress code included a dress and hose for women, and she expected her facilitator to dress accordingly.
- **Share lunch with participants.** The networking is great, and local participants know the best places to eat, including when the food trucks visit their area. An excellent way to connect is to ask participants to share a list of must-go-to restaurants or local activities to do in the evening, and then include stories and examples to "localize" the presentation.

Getting Started: Conduct a Needs Assessment

While surveying colleagues across the United States, reduced life cycles for instructional design and delivery processes is one trend I've seen. Talent development professionals tackle training requests of all types from all levels of the organization. Whether the request comes from a training director, a department manager, or an advisory committee, trainers are being asked to fix organizational problems "yesterday." It may be as simple as corporate decisions to cut training budgets, or it may be workplace trends affecting U.S. talent development. These trends continue to demand just-in-time delivery, which puts pressure on time and financial budgets.

Here are two suggestions for practical needs assessments.

Ask Direct Questions

In U.S. corporate environments, people tend to be straightforward. As a training consultant partner, you are expected to respond in an assertive manner as you move through the needs assessment discussion. For example, a decision maker may make a specific request such as, "We need team building." As a consulting partner, you should be sure to clarify their requests, not just say yes.

A client recently asked for help designing an influence program. Influence is a broad and vague topic. Asking questions like, "What do you mean by influence?" "What sort of situations do these participants need to influence?" "What business goals are driving this need?" and "What performance gap are you seeing?" all helped clarify the request. It takes patience and courage to have these discussions, but they often lead to targeting exactly what the client's goals are and the results they need.

It's not enough to end the discussion when the topic is clarified. You need to continue to advocate for other elements of the program that are essential based on your design knowledge, whether it is delivery methods, assessment tools, or an off-site location. For one client, we were inviting senior executives to be part of the kickoff for a program. Having a C-level manager kick off a program supports the learning. Suggesting that the senior executives be part of a panel discussion and stay for lunch to get to know participants informally was an even better idea. The discussions were the hit of the program for participants and executives alike.

Summarize Results

Most U.S. managers prefer a big-picture view with supporting evidence as a backup. Prepare a summary document to ensure buy-in. The document could include the following:

- Make recommendations quickly when presenting ideas. Be prepared to circle back with more details if the requester asks for more information.
- Get approval on the learning objectives discussed.
- Justify any actions you decide not to take.
- Confirm budgets.
- Share any concerns over budgets. Especially share concerns if constraints cannot be met. Don't just say yes. Remember: Honest, direct communication will be most valued in the United States.
- Use a multipurpose summary template.

Itineraries: Plan the Learning Journey

Planning a journey can be a daunting task. It is easy to get overwhelmed. The following simple steps will help engineer a well-planned learning journey, so less time is spent worrying about smile sheets and more time is spent transferring knowledge.

Decide Where the Learners Are Going

Identifying the destination is the first planning step for any journey. A good needs assessment conversation will assist in determining the purpose, learning objectives, and direction of the training program.

The co-pilot for any learning journey should be the learners' manager. In a recent study done by DPG Plc. titled *Transforming Formal Learning,* 45 percent of the 5,000 employees surveyed reported that their managers discussed learning objectives with them before they attended training (Overton and Dixon 2016). What I have found is that U.S. managers are willing to have discussions about objectives and learning goals if they are coached by talent development professionals to understand the benefits of those conversations. You need to provide managers with pre- and post-course tools such as job aids, coaching tips, email templates, and quizzes to reinforce what their direct reports learn in training.

Select Delivery Methods

Think of your last vacation. Did you use only one mode of transportation, or did you use a combination of car, plane, ship, and Segway to get to your destination? Combining or blending approaches is a good idea for the learning journey, too. Looking at current North American training trends from ATD's (2015) *Global Trends in Talent Development* report can you help plan the right blend for learners:

- Currently, a little over 50 percent of learning hours available are instructor-led classroom hours.
- Synchronous, instructor-led online learning accounts for about 25 percent of instructor-led training. The United States boasts the highest levels of this type of training.
- Self-paced online learning accounts for about 34 percent of learning in North America.
- Use of mobile learning is under 5 percent in the United States. This could be because the United States does not fall into the top 10 countries for mobile smartphone use.
- Twenty-one percent of training in the United States utilizes a blended approach.
- Social learning is a growing trend, with approximately two-thirds of U.S. companies saying they use the method. Social learning is an activity where participants learn by watching and modeling what others do, including

watching videos, observing tasks, answering questions, and posting in discussion forums. Both younger and older employees enjoy learning this way.

Plan Activities

Simulations and games have been standard training tools for more than a decade, and U.S. audiences have come to expect them. Listening to a lecture becomes annoying. The average adult attention span is only about 20 minutes (Cornish and Dukette 2009); however, my observation is that attention spans in the United States seem shorter than that. Plan a break from face-to-face lectures with U.S. audiences every 12-15 minutes. For synchronous online learning, expect attention spans of three to five minutes.

Training technologies are becoming more advanced, and companies are seeking more ways to have an impact on learning. Whether using games from U.S. television shows like *Jeopardy!* or *Family Feud* or activities found in game books like *Games Trainers Play* by John W. Newstrom (1980), computer simulations or scenario-based role-plays do not drift too far away from learning content. U.S. audiences quickly become disinterested and unreceptive if they do not see the connection to what they're learning before, during, and after the activity.

When planning activities, be sure to:

- Select an activity that will drive performance on thejob.
- Start the game by sharing the learning objective connected with the game.
- Debrief with questions:
    - o "How does this activity relate to the content?" If the participants cannot see the connection, the activity didn't work.
    - o Don't be afraid to ask, "How did this activity's challenges connect to real problems in the workplace?"
    - o Remember to ask, "How will you apply what you learned?"

Evaluate Success

The Kirkpatrick levels of evaluation are essential. Know which level the organization currently measures and then urge the organization to go further. Create additional ways for knowledge to be measured in class and after class. What else can be done to measure results and return on investment?

Sometimes, even when everything is done right, unsurpassable roadblocks may be reached. In one instance, the Super Bowl was coming to town, and a media company that wanted to cash in reached out to me. My team and I planned the perfect learning journey:

- We helped with the needs assessment and identified the corporate goal: Increase sales for the Super Bowl.
- The learning objective for the Sales Manager Coaching Program was also clear: Coach sales staff through the new sales process.
- We designed and delivered an excellent program. Managers enjoyed the program, and it earned 4.8 on a scale of 5.
- We videotaped the coaching role plays and gave managers feedback on their performances, so we knew they could demonstrate the proper coaching skills.
- After 45 days of delivering coaching to their sales staff, we surveyed the sales staff. We used the learning objective language on the survey so we could be sure managers were demonstrating successful coaching behavior changes. Survey results were good.
- Our learning journey was going in a straight line following all the measurement signposts. Sales were also increasing.

The end results would have been spectacular if Mother Nature had not decided to dump an ice blizzard on that warm-climate city for Super Bowl weekend, destroying last-minute advertising and halting print delivery.

Packing Lists: Logistics, Technology, and Resources

In the United States, technology is reliable, so technological difficulties are easier to handle. Prepare by packing extra batteries, power cords, multiple copies of materials, and a few extra supplies, and you shouldn't have to worry about technical problems.

During a recent situation, a client forgot to rent a projector. Fortunately, we had packed one of the new HDMI pocket projectors. The hotel had extra adapter cords and could reproduce a handout. Reliability is a common experience with most on-site and off-site venues in the United States.

Preparation and additional resources are still key. At a recent conference I attended, the speaker's remote slide advancer went dead in the middle of her train-the-trainer presentation. She probably had extra batteries but did not stop her presentation at that moment. A participant in the front row replaced the presenter's batteries, so the presenter did not miss a beat.

For a synchronous, online environment, get online early, test equipment, and work with a producer whenever possible to reduce technical difficulties. Bandwidth can still be a concern in the United States if too many people are online and try to run video and cameras all at the same time. Having a good checklist is still important.

Customs: Body Language Dos and Don'ts

Being on the Second City stage in Chicago, where the likes of Jim Belushi, Gilda Radner, and John Candy had performed, was one of the most fun experiences of my life. Only after taking the Second City improvisation classes and applying my new skills to the training profession did I realize their real benefits. U.S. training audiences enjoy a little drama, or "edutainment," with their lessons. Projecting your voice, feeling comfortable while acting out stories, or experimenting with physicality to emphasize a point are all vital skills to have for a U.S. instructor. Finding the right fusion of theater and lesson is the challenge.

A sign in front of Chicago's Second City comedy theater. U.S. audiences enjoy a little edutainment in their training, so improv techniques might serve you well with these participants.

The following outlines important body language dos and don'ts to keep in mind:

- **Move around the room.** Education in the United States is informal, so training needs to be informal, too, or seem informal. However, it is still important to be completely prepared. If not tethered to technology, survey the room for possible traffic patterns and move around the space.
- **Sit occasionally, perhaps on a tall stool.** Equality is important in the United States, so participants believe that they are equal to you, the presenter, and do not want to feel like you are standing over them during discussions. However, standing up while facilitating online helps with voice projection and energy.
- **Respect personal space.** Comfortable social boundaries in the United States are three to four feet apart. However, classroom and conference chair arrangements in the United States are closer than in some other cultures. A handshake or a touch on the shoulder is OK, but nothing else. Participants may hug each other occasionally, but

don't initiate a hug. If someone gives you a hug, it is OK to respond warmly.

- **Gesture naturally.** Practice gesturing in front of a mirror to look natural. For smaller audiences, keep gestures between your waist and shoulders. For audiences with more than 30 participants, your gestures can be bigger. As a U.S. audience gets comfortable, they will accept exaggerated gestures that reach beyond your shoulders.
- **Make eye contact.** Most U.S. audiences expect to make eye contact with the instructor and hold it for approximately three seconds. There are always exceptions. Native Americans' communication style is influenced by values that emphasize humility, respect for elders, and concern for group harmony (Chiang 1993). They prefer minimal eye contact.
- **Stand confidently.** Feet should be shoulder-width apart. Spend most of the lecture time standing on both feet. It is OK to sit down when you are facilitating a discussion and want the focus to be on the participants instead of you. Genuinely confident people speak with certainty. Participants in the United States appreciate the confidence.
- **Project your voice.** Americans are known for being loud. It is OK to use voice projection occasionally for vocal variety. It adds to the edutainment effect.
- **Pace yourself when speaking.** The average rate for English speakers in the United States is about 150 words per minute (National Center for Voice and Speech n.d.). Speaking too quickly is one of the most common speech problems. Perhaps it is because most of us tend to speed up our speech when we are stressed or excited. Focusing on your enunciation is a good way to slow down your speech. Practice reading out loud with a timer.
- **Smile and use humor.** A friend once came to watch me present. She was there for the grand finale, which

included a summary and driving home the learning objectives. She described the closing as passionate. Then she mentioned that she had not seen even one smile throughout the entire ending. Human faces are capable of more than 10,000 different expressions. Be sure to use some of them. As for humor, the safest to use in the United States is a little self-critical humor. Avoid humor about religion, politics, gender, or ethnicities. U.S. audiences are very sensitive to those topics.

Climate:
Create a Warm Learning Environment

A warm learning environment in the United States must be more than just edutainment. It does not happen accidentally—it happens by design. Creating a positive, engaging learning environment comes down to relationships: the participants' relationship to the learning environment, their relationship to the content, their relationship to one another, and their relationship with their instructor.

Create a Connection With the Environment

- Arrive 45-90 minutes early and prepare the learning environment, whether online or face-to-face. Distribute training materials, test equipment, and arrange for open discussion spaces.
- U.S. learners have come to expect fidgets and stress toys on the tables. These toys enliven learning, stimulate the senses, and keep kinesthetic learners engaged.
- Provide refreshments when possible. U.S. audiences love chocolate in the afternoon and expect coffee and tea all day long. I have worked with some companies that have eliminated food for budgetary reasons. It is risky to be the facilitator when there is no food or coffee.

Create a Relationship to the Content

- Send an invite to the learners before the event communicating learning objectives—what participants will be able to know and do by the end of class. Millennials, especially, are motivated when they know how they can make a difference.
- Invite learners' managers to be part of the pre-class discussion. Send out pre-work. U.S. audiences are more likely to do pre-work if their manager mandates it.
- Celebrate learner success.

Create Relationships With One Another

- Learn and use participants' names, so they get to know one another.
- U.S. audiences value networking. Mix up participants into different groups using pair-share, triads, small groups, and breakout rooms in online environments.
- Most U.S. audiences enjoy sharing their experiences and stories. In one class design, the instructor was supposed to describe the "challenges of the job," but the feedback suggested that the instructor gave too many examples. By changing the module to allow participants to identify their own challenges and to role-play solutions, we were able to better engage the audience, and evaluation and retention scores went up.

Create a Relationship With You

The role of a teacher in U.S. classroom environments has changed. Years ago, student-teacher relationships were more formal, and the teacher's judgment was accepted. Today, students take the leadership role in creating and leading discussions. Because of the educational system, these changes affect what happens in U.S. training environments:

- Greet participants early and ask them about themselves. Share facts about yourself that align with their interests.

- U.S. participants expect you to have a mindset of "serving your learner."
- Have faith in people, and they will rise to the level of expectations.
- Treat everyone with dignity.

Things to Consider: Handle Classroom Challenges

Americans believe time is money, and they hate to waste time. If a participant must attend training without knowing its relevance to their job, they become frustrated. Partner with managers throughout the entire instructional design process, from needs assessments to sending the training invite, to minimize the potential of participants coming to a training session ill-prepared. Discussing the learning objectives and job relevance often throughout training is also essential for defusing potential classroom frustrations.

I do not think people intend to be difficult in training classes. Indeed, the difficult personality exists, but more frequently, a challenging situation is due to recent organizational changes. People from the United States are not afraid to speak up and voice opinions. Often the classroom becomes a public forum for expressing concerns about changes. Participants may be frustrated by a new process that they were sent to class to learn.

The worst situation I faced was a government shutdown. The news came over the weekend. On Monday morning, welcoming participants to "When Bad Things Happen to Good People" was not easy. Participants were hostile. The fact that I had nothing to do with the situation did not matter to them. Being the only person of authority present made me the target of their venting. We did not cover any content until after lunch. They came back from lunch and, as a group, decided to turn their backs to me. I read material aloud until the end of the day to the back of 25 angry heads. In the United States, conflict is often dealt with openly and directly.

The situations may not be about us as the trainer. However, it is our responsibility to address any situations we face. It is our duty to treat each participant with dignity while we defuse challenges. There are three available tools for handling difficult situations with people.

Verbal Responses

- A favorite is the "yes, and . . ." response. The agreement disarms people and gives the floor back to the instructor.
- Paraphrase but repeat a milder version of what they just said. U.S. participants realize the HR consequences of not "toning down" their remarks. The milder paraphrase will send a clear message.
- Verbal responses can also include private conversations you have with participants on break. Communicate kindly but firmly the behavior expected. Politely telling even managers, "I need you to listen to allow space for your team to speak up," is acceptable in the United States. Professor Geert Hofstede's work on cultural dimensions describes the Power Distance Index (PDI), which measures the equality of workers and supervisors. The United States is a low-barrier culture, where it is OK to speak up, so giving private feedback to a manager is fine.

Body Language and Movement

- Move slowly and carefully toward a difficult participant. Keep hands down by your side and open, which is a universal sign of peace. Nod your head yes, using the "yes, and . . ." verbal approach. Back away slowly as you begin to speak. Finish remarks facing away from the difficult participant. Ask another question of someone from the other side of the room.

Authority

- As a last resort, use your authority and privately ask a participant to leave class. If you don't have the power, call a manager to handle the situation. During one four-day class, one of the participants was repeatedly late due to work obligations. Reviewing ground rules and a private, friendly conversation with him did not help. He intended to fit the program into his workday schedule rather than delegating work to someone else. Talking with his manager in the evening allowed me to have the day-three conversation. When the participant showed up late on day three, he had a choice: Be on time or sign up for the class next month.

- When there are difficulties, participants expect the facilitator to manage the situations that may be interrupting their learning. Manage situations with dignity and participants will appreciate the professionalism, even if the situation cannot be remedied. However, if a facilitator loses their cool, participants will most likely turn against the instructor. The training development professional is expected to keep the learning environment safe for learners.

Tips and Warnings: Advice for Nonnative Trainers

When coming to the United States to facilitate, or even when meeting U.S. participants in a local classroom or online, here are a few ideas to keep in mind:

- **Build credibility with an opening story that includes credentials that matter to the participants.** Share the reason you were invited to teach this topic in this location. Tell audiences your connections to the content and them. Look them in the eyes when telling the story. U.S. audiences also like a little self-effacing humor. Let them laugh at you about things that are uncomfortable about our culture. Laughter connects us and allows us to be human. It can lighten any situation and reduce stress.
- **Ask difficult questions in the needs assessment.** People in the United States are direct and respond well to direct

questions. Being indirect will probably not generate complete answers about performance gaps or business goals. Also, ask clients what they mean when they use business buzzwords. The clarification will help training be a success.

- **Speak slowly and clearly.** People in the United States tend to be lazy listeners. Give audiences a chance to get accustomed to your accent, speaking style, and cadence.
- **Do not assume all members in a U.S. audience have the same needs and interests.** Do not believe the generalities and clichés seen in movies. Get to know people as people. Learn a little about the region of the country where the class is held. Do not assume that if participants are in the United States and speak English they are Americans and adhere to all U.S. beliefs.
- **Do not hesitate to manage difficult situations.** Participants may challenge you early. Be respectful but control the situation. People will be watching for coolness and poise. Call for a break, or have students change seats to prevent talking. Saying, "Let's agree to disagree" is a good way to gain control of a discussion.

Bon Voyage

Remembering back to that day, looking from the classroom window and seeing the breathtaking view of the sun setting over the Statue of Liberty, I realized that her symbolism still holds true. Liberty's image is one of welcome, strength, majesty, and hope. Get to know U.S. audiences when training with multinational organizations. The Statue of Liberty is more than a monument; she is a beloved friend.

About the Author

Donna Steffey is an international trainer, author, facilitator of the ATD Master Trainer Program, and adjunct faculty member at Lake Forest Graduate School of Management.

References

ATD (Association for Talent Development). 2015. *Global Trends in Talent Development.* Alexandria, VA: ATD Press.

Bernardo, R. 2017. "2017's Most & Least Culturally Diverse Cities." WalletHub, February 22. https://wallethub.com/edu/cities-with-the-most-and-least-ethno-racial-and-linguistic-diversity/10264/#methodology.

Chiang, L.H. 1993. "Beyond the Language: Native Americans' Nonverbal Communication." Paper presented at the 23rd Midwest Association of Teachers of Educational Psychology annual meeting, Anderson, Indiana, October 1-29. http://files.eric.ed.gov/fulltext/ED368540.pdf.

Cornish, D., and D. Dukette. 2009. *The Essential 20: Twenty Components of an Excellent Health Care Team.* Pittsburgh, PA: RoseDog Books, 72-73.

National Center for Voice and Speech. n.d. "Voice Qualities." National Center for Voice and Speech. www.ncvs.org/ncvs/tutorials/voiceprod/tutorial/quality.html.

Newstrom, J.W. 1980. *Games Trainers Play.* New York: McGraw-Hill.

Overton, L., and G. Dixon. 2016. *Transforming Formal Learning: Principles for Delivering Results in the Modern Workplace.* London: Towards Maturity.

14

Western Europe

Deniz Şenelt Kalelioğlu

At 6 a.m. in the lounge of the Waldorf Astoria Hotel in New York, my career changed for the better. I was already delivering training locally, and sometimes nationally, in Turkey. My desire for international work was about to become a reality, finally. As a member of Junior Chamber International (JCI), a worldwide federation of young leaders and entrepreneurs, I was attending the 2004 Leadership Summit at the United Nations headquarters in New York City. The JCI president leading the summit was an excellent trainer from Venezuela. After his presentation, I asked him for a few mentoring moments. He said he could spare 15 minutes at breakfast the next day.

That is how I ended up at the Waldorf Astoria, with its shiny silverware, yellow flowers, and smell of fresh bread. His advice was to join ATD. In 2006, I was awarded the Most Outstanding Trainer in Europe, the first Turkish trainer to receive that honor. In 2015, I was appointed as the JCI training commissioner, who is responsible for training activities in European countries.

Since that breakfast in 2004, I have delivered training programs in 31 countries at various multinational events, extending from the United States to Japan to Denmark to Syria. Being an international trainer is challenging, so prepare for mental barriers. Some of my own challenges have derived from the fact that I am young-looking, Turkish, and a woman. To bypass these obstacles, I confidently demonstrate experience and expertise and keep a sense of humor and a positive attitude. "Turkey is where east and west meet, living on two continents," I would say. Then humorously I would end with, "No, I do not ride a camel to work."

People and Culture: Get to Know Your Audience

Determining which countries are included in Western Europe can be complicated. It could be mostly the western part of Europe, like France, the Benelux countries, and maybe Spain and Portugal. Alternatively, it could be the limits of the European Union or the division of Europe that United Nations agencies use. All that said, I have training delivery experience in many of these areas and have traveled all over the region, so here is the list of countries this chapter will look into:

- **The German-speaking:** Austria, Germany, the majority of Switzerland, and Liechtenstein
- **The Francophone:** France, parts of Belgium, parts of Switzerland, and Monaco
- **The Benelux:** Belgium, the Netherlands, and Luxembourg
- **The Nordic:** Finland, Sweden, Norway, and Denmark
- **The Mediterranean:** Turkey, Greece, Italy, and Spain.

Western Europeans are like a colorful mosaic. When talking about the 18 nations listed, their groupings can summarize their cultural differences. The Mediterranean people are dynamic, very talkative, and loud. The Nordics are patient and questioning. Benelux needs the fun element, while Francophones seem reserved. Germans are sharp and by the book. More broadly, according to the *Global Trends in Talent Development* report (ATD 2015), a top content area in Europe is interpersonal skills.

Experiential learning experts Simy Joy and David Kolb (2009) have a cultural learning style preference model that can help you understand Western Europe better. The model says that transformative experiences create learning. They include concrete experience, time for abstract conceptualization, reflective observation, and active experimentation—in other words, experiencing, reflecting, thinking, and acting.

Peter Honey and Alan Mumford (2000) identified four learning styles—reflector, theorist, pragmatist, and activist—that you'll see throughout Western Europe. For instance, I have a dynamic delivery style that fits perfectly with Spain and Turkey, so I prefer to have learners jump right in with lots of hands-on experiences. However, that method may not work throughout Western Europe.

In Germany or Austria, they like to understand the reasoning behind the actions and are known as theorist-style learners. In Norway and Denmark, learners are more pragmatic. They do not like games for the sake of games, but enjoy activities where they can discover a direct application back on the job. Francophone and Benelux learners prefer to learn not by jumping in, but by collecting data and reflecting.

My first time presenting in Denmark was in Aalborg while teaching a training design class. Explaining directions for an exercise took longer than expected. There were so many questions, as if participants were judging every word. I did not feel comfortable until I remembered that Nordic people do not like activities unless they understand the purpose. Surprisingly, when explaining the same content in Spain, participants barely listened to directions and jumped into the role-play exercises. As international trainers, particularly in Western Europe, we need to have a global mindset and employ our observational ability to understand participants better and adjust our style to their needs.

Aalborg, Denmark

Getting Started: Conduct a Needs Assessment

Tolerance for uncertainty is essential when analyzing the various success factors for being a trainer in Western Europe. A thorough needs assessment is key to identify business drivers to target training and understand the audience.

Conducting needs assessments will be different in various part of Western Europe. For instance, German-speaking countries and Nordics will be ready to answer questions openly and may even provide reports to give an insider view. When I was training German doctors on how to talk with patients, the HR department provided a detailed report about the participating physicians. When I delivered the same course in Turkey, the needs assessment process was completely different. There were no reports, so I asked permission to go directly to the clinic to observe doctor and patient conversations to get information.

Francophone, Mediterranean, and Benelux countries will give only hints about the big picture, making it necessary to use more direct questions to uncover what is truly a training need. In one case, I was approached for sales enhancement training, only to discover that customer relations skills were needed instead.

The data-gathering tools to use in the countries where systematic thinking is dominant—like Germany, Denmark, Norway, and Sweden—could be questionnaires and surveys or focus groups. However, in more emotional cultures—like Spain, Turkey, Italy, Greece, and even Austria—using on-site visits, observations, and one-on-one interviews will result in more accurate data. In Western Europe, custom-designed data-gathering tools will allow you to dive deeper into the needs assessment.

Regardless of the data collection tool, frontline managers are as important as the HR manager in this needs assessment phase. Approach each of the related directors in a polite way, and emphasize that their support and comments are valuable. Conversations might need to be more aggressive in the Mediterranean (insist on receiving their active participation) and more assertive in the Nordics (demonstrate standing as an expert), while softer tones would be sufficient in the Francophone and Benelux countries.

Itineraries: Plan the Learning Journey

As a trainer, there are four dimensions on which to focus during training delivery: content, process, task, and people. Because I'm from the Mediterranean, my preferred style as a learner and as a trainer is to be active and focus on people and process dimensions. German-speaking nations might prefer the trainer's attention to be on the process and task. Nordics would expect content focus. As talent development professionals, you need to concentrate on all four dimensions, but it is important to recognize your natural tendencies and the preferences of the learners.

All methods—lecturing, discussion, and case studies; interaction and activities; and simulation and hands-on practice—fit well with Western European learners as long as you plan their timing to match your learners. Another good idea is to use blended learning to enhance adaptability for the culture and European locations. Keep in mind the objective, timeframe, and participants.

Tactically, when training in Europe, start with pair work, follow with group work (changing team members between assignments), and end with pair work again. This pattern starts the interaction in a safer zone, opens discussions that ignite group thinking, and finishes with sharing the action plan with a partner. From time to time, decide if adding competitive energy would have a positive or negative impact on the particular group. The cool Nordics or goal-oriented Germans might need the liveliness, but the energetic Turks or Italians might forget that it is just a learning activity.

In addition to these interactive discussions, include quick review activities to energize participants in each module. Conduct relay races or have participants go up to a flipchart to draw a picture of what they learned. Include a longer, more challenging activity each day to get participants thinking more deeply. Remember to close the activity with good debrief questions such as, "How do these challenges relate to the workplace? What was learned? What will be applied back on the job?"

Here are some additional tips for a smooth learning journey:

- **Match the schedule to the country.** While designing or delivering a classroom-based workshop, even the schedule needs to align with the routine of the country. In Benelux or Mediterranean countries, start the training with a fun activity related to introducing the participants, but make sure to limit the timing per person and the scope of the introduction. In German-speaking and Nordic countries, introduce the subject efficiently, and then have them discuss some content in pairs or groups, starting with their introduction.
- **Get participants involved.** Choosing the spokesperson of the group discussion also matters in different parts of Western Europe. German-speaking and Nordic countries will decide among themselves without losing time. However, the best method to use in Benelux or Mediterranean countries is to throw a ball to a group member to have them start, then select the next speaker by tossing the ball again.
- **Nail the closing.** The closing is also crucial. It should summarize the course content, the objectives, and what the participants need to apply back on the job. Decide how to summarize—preferably let the participants interactively do that—and how to leave them with their next steps. Prepare the setting for them to come up with an action plan for themselves.
- **Explain the purpose of pre- and post-work.** Collaborate with the HR department or the organizers to get help with the pre- and post-work assignments. For German-speaking countries, just send them the guidelines about the assignments and let them know the deadlines. For Nordics, provide arguments about the reasoning.

For Francophone and Benelux countries, explain the benefits. For Mediterranean countries, explain what could go wrong if they do not do the activity.

Creating an online group may be a useful tool for pre- or post-work. You will recognize the cultural differences even in the active use of social media. For example, it might not be easy for talkative Mediterranean participants to keep messages focused on the training subject. If this is a multinational group, expect Norwegians or Germans to become frustrated with the off-target conversations and perhaps even withdraw from the team.

When it comes to evaluation, the Kirkpatrick evaluation model (where reaction, learning, behavior, and results are the four levels) is widely used. In the Mediterranean and Benelux countries, the general measurement of training goes to Levels 1 and 2. A Level 1 technique is to hang a flipchart with colorful sticky notes—one with a smiley face and one with a thought bubble—on the inside of the room close to the door, where participants will see them while exiting. Ask participants to give feedback under each heading. German-speaking countries and Nordic people skip Level 1 and measure learning and behavior, and may even go to the results level for the long term.

To obtain valuable evaluations, give participants forms to use, which German-speaking and Nordic participants will return with solid points and comments. However, other countries might include smiley faces and soft words. A better idea is to approach these participants and have a personal chat to get real feedback. Cultural variances explain these differences in power or how individualistic or collectivist the nation is.

These cultural characteristics will also be visible in the training session if the participants are asked to give feedback to one another. After an activity, it is more productive to ask the participant to evaluate themselves first, and then ask others to provide additional feedback. While conducting this debriefing, it would also be helpful to use a frame, like what was good and what could be improved. The structure will help keep the audience focused, and help you finish on time.

Packing Lists: Logistics, Technology, and Resources

When working with international organizers at a foreign location, it is unrealistic to expect the correct setup and all needed materials to be ready. Logistics, technology, and resources will often be issues. When trusting everything to be set up, Nordics or Germans will not disappoint. However, with Francophones and Benelux, be sure to check everything. With Mediterranean countries, to be on the safe side, bring extra materials, such as cables, adapters, batteries, pens, and sticky notes.

When I was training on public speaking in Luxembourg, every detail was perfectly organized: the facilities, room setup, and materials. The same training course in Spain had some delay due to unavoidable adjustments to the room setup; my toolbox came in handy because the organization's assistant was having a siesta.

Electrical outlets are different in Europe than in the United States and the United Kingdom, so be sure to carry an adapter just in case. The Internet in Western Europe is reliable, and there are many Wi-Fi spots. However, mobile-phone roaming is expensive, so either buy an international package from your provider or get a temporary SIM card for use in that country.

Customs: Body Language Dos and Don'ts

Mediterranean people often talk with their hands, especially Italians and Turks. Big hand gestures do not mean excitement or anger; it is just part of normal conversation. So for the Mediterranean participants, the more animated a trainer can be, the better. Conversely, keep calm in the Nordic or Francophone countries so as not to seem nervous or incompetent.

The Turks make a noise between their teeth that sounds like *thic* or *chik* and means *no*. It is sometimes accompanied with the head moving upward. They shrug to say either "I do not know" or "I do not care." These are very common gestures for Turks and confusing to foreigners until they are understood. Observe and ask a local for an explanation about these and other gestures.

Eye contact also needs consideration. Eye contact might mean attentiveness or engagement to some groups, but it can feel like a penetrating gaze to others. While an intense look between people of the same gender might suggest a high level of trust, that same look between two different genders might be inappropriate. For instance, a man in Germany looked intently down at the floor versus giving any eye contact during a training course I was facilitating. Later on, I learned that he was a Muslim who respected strict separation between genders. However, lack of eye contact does not apply to all Muslims, so don't generalize.

Here are more general suggestions for Western European body language dos and don'ts:

- Pointing with your finger is seen as aggressive. Forceful tones might be common in the Mediterranean, but aggressiveness would not be typical for a trainer. Ask for a volunteer or invite participants to respond to questions.
- You might see some men in Mediterranean countries put their hands in their pockets while standing or cross their arms behind their heads while sitting. If participants display those postures, do not be offended by it. It shows male domination. Still, it is not well received, so do not try to fit into the culture to that extent.
- Physical touch is a delicate issue. In the Mediterranean, close physical contact is common, including extended handshakes and pats on the shoulder. These gestures demonstrate friendship and encouragement. However, the farther north you travel, the more personal space there is between people. You may be able to sense the difference while in the elevator to the training room:

Swedish and Finnish participants are pressed to the wall, while Greeks and even some Austrians have no problem being close. Make sure to observe customs and respect comfort zones so participants will be relaxed.

Climate: Create a Warm Learning Environment

The learning environment is critical. It is a good idea to use customized accelerated learning tools to create an appealing and friendly learning environment to fit different cultures. Use tools like local quotes, music, news, people, and places. Colorful photos would also work well. Research the area and keep up-to-date. For example, do not play Tarkan's songs in Turkey just because he is a famous Turkish singer; he's not as popular now. Catch up with what is new in the country where the training course will take place.

Corporations' and participants' motivations for attending a training session also differ by country. In German-speaking and Nordic countries, companies usually send their employees—including management level—to training programs to learn and network. In Mediterranean countries, praise or rewards are common motivators; participants are chosen because they are good at their jobs. These motivations affect the intentions or the expectations of the participants.

Even what happens after the training session varies. Participants may come up to talk, ask questions, or just exchange business cards or take a selfie. A warm environment means cooperating with their requests. I once watched a trainer read a book during lunch while sitting at the table with participants but ignoring them. Yes, the instructor probably needed the mental break during lunch, but if you need to recharge, leave the room. Ignoring participants who want to chat doesn't create a warm learning environment.

Concerning the starting time of the training, consider traffic and transportation possibilities. For example, if your training course is in Istanbul, a city on two continents with 15 million inhabitants, a start time of 9:30 a.m. is preferred. In Switzerland,

Germany, Luxembourg, and Belgium, 8 a.m. would be typical. Find out the best starting time during the needs assessment.

One thing to keep in mind is that some participants might find a reason to leave class early if there is no certificate or group photo at the end. Tell participants that you have a treat for them at the end of the day to encourage full participation.

Things to Consider: Handle Classroom Challenges

The classroom might contain participants from across Western Europe. Most Western European countries border one another closely, so people are aware of different cultures. Nevertheless, be prepared to handle different kinds of training challenges.

First, participants from different countries often have different concepts of punctuality. Germans are business-minded and arrive exactly on time. Austrians, the French, and the Dutch arrive early to mingle. Italians, Greeks, and Turks may be slightly late. While we are talking about time, a longer lunch break is necessary for Turkey, because Turkish participants like to enjoy Turkish coffee after their meal. Make use of this time by assigning participants to small group discussions.

There might also be gender differences. Mediterranean men might talk over Mediterranean women. And Mediterranean women might not be as bold as Danish or Swiss women while defending an opinion or questioning an argument. Women or men might want to sit in groups divided by gender, out of tradition or just because they know one another better. If they do divide by gender, decide strategically if mixed groups are needed, and if so, explain the reasoning well. I often encounter a room with tables of men and tables of women. Ask them to count off from one to five and then have them sit with a new group to discuss the subject. This way, people are mixed for the sake of learning, so no one objects.

Be careful with activities that require touching. Nordic and Benelux people won't have a problem at all, while Austrians and

French people will likely accept it, even though they do not like it. Be attentive and recognize the mood.

Religion might be an issue to keep in mind as well. Muslims may leave for midday prayers on Friday. I experienced this in Turkey: Some of the male participants asked permission to have time to go to the mosque. You can plan group work for such occasions, so the mosque-goers can quickly catch up by listening to the results of the discussion when they return.

Finally, in Western Europe, many participants will still be responsible for their daily work. To handle this potential distraction, contact the participants' direct managers, and help them understand that it is important that the participants' attention be on the session. After getting the approval on this, write a short email that managers can send to the participants explaining how important their full concentration is during the training session.

Tips and Warnings: Advice for Nonnative Trainers

When designing or delivering training for participants from Western Europe, here are a few things to keep in mind:

- **Learn some words from the local language and use them, especially in the beginning and at least once more toward the end.** Francophones, in particular, appreciate an attempt at French.
- **Bring something local from your home country to share with participants.** I offer Turkish delight—a traditional sweet from Turkey—and evil-eye pins called *boncuk*, which are an important part of Turkish culture.
- **Bring some items to attract attention and to create curiosity.** Put them somewhere visible.
- **Let them share.** Open the workshop with introductions, allowing time for participants to talk about themselves. A favorite icebreaker is to ask participants where their ideal holiday location is, because Europeans love to travel.

- **Don't joke in a new culture.** Hazardous conversations include religion, politics, and even football. In the Mediterranean, football is a no-joke zone.
- **Don't put participants on the spot by calling them directly by name to answer or give their opinion.** This behavior makes the participant uncomfortable, and will make other participants nervous that they'll be the next one called. Instead, find creative ways to invite people to respond.

Boncuk, or evil-eye pins, are an important part of Turkish culture.

Bon Voyage

The main highlight I learned over training hundreds of hours internationally is that all the differences are stereotypes in the end. The most significant memory of my career occurred during a team-building training workshop in the Austrian Alps. While we were debriefing the learning points, a German man in his thirties burst into tears about how touched he was. He was not acting like a typical German man. Just remember to pack a global mindset, make use of cultural intelligence, and respect the fact that, in the end, we all are human.

About the Author

Deniz Şenelt Kalelioğlu is an international trainer, executive coach, learning and development consultant, and founder of ProAkademi consulting firm. She has designed and delivered training programs in more than 25 countries, reaching 100 nationalities on five continents. Deniz has participated in the ATD International Conference & Exposition eight times as a speaker and three times as a panelist since 2007. She was also a speaker twice at the ATD Asia Pacific Conference in Taiwan, and at ATD regional workshops in Istanbul and Denmark.

Deniz served as head trainer at the European, Norwegian, Russian, Estonian, and Austrian International Academies, leading diverse trainer teams. She was designated Most Outstanding Trainer and appointed training commissioner for Europe by Junior Chamber International. She also earned the Distinguished Toastmaster title from Toastmasters International. The first Turkish trainer certified as an ATD Master Trainer, Deniz holds certifications in coaching, consulting skills, instructional design, blended learning, and accelerated learning.

References

ATD (Association for Talent Development). 2015. *Global Trends in Talent Development.* Alexandria, VA: ATD Press.

Honey, P., and A. Mumford. 2000. *The Learning Styles Helper's Guide.* London: Peter Honey Publications.

Joy, S., and D. Kolb. 2009. "Are There Cultural Differences in Learning Style?" *International Journal of Intercultural Relations* 33: 69-85.

15

The Virtual Classroom

Demetrice (Denise) Walker

In the late 1990s, my career was in the field of training for disaster recovery. Lives and company success depended on how fast we could get employees up to speed on handling natural disasters and keep our customers' businesses going with minimal disruption. Then, in 1999, my co-worker suggested that I conduct a virtual training session using a new software technology called WebEx. Previously we trained using a traditional conference call. One exposure to WebEx's visuals, two-way communication, and engaging tools to involve the learner, and I was hooked.

Technology provides talent development professionals with the ability to learn on the go and in any location with an Internet connection. It will continue to connect people from around the globe to knowledge and to one another; that is why I am a tech junkie when it comes to talent development. If it can happen with technology, I will make it happen. I am always testing new equipment, using proofs of concept, and learning which new technology is on the rise. I learn by testing the technology until it breaks. If it is unbreakable, then I put together a process for using the technology more efficiently with the correct tools.

This chapter is about navigating the virtual classroom and getting to know the people and the equipment you will meet along the way. Anything is possible if you have the Internet and a computer.

People and Culture: Get to Know Your Audience

To make technology work as a tool to transfer knowledge, knowing who is in the audience is a must. Moreover, because trainers need to keep the attention of learners who are not sitting in a classroom, you'll need lots of illustrations, activities, videos, and interactive participation to keep everyone engaged. You may also want to use a producer to help facilitate the technology. To allow trainers to concentrate on content delivery and keep people involved in a two-way conversation, a second person to support technology efforts is crucial.

Anytime technology-based delivery is a potential solution, trainers must consider their audience. There are different types of learners, which might include:

- **Technophobes.** These people fear technology. To help them, provide guidelines at the beginning of class and review how to use the technology. Before beginning an activity, remind participants how to use individual software tools. For example, remind the learners to use the "raise the emoticon hand tool" to ask a question.
- **Technology experts.** This audience loves technology and may even know more than you. To keep them engaged, use them as team leads to direct activities. Show respect for their knowledge.
- **Audio, kinesthetic, or visual learners.** For audio learners, make sure to include video pre-work and post-work. During the session, play videos and use prerecorded audio clips. For kinesthetic learners, use whiteboard activities where the learners will have to write answers, ask questions, and contribute to the session. Also, use polling and quizzes to keep their hands busy. For visual learners, use lots of illustrations, graphic designs, and videos.
- **English as a second language (ESL) learners.** Because this audience may struggle to understand written or spoken English, employ lots of meaningful graphics within the session. Allow them time to ask and answer questions. Send out materials and assignments early to give ESL learners time to process the content and come prepared for the session. Use teams and partnering to pair ESL and non-ESL learners.
- **Diverse global audiences.** Select the time zone that is preferable for most of the learners. Use translations within the content when available. Allow learners to

explain the similarities and differences within their regions. Keep diversity in mind when creating group activities, such as using multilingual icebreakers. An example might be: Finish the statement, "In my country, my favorite ice cream flavor is pronounced . . .; in English it is pronounced . . ." The more learners connect and close distance gaps, the better the learning experience will be for everyone.

Getting Started: Conduct a Needs Assessment

To use technology appropriately, perform a thorough needs assessment in the standard way used for any new training initiative. Focusing on a technology needs assessment will help identify available technology, match the technology to the topic, and troubleshoot possible limitations for that region. There are pros and cons for each technology delivery method. Here are some steps for conducting a technology needs assessment:

1. **Determine management's attitude toward technology.** If management prefers classroom training, start by explaining the cost benefits of using technology rather than sending participants to a training program, and account for the resource savings of learner time and effort. Use persuasion skills if management insists on using a particular type of technology because they just bought it. If the technology is not right for the topic, offer to conduct a pilot program, then explain the pros and cons of the technology and the results. Become the expert so you can speak to any objections that may arise.
2. **Assess audience knowledge of technology.** Participants should take a technology skills set survey before the start of any technology-based course. Include questions about how many webinars or interactive virtual sessions they've attended and what operating system and browser they use, and ask them to rate themselves on their level of

comfort with technology. Offer a few courses at different times to train learners on the technology. Remember to record the courses for learners who cannot attend.
At the start of each session, discuss guidelines for how to use chat and how to answer questions using the tools within the system (polling or quizzing). Incorporate icebreakers and brief activities that include the use of the software. If learners have challenges, the producer should take them into a breakout session and troubleshoot the problem. The facilitator should start the session but recap what was learned at the end of each topic to catch up the group. Recording the session and sending the link to the participants is a great way of providing follow-up information to participants having issues with the technology.

3. **Assess available technology.** There are many virtual training software companies available, such as Zoom, Adobe Connect, and WebEx. Table 15-1 lists some pros and cons for these virtual software offerings.

Table 15-1. Pros and Cons of Available Virtual Software

Virtual Software	Pros	Cons
Zoom	• It is user friendly • It has audio and video capabilities • It distributes bandwidth according to learners' bandwidth settings • The app software is mobile and tablet friendly • Sharing content is easy • Video can be played through learners' computers • It allows breakout and whiteboard sessions • It allows trainers to see if participants are actively engaged	• Annotation writing is hard to use • Whiteboard integration within the software does not exist • Multiple windows are needed to see chat and participants simultaneously

Table 15-1. Pros and Cons of Available Virtual Software (cont.)

Virtual Software	Pros	Cons
Adobe Connect	• It has video and audio • Pushing out e-learning created with Adobe Presenter and Adobe Captivate during the session is easy • It can push URLs to the audience • Learners control videos during the course • It allows breakout and whiteboard sessions	• Admin dashboard is hard to use • System setup can be time-consuming • Multiple layouts and windows are allowed to be opened at one time, causing confusion • First-time users can get lost in the session • Keeping track of the session is challenging with the many views available • There are different experiences for mobile and tablet users; for example, chat and polling may work differently on mobile and tablet versions, versus the desktop version
WebEx (must have the training tool enabled)	• It has a user-friendly environment for the host, producer, and panelist • Chat window, presentation screen, and participant list location are in one window • It has emojis that participants can use to increase engagement • Quizzing and polling are available • Many users are already familiar with this platform for conference calls • It allows breakout and whiteboard sessions	• Videos played within a session cannot be heard on the user's computer • There are meeting size limitations for interactive sessions

Keep in mind that when using technology for any topic, conducting a thorough needs assessment is essential. However, going that extra step by assessing the manager's and learner's attitudes and skill levels regarding technology will guarantee a better chance of success and learning transfer.

Itineraries: Plan the Learning Journey

When planning the learning journey, consider how a learning management system (LMS) can help. A learning management system can hold e-learning training content, including videos and PDFs, and pre- and post-assessments. The right LMS will allow facilitators to use an email generator to send out emails to the audience, register participants for the course using the calendar and event functions, and send a welcome email along with the pre-work assignments or assessments. Depending on the results of the knowledge assessments, participants can be invited to take additional courses. A learning record can now follow a student and give insights into training engagement and performance.

Match the Topic to the Available Technology

Using a blended learning approach—combining two or more delivery methods—is an excellent way to use technology. For example, the facilitator can set up a training session on a virtual platform, and once the learners have attended the first course, they can be registered in a virtual learning path. Once complete, the participants may be invited to a live training session as a follow-up to the virtual training one.

Blended learning can comprise online training, live facilitation, and remote broadcasting. For online training, participants can use an LMS to complete their online modules. Online courses can include practicing and role-playing, and some systems will allow for quizzes to be built right into the system. After participants complete the online course, they can attend a live facilitated class or broadcast. This is a way to expand the topic and share best practices. After the online and live classes are finished, the participants can complete a post-assessment to measure the effectiveness of the training initiative.

Once the post-assessment has been completed and passed, an additional assessment surveying the participant may be sent two weeks after the post-assessment. The survey will ask questions such as, "Did you feel confident applying the gained knowledge of the topic?" An assessment can be sent to the person's manager as well, asking questions about the participant's improvement.

Six months later, the participant can be assigned another assessment regarding the application of the topic within the training initiative. An LMS can be used both for assessments and as a survey tool for polling sent through a delayed email process.

Include Visuals, Activities, and Tools

One activity to use during a virtual training session is to separate learners into two teams. Using the whiteboard function, present a list of 20 questions on topics that were covered and have teams race to complete the answers. The producer will count the questions and grade the document by giving points to the teams, with winners announced after tallying the score. Another activity is a virtual tag game. Show a group of applicable pictures, and "tag" or select a participant to describe an image's relevance to the topics discussed. That person will tag the next person.

Two great books that can help you get started are *Michael Allen's Guide to eLearning,* 2nd edition (Allen 2016), and *Virtual Training Tools and Templates* (Huggett 2017).

Measure Online Learning Effectiveness

Research has found that e-learning is the second most valuable training method used in corporations (Pappas 2013). Companies can use an LMS to send out surveys about learner reaction to the training experience (Level 1). A pre-assessment before the training session to test the learner's knowledge of the subject, and then again, several weeks after, is a convenient way to measure what was learned (Level 2). After six months have passed, send an observation checklist to learners and managers of desired competencies to measure behavior training (Level 3). On-the-job application assessments and self-reporting surveys can be completed by managers and learners to measure if the expected changes took place over time (Level 4). Finally, training can be tracked by measuring efficiency, effectiveness, sales, or increased production as compared with stated objectives to assess if ROI goals were met (Level 5), thus encompassing all of the Kirkpatrick and Phillips levels of evaluation.

Follow Up With Social Learning

Following up with social learning is a great use of technology. Some learning management systems use collaboration tools, such as connecting between Facebook and LinkedIn. A community of practice can also be built within the LMS. Twitter, WhatsApp, Google Hangouts, and Skype are great collaboration tools that learners can use to share their expertise and experience during and after the learning sessions to connect and keep on learning about the subject. Some companies use Yammer; this tool is a safe, internal way to collaborate and share documents, articles, and projects. Social learning can create communities where learners can keep in touch, build great relationships, and grow by learning from one another.

Packing List: Logistics, Technology, and Resources

One of the biggest virtual training resource challenges encountered around the world is bandwidth limitations. Designing for multiple types of learner devices and browsers can also be a problem. In many cases, the trainer cannot mandate what device should be used, and has no control over these issues.

Technology Resources

Important resources to consider are Internet services, conferencing services, webcams, cell phones, tablets, two laptop or desktop computers, landline bandwidth, two monitors (to view participants and chat or present material), a mouse, and content in the form of documents or PowerPoint. Use a USB drive or Google Drive to save the recording. A projector or TV is needed if the facilitator will be on-site at one location teaching a group while broadcasting to another location.

Just as useful is having a second person, called a producer, to help run the virtual classroom. A producer runs the technology and is vital to success. They have many responsibilities, including:

- uploading the content while advancing the PowerPoint slides for the facilitator
- monitoring the chat window and setting up activities like polling and questions
- troubleshooting and resolving technical issues behind the scenes so the facilitator can concentrate on the learners
- monitoring session timing and keeping the facilitator on schedule
- taking over if the facilitator has technical troubles
- maintaining audience engagement by including activities if engagement levels decrease
- editing the recordings before distribution.

Backup Plans

Be ready to use the second set of devices if the first fails. The producer is the backup for the facilitator, and both should be able to fill in for one another. If bandwidth is an issue, select a different location ahead of time. If there is a power outage, another facility or a library with a training room can be a substitute. A generator is a good way of maintaining power if the producer or facilitator works from a home office.

Resources Learners Need

Learners need Internet capability and a mobile phone, tablet, or computer and monitor. They also need a webcam, a computer mouse, speakers, and a microphone or headphones with a microphone. Software needs to be downloaded onto their device before the start of the session.

Also, have learners go to www.speedtest.net to check their bandwidth strength before the training course. Have learners join at least one test session before the start of the meeting to ensure that everything will work as expected. They should download the app where necessary and sign in before the onset of the session if the software technology uses a mobile app.

Customs: Body Language Dos and Don'ts

As a virtual trainer, remember that you are still in front of your audience whether or not the camera is on. Participants are watching or visualizing you, so smile and use friendly facial gestures. Turning the camera on is helpful because learners can view the instructor, producer, and one another, and get to know everyone better. Here are a few additional tips:

Pair Your Verbal and Nonverbal Behaviors

Smiling, nodding, and complimenting good answers acknowledges that a reply is correct and encourages students. Voice fluctuations should be used to stress points and ideas while looking directly into the camera so that the learners will understand that this is a crucial topic. Hand movements can be used to stress points. However, they should be used carefully and with an appropriate tone. Note that gesturing too quickly can make learners feel ill. Facilitators should not turn away from the camera quickly or bend down so that the learners cannot see them.

Your eyes should be focused on a location in front of the webcam so that learners think that you are speaking directly to them. Place the webcam on top of the screen and use well-placed cues to remind yourself to look up. If using a laptop, make sure to put a monitor behind the laptop on a stand. Tilt the laptop back so that it appears that the facilitator is always looking at the group. If you are going on break, cover the webcam. Do not walk away from the camera in front of the learners. Do not use the camera as a mirror; others are watching. Do not whisper, and minimize background noise and distractions where possible.

Partner With Your Producer Seamlessly

Use private chat or texting to correspond, particularly if the producer is occupied assisting with a technology issue or setting up activities. Producers should monitor the agenda, activity schedule, and time spent on a topic. They should notify the facilitator if the session is running behind, and they should communicate schedule adjustments as well.

Manage Participant Noise

If learners aren't speaking, keep phones and microphones muted. A hand-raising emoji can be used to ask a question. Use emojis, such as a coffee emoji, to indicate breaks. Alternatively, chat boxes can be used if there are no emojis for breaks or questions. Respond to participants who answer questions when not called. Politely remind them to use the hand-raising emoji or other means as established in the guidelines.

If learners interrupt you or the producer while the session is taking place, politely tell everyone that interruptions are challenging and they need to allow everyone else to finish. If this continues, you or the producer may need to address the participant on a private chat or phone call.

Engage participants frequently in an activity that requires them to put their hands on the mouse or keyboard. Keep them too busy to be distracted.

Climate: Create a Warm Learning Environment

Virtual instructor-led training is different from face-to-face because it is harder for the audience to stay focused and avoid distractions. The facilitator and producer have the shared responsibility of engaging the audience with interactivity every five to seven minutes. Create a warm virtual learning environment by having the learners interact with one another and by keeping the environment informal and respectful. Let students share photos during the training session. Create a collage as each learner posts their picture and send it to the group. Take screenshots of their pictures and send them to the group to create a class photo.

More activities and icebreakers may include a "name my country" guessing game with clues. PowerPoint bingo and Jeopardy are fun ways to engage the learners. For the Jeopardy game, create a PowerPoint resembling the game show's big board and break the participants into groups depending on the size of the class. The group sizes should remain small—no more than five in a group. Use breakout rooms for discussion. Give the teams five minutes to chat and come up with a correct answer to win that round. The winners will pick the next topic. For bingo, send a word document with the bingo card numbers to each participant. Have the producer post the numbers, and have winners use chat to announce they won. The first one to get bingo wins. Games start a competitive atmosphere, and they are a fun way to teach learners how to use the chat box and breakout rooms effectively and efficiently.

Here are two additional tips you can use to create a warm virtual learning environment:

- **Send welcome instructions before class.** These should cover how to log on to virtual training and use the tool. They should also include bandwidth testing directions and required specifications. Also send a short biography to the learners along with social media information (LinkedIn or Twitter). Communicate to participants how absences need to be handled. Provide telephone numbers and email addresses for you and the producer.
- **Explain the producer's role as helper.** Tell learners that the producer is another set of eyes and ears for the instructor. The producer can also identify learning gaps and provide details to the facilitator so that they can fill in the gaps.

Things to Consider: Handle Virtual Classroom Challenges

Technology can be complicated, and sometimes it does not work the way we want it to: computers going dead, Internet interruptions, the volume dropping out in the session. Many of us have been in these situations.

As a facilitator, you should use two computers if possible. One computer can be used to conduct the training course, and the second computer can be used to view the training course from a participant's perspective. Most important, the second machine is also available as a backup.

If participants are having difficulty connecting to the session, ask them to change Internet browsers. If they lose connection during the session, have them shut down their computer and attempt to rejoin the class. Make sure the audience has contact information for the facilitator and the producer.

Inevitably, you'll have to deal with participants who refuse to mute their microphones or who use the chat window for non-training-related discussions. Here are a couple of ways to handle difficult people:

- For learners that talk out of turn, use "mute all" during your session and unmute participants who use the hand-raise emoji or whom you want to speak.
- For participants who do not participate in class, give them a leadership role by asking them to lead a breakout session.

I once had a student who was not well versed in technology and held up the first 20 minutes of training with questions on how to post pictures to the group using chat. In these cases, ask the producer to assist the participant separately from the general group discussion.

Another time I had a learner start the session, stay for about 15 minutes, and then come back five minutes before the end. In this instance, I did not give the participant credit for attending the session, and I notified the person's manager. I also reminded the learners that if they did not participate for the entire session, they would not get credit. Several virtual training platforms will notify you if someone has left the meeting and how much time they spent in the session. Tracking learner engagement is important for the facilitator and the producer. For example, the producer can include more interactions if the participants are not as focused as they should be during the session.

Tips and Warnings: Advice for New Virtual Trainers

Remote webinar training is different from live training. It has a faster pace, it is hard to keep the attention of the participants, and it takes time for even experienced trainers to adapt to the platform. Here are some important points to keep in mind when conducting virtual training:

- **Use a producer.** It cannot be said enough. A producer is a vital part of the training team, so always include a producer in any plans to deliver a virtual class.
- **Engage audiences.** Use emojis, questions, polling, and the whiteboard. Keep your audience motivated with surprising music and pictures. Interact with them every three presentation slides or between each training topic.
- **Connect learners with their peers.** Before the training course, send a group email to all participants and ask them to introduce themselves. Use icebreaker questions in the chat box during training so the learners can get to know their peers. Separate learners into groups and use breakout rooms for them to complete assignments together.
- **Know your material.** Research says that trainers who use virtual training practice their material less because they believe they can keep their notes in front of them and they do not need to study. The fast pace of online training prohibits this practice.

- **Use a world clock.** If your audience is in different parts of the world, use a world clock to schedule your training sessions. Plan the training sessions during a time when most people can attend.
- **Don't lose control of the session.** Use mute upon session entry and unmute only when participants should speak. Use housekeeping rules to remind learners to use the raise hand emoji. Teach them to type questions in the chat box. Ask the producer to read the questions for the students and post the questions and your answers on the virtual whiteboard to keep learners focused on the topic.
- **Don't assume that the technology will work.** Before your session starts, test all computers. Make sure you have power. Make sure monitors are working correctly. Check Internet connectivity. Check virtual webinar software and schedule a walk-through with your producer.
- **Don't take a simple presentation slide deck and drop it into new technology without changes.** For virtual webinars, it is best not to use animation; some animation will not work, and iPad and mobile users will not be able to see it. Enlarge text to a 14-point font or bigger. Use vibrant primary and secondary colors and pictures. Consider your audience, their devices, and their bandwidth.

Bon Voyage

While virtual training can be a cost-effective way to train many participants quickly, a trainer must be prepared to handle the many situations that can occur. As with any good training program, awareness of potential issues, a strategy to control them, and practicing for all possibilities, including your delivery portion, will ensure you are prepared to handle training in a virtual environment.

About the Author

Demetrice (Denise) Walker, a Master Trainer, is the president of D5 Walker Group. A techie, she develops best practices for using technology for training and identifies the best technology to fit the needs of generational learners. She has transitioned training to the growing trend of virtual training and microlearning while saving companies time and money.

Denise loves learning about new technologies and transferring the knowledge to technophobes. She teaches and supports anytime, anywhere learning. She embraces learning on the go on whatever device is available, from virtual reality devices to mobile devices to Xbox gaming devices. Her background includes disaster recovery, business consulting, and marketing.

References

Allen, M.W. 2016. *Michael Allen's Guide to eLearning,* 2nd Edition. Hoboken, NJ: John Wiley & Sons; Alexandria, VA: ATD Press.

Huggett, C. 2017. *Virtual Training Tools and Templates.* Alexandria, VA: ATD Press.

Pappas, C. 2013. "Top 10 e-Learning Statistics for 2014 You Need To Know." eLearning Market blog, December 1. https://elearningindustry.com/top-10-e-learning-statistics-for-2014-you-need-to-know.

Afterword

Learning Trends Around the Globe

Fady Kreidy

"Put a dent in the universe," said Steve Jobs circa 1985. This quote has many interpretations. For me, it speaks about touching the lives of the people in our sphere of influence. That circle includes my children, colleagues, and the learners I meet in training.

It's no surprise that I would admire Steve Jobs. As a child, I loved to disassemble any electronic device and create something different out of it. I got a computer in 1991, a few years after Steve Jobs made his comment. My first teacher was a younger brother—he used to crush the computer system, and I would have to rebuild it. Although it was not his intention, he provided the opportunity to learn perseverance, creativity, logic, and problem solving.

My love for technology continued into college, where I studied computers and communication engineering. After graduation, I worked in a training center as a technician, then an IT administrator, before becoming a manager. Then one day, one of the trainers got sick. The learning manager asked if anyone could deliver the course. I was speechless but somehow nodded my head yes. After that, my life changed. I became a trainer and discovered a new passion: developing people.

During this career journey, I was exposed to different cultures, meeting with people from all around the globe, from East Asia to Central America. Still influenced by Steve Job's passion for doing what you love, my purpose in life became to nurture future generations and discover tools and technology to help them. It is amazing to have a passion for people and an addiction to systems at the same time. With this competency combination, there is no better time to be in the talent development field.

This chapter is about the future of talent development. What we see through research and surveys is a strange mix of people and systems, education and technology, emotions and logic, and the reality of how it is affecting organizations. Today's organizations face a business environment characterized by increasingly complex and rapid changes. Different industries face different challenges, but all conclude that change is becoming a must for companies to survive. The learning paradigm is no exception and has to go through its set of changes to support businesses' bottom lines and retain talent.

Everything around us seems interconnected now; all that used to be disconnected is now wired and intelligent. Cities, transportation, and technology increasingly influence every aspect of our world, and the workplace is no different. Fueled by digitization, mobilization, augmentation, and automation, the skills we need will be dramatically different, and our way of work will never be the same.

According to ATD's 2016 *State of the Industry* report, in 2015, 41 percent of learning hours used technology-based methods, compared with 38 percent of hours used in 2013, an upward trend in average learning hours. Moreover, the ongoing evolution of mobile technologies is driving continuous changes in the ways organizations do business, nurture talent, and communicate with customers and employees.

Independent research firm eMarketer (2017) estimates that "in 2017, 2.73 billion people worldwide will use a mobile phone to access the Internet." The firm also estimates that tablet users will top 1.4 billion by 2018 (eMarketer 2015). The widespread popularity of smartphones and tablets has powered extensive interest among learning professionals about the use of mobile devices for training delivery.

By looking at key metrics, this chapter will help talent development professionals benchmark practices against those of regional peers. It offers assistance to evaluate what could be applied and how to apply it based on the readiness of their audience. It suggests tailored learning offerings to each unique learning environment, offering comparisons across the global regions of Africa, Asia, Europe, the Middle East, and North and Latin America.

Learning Methodologies

Face-to-face classrooms are still the most used learning method worldwide. According to ATD (2016), the classroom was still the delivery mechanism for 49 percent of learning hours used (and available) in 2015, but this number is down from 51 percent in 2014 and 55 percent the year before. This figure has dropped over time: In 2009, 60 percent of hours used were delivered in a classroom. For the first time, in 2015, less than half of available learning hours at the average organization were offered in a classroom setting.

Instructor-led online training programs, or synchronous learning systems—such as WebEx, Centra, and Adobe Connect—are real-time, online learning events. All participants are logged in at the same time and work together as the instructor leads the class. According to ATD (2016), 10 percent of learning hours at an average organization were delivered using the instructor-led online method in 2015.

Instructor-led remote (satellite, video) is a method where a live instructor delivers the course from another location using video-conferencing software, such as Skype or Cisco. This approach was used about 6 percent of the time in 2015 (ATD 2016).

Asynchronous learning systems, such as e-learning, videos, and on-demand modules, allow the instructor to provide course materials that learners can access at any time within defined limits. This method does not require trainers and learners to participate at the same time. Some examples include online and self-paced courses, online discussion groups, and email. Asynchronous learning systems averaged 18 percent of learning methods in 2015 (ATD 2016).

Blended learning is a planned combination of training delivery options such as coaching, participation in class, reading, reference material, and involvement in workshops or online communities. It is worth noting that technology capabilities can drive some portion of a blended learning solution.

Self-paced online, such as platforms like Udemy, Coursera, and EDX, allows participants to take web-based courses at their pace. This method does not require the trainer and the learner to participate at the same time or to follow a strict structure. Self-paced online delivery continued to be the most widely available and used technology-based method in 2015, accounting for 19 percent of learning hours available and used, up from 16 percent in 2013 (ATD 2016).

Self-paced, nonnetworked computer is a methodology that only requires the availability of the training content on an offline storage, like CDs or DVDs. This kind of learning averages around 4 percent of learning hours used (ATD 2016). Self-paced print, such as books and written articles, took 5 percent of learning hours used in 2015. Noncomputer technology (DVD players, overhead projectors, TVs) is slowly decreasing, comprising 1.4 percent of learning hours (ATD 2016).

Mobile learning (including gamification and business simulations) is showing a slow increase in popularity over the past few years, garnering around 3 percent of learning hours used in 2015. Although this figure remains small, it represents an increase from 2013, when mobile learning averaged 1.2 percent of hours used (ATD 2016). A third of organizations have mobile learning programs (ATD and i4cp 2015).

Other methods, like assessment centers, in-person coaching and mentoring, and structured on-the-job training, are currently growing in popularity, from almost nothing a few years ago to 4 percent of learning hours used, according to ATD and i4cp (2015).

Learning Content Areas

Although the number of annual learning hours is not notably different across regions, with a worldwide average of approximately 34 hours annually, some regional differences emerge when looking at expenditures, outsourcing activity, content, and delivery methods (ATD 2015). These variances may reflect cultural factors of desired knowledge and skills. As in previous years, managerial and supervisory content made up the largest share of the total courses offered in 2015: 12 percent on average across all organizations (ATD 2016). Table 16-1 shows it by region (ATD 2015).

Table 16-1. Top Learning Content Areas

Asia-Pacific	Europe, the Middle East, and Africa	Latin America	North America
1. Managerial and supervisory	1. Interpersonal skills	1. Professional specific or industry specific	1. Interpersonal skills
2. Interpersonal skills	2. Managerial and supervisory	2. Interpersonal skills	2. Processes, procedures, and business practices
3. Executive development	3. Customer service	3. Managerial and supervisory	3. Managerial and supervisory

ATD (2015).

Afterword

Global Survey

The contributors to this book ran a small, practical survey with trainers in 25 countries and territories, divided into five training regions: North America, Central and South America, the Middle East, Asia, and Africa.

The survey asked professionals to consider the current methodology usage in each country or territory where they delivered training. Then, it asked them to use their network, experience, connections, and other data science to give a rough estimation on its anticipated usage in 2020.

The results indicate that there will be a significant decrease in the use of traditional delivery learning—from 73 percent in 2017 to 53 percent in 2020—in contrast with an increase in learning using technology, from 16 percent to 32 percent (Figure 16-1).

Figure 16-1. Learning Methodologies: 2017 vs. 2020

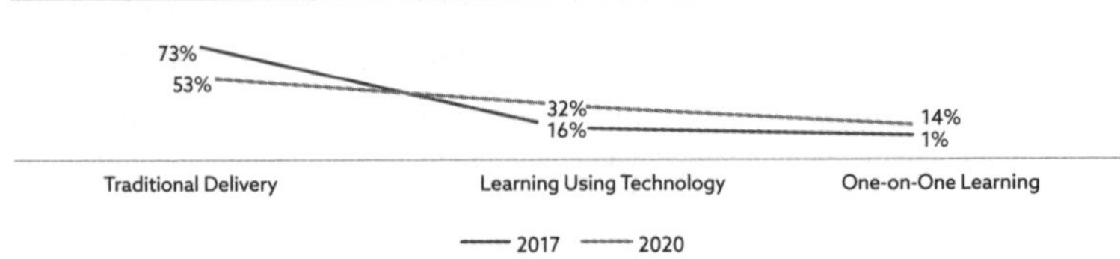

Figure 16-2 shows this trend broken down by region.

Figure 16-2. Learning Methodologies by Region

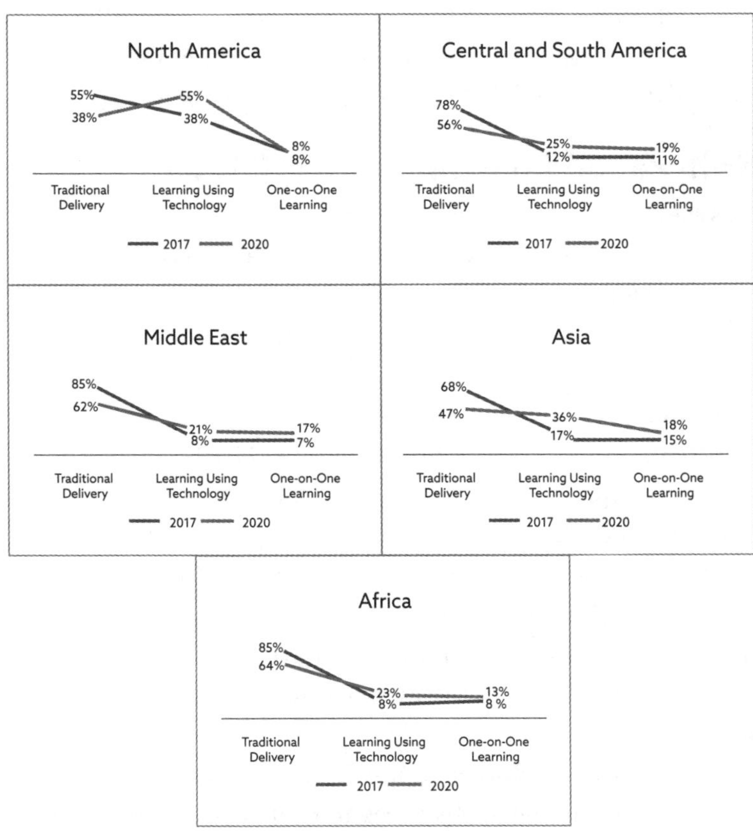

North America leads the regions in integrating technology with learning, and is predicted to remain at the top for the next three years. Asia is second, with a promising use of technology in 2020, even though only Japan and India were surveyed. Central and South America, Africa, and the Middle East are almost the same. Learning continues to rely on traditional methods, such as instructor-led classrooms; however, this does not eliminate the fact that technology will be playing a bigger role in 2020. The figures also show an interesting point about how the use of technology is related to how developed the country is, which could be because of the broad availability and length of time technologies have been available.

Another means of learning delivery involves one-on-one learning. Although this technique was not among the leading tools and approaches noted in the research, the survey found that it will be used more in the future, especially in emerging countries.

Self-Paced Learning and MOOCs

Massive open online courses (MOOCs) have experienced varying levels of attention over the last few years. Recently, interest increased for several reasons. The ability to access MOOCs whenever and wherever encourages companies to shift more toward online learning, giving learners autonomy. For many employers and employees, their cost effectiveness is also attractive. And now Coursera, EDX, Lynda.com, and many other MOOCs offer learners an array of options accredited by well-known universities, so you have greater choices while meeting needs and expectations.

Furthermore, according to our survey, self-paced learning shows a promising growth worldwide, moving from 4 to 6 percent in 2020, with all regions on the rise. Here are some best MOOC practices gathered from the master trainers who conducted the survey:

- Identify employees' desired learning outcomes. Create a list of learning objectives and outcomes desired by the organization and its employees. If possible, define which competencies to improve and the success measures.
- Identify and screen appropriate MOOCs. Look for providers that offer single sign-on options, a defined and on-demand catalog, and an administrative dashboard for monitoring. It will limit the vast choices of courses to only 40 or 50. Involve staff in the selection to gain their ownership.
- Define the pool of employees who are eligible for self-paced learning. Each learner has a different learning

style; some will benefit from self-paced learning and others will prefer traditional methods. Make it worthwhile for the intended audience. If the provider is offering a package encompassing X number of hours for X number of employees, try to decrease the number of hours per employee and widen the number of staff.

- Use employee development plans and performance appraisals to determine the skills and competencies each employee needs, enabling a match with a particular program.
- Assess the course. Employees should report course completion and submit any certificate they receive for their personnel file. Course completion should trigger a survey that asks learners to assess their satisfaction with the course based on meeting their learning goals. Compile these data to create more robust information and analysis.
- Recognize employee activity and reward employees who have completed a course. Awards will differentiate a company that has a keen eye on people development.
- Share the employees' experience and organize knowledge-sharing sessions to benefit others. Research shows that courses completed in teams have higher completion rates. Therefore, if possible, let the team who attended the course lead these knowledge-sharing sessions.

Gamification

Gamification is the process of using game thinking and dynamics to engage audiences in learning a subject in an innovative way. With its ease of use, flexibility, and low cost, it is gaining popularity in the learning industry and allows learners to have fun while attaining information and building skills.

My company introduced gamification to its markets. The gamification elements were an instant hit and drove employee engagement. The idea that participants are building competencies or changing a habit while having fun is proving to be effective, and it is increasing participants' acceptance of innovative learning solutions. Most important, managers have witnessed behavioral and habit change.

Yet according to our survey, use of gamification is growing slowly, comprising only 2 percent of overall learning usage currently; it's projected to increase to 3 percent in 2020. North America is at the top, but use in Asia, Africa, and the Middle East is growing fast.

When using gamification, consider these suggestions:

- Look for providers that offer an administrative dashboard for follow-up and monitoring, full-time support, and thorough reports on participant results. The latter should include the strengths and the weaknesses of each.
- If the game needs a certain amount of time to be completed, insist that participants finish in less time, and grant them an extension as a "special exception." Many will wait until the last minute if given an extended period to complete the games.
- Be careful about candidate selection and use a pilot group to test the solution. If an employee is interested in or has been suggested for this course, forward contact details, if possible, to the provider alumni so they can exchange info and evaluate whether this approach will fit or not.
- Clearly communicate objectives before the training program. Run an introductory session for participants to orient them to the game.
- Again, be careful with the selection. Trainers cannot, for example, engage people for a time management course who usually can't commit due to their busy schedule. It is better to engage them in traditional face-to-face sessions.

- Reinforce learning by sending refresher emails at regular intervals after the training course.
- For participants who complete the game, offer a prize that is related to the topic as an encouragement for their efforts and to use what they learned. As an example, for a time management course, offer an agenda with their name engraved on it or a one-year subscription to a productivity tool.

Mobile Learning

Mobile learning is the ability to provide educational content on personal pocket devices, such as smartphones, which accommodates people on the move. Not included in this category are tablets, laptops, or mini PCs. Another important aspect of mobile learning is it encourages social interactions by promoting and fostering collaboration and communication.

The primary objective of mobile learning is to encourage anywhere, anytime learning, allowing participants to gather, access, and process information outside of a traditional context. My CEO uses mobile learning during airport layovers, and other colleagues use it while they are in the field.

Our informal survey confirms that mobile learning usage is on the rise, even though it is minimal. Now it accounts for 1 percent of the current education usage, mainly coming from North America with 60 percent share, but the outlook shows that it will reach 3 percent usage in 2020, with Asia topping the list.

Based on the experience with mobile learning implementation of the surveyed regions, there are several issues to note:

- Consider how to integrate mobile learning into your formal training programs. Is it for homework usage only? Is it going to be controlled in the classroom? Is it going to be used for mentoring purposes? For the latter, there are several smartphone apps in the market. I used one called Mentor, and it proved highly effective. It is a web and mobile application that gives participants the ability to upload videos to designated experts for evaluation, coaching, and feedback. The expert reviews the videos and can annotate or record audio comments. This would be ideal for salespeople, who could take videos of their product pitches, upload them, and ask for advice.

- Determine user readiness. With the increasing use of mobile devices for social networking, it seems evident that employees would welcome mobile learning opportunities, but not necessarily. Some employees know only the basics. Conduct orientation sessions before each new release.
- Begin by launching pilot programs to verify technologies and delivery methods and to get buy-in.
- Keep content fresh. Users will immediately drop out when the info becomes outdated.
- Provide support, either internally or from the provider.

Business Simulations

Business simulations are applications used mainly on tablets or smartphones for training or assessment. Most simulations are scenario based, with learning objectives that include strategic thinking, entrepreneurship, leadership, decision making, problem solving, financial analysis, market analysis, operations, teamwork, and time management. It provides interactivity and collaboration, as opposed to similar on-paper methods. Business simulations' current usage is limited, with only a few organizations benefiting from them. The methodology is new and the cost is not competitive. However, our survey predicts a fast growth rate for business simulations in 2020, reaching almost 2 percent of learning hours used, with North America, the Middle East, and Africa topping the list.

Before deciding to implement business simulations, consider these points:

- The use of business simulations is linked to tablet usage. Once tablets are in the hands of more people, business simulations will increase in market share.
- Good business simulations are costly compared with other technological approaches. The cost is typically per user and still needs to be controlled. However, with a rise in competition, expect a drop in prices similar to the one that occurred with self-paced learning.
- Business simulations should be related to relevant content and should link to a purpose. For instance, I once used a simulation for teaching performance management. In this simulation, I played the role of a manager and guided the discussion out of the given options toward achieving a productive meeting with the appraised person. The outcome of this simulation was highly effective.
- An orientation session should occur before the implementation. Are the users technologically ready for complex business simulations where you virtually answer a phone, drive a car, ask for a meeting, or create a company?
- Provide good-quality tablets with large screens (no less than nine inches) and have enough technical support.

Conclusion

Change is coming. Some countries are currently more advanced in technology usage, but others will be topping the list soon. Whether you're an investor, a learning specialist, or a learner, carefully select which approach to adopt to deliver the right message.

I'll leave you with a set of questions to consider when developing a strategy to cope with future trends:

- Do trainers know what will shape the decisions of organizational training and development functions in the future?

- How will technology affect talent development teams?
- Are instructional designers ready for the future? Do they know now what it takes to be there?
- Is your organization ready for change?
- Will these learning trends produce better learning results?
- What kind of budget will you need?
- Do you have a place for Millennials?
- Are you innovative and creative enough to lead the change? Do you have the transformative power?

As Gerd Leonhard mentioned in his book *Technology vs. Humanity* (2016), "The future is in technology, yet the bigger future lies in transcending it."

***

About the Author

Fady Kreidy is a computer and communication engineer from Lebanon who has more than 15 years' experience in the fields of IT and HR. His passion for developing people led him to make a surprising shift from operations to HR, believing in human assets as the main drivers for many businesses. His long and extensive role in HR has exposed him to different cultures, especially during his time at Nestlé, meeting with different generations from all around the globe. He is a Microsoft Certified Trainer, a CCC Certified Trainer, an ATD Master Trainer, a Hay Group Emotional Intelligence Certified Trainer, a Profiles Certified Assessor (PCA-Profiles Psychometric Academy), and a FISH! Philosophy Trainer (ChartHouse), and is in the process of getting his coaching certification from the International Coach Federation. He is well known in his region as a distinguished trainer, commended for his high performance and proven results, coupled with an extensive background in HR generalist affairs.

References

ATD (Association for Talent Development). 2015. *Global Trends in Talent Development.* Alexandria, VA: ATD Press.

——. 2016. *State of the Industry.* Alexandria, VA: ATD Press.

ATD and i4cp (Association for Talent Development and the Institute for Corporate Productivity). 2015. *The Mobile Landscape 2015: Building Toward Anytime, Anywhere Learning.* Alexandria, VA: ATD Press.

eMarketer. 2015. "Tablet Users to Surpass 1 Billion Worldwide in 2015." eMarketer, January 8. www.emarketer.com/Article/Tablet-Users-Surpass-1-Billion-Worldwide-2015/1011806.

——. 2017. *Worldwide Internet and Mobile Users: eMarketer's Estimates for 2016–2021.* New York: eMarketer.

Leonhard, G. 2016. *Technology vs. Humanity: The Coming Clash Between Man and Machine.* London: Fast Future Publishing.

Appendix

Assessing and Developing a Global Mindset

Donna Steffey

At this point, you may be wondering if you have a global mindset? Here are some questions to ponder; there are no right or wrong answers. The four CQ competencies mentioned in the introduction serve as a base for these questions. To get a truer picture of CQ, use one of the instruments discussed later in this appendix. These questions have been designed to be introspective and stir thinking about personal global mindset capabilities.

CQ Drive

The Interest, Confidence, and Drive to Adapt to Cross-Cultural Situations

- Which cultures are you uncomfortable with or naturally drawn to? CQ drive includes admitting the inherent prejudices and biases we have toward particular groups of people and working to overcome those biases.

- What level of confidence do you have in your ability to function well in cross-cultural situations? Why?
- What will be gained from functioning effectively in situations characterized by cultural diversity?

CQ Knowledge

Understanding Culture and How It Shapes Behaviors

- Can you compare the values, norms, social etiquette, and religious perspectives of other cultures with your culture?
- Considering the cultures you most frequently work with, can you demonstrate some of the business etiquette rules for acceptable verbal and nonverbal communication?
- Can you coach someone else on how to effectively manage people and relationships in a different culture?

CQ Strategy

Using Self-Awareness and Knowledge to Manage Cross-Cultural Experiences

- Would you know how to plan an effective dynamic cross-cultural meeting or training course?
- Can you anticipate what to expect, based on your level of intercultural knowledge?
- Are you aware of how you come across? Can you adjust behaviors if the situation is not going as planned? Making self-aware adjustments is called "reflection in action."

CQ Action

Acting Appropriately in a Culturally Diverse Situation

- How naturally can you adjust your verbal behaviors, such as accent, tone, pronunciation, or cadence, without coming across as mimicking another culture?
- How adeptly can you adjust communication styles in stressful situations, like reaching agreement during discussions or managing classroom challenges?
- Can you list nonverbal behaviors you might need to adjust?

Assessing the Organizational Global Mindset

Some organizations dismiss global mindset or CQ competencies as a set of mysterious, soft skills that cannot be measured or taught. That is not the case; these skills are being developed by smart organizations globally.

In recent years, there has been a flurry of inventories that assess intercultural competencies. Organizations use these assessments to develop cross-cultural awareness and skills in staff. They can highlight which competencies need the most attention and can benchmark performance. Other appraisal inventories include multirater assessments so users can see how their colleagues, supervisors, and customers perceive their CQ. Some intercultural inventories assess individual traits, demographic characteristics, attitudes, beliefs, or implicit biases.

When selecting an intercultural assessment, be clear about what needs to be measured. Investigating the reliability and validity of the instruments is important. A useful way to do this is to read published articles that compare the different assessments. Table A-1 gives a quick overview of various instrument types.

Table A-1. Selecting an Intercultural Assessment

What Do You Want to Measure?	Sample Assessment	Ideally Used For
Individual preferences (personality traits, cultural values, beliefs, etc.)	• Cultural Values Profile • Culturewise • GlobeSmart • Multicultural Personality Questionnaire	• Individual contributors • Self-awareness • Hiring (for "fit")
Cultural awareness and readiness (attitudes and worldview)	• Implicit Association Tests • Intercultural Development Inventory	• Diversity programs • Overseas assignments
Intercultural skills	• Cultural Intelligence Scale	• Inclusion initiatives • Multicultural teams • Global leadership roles

Livermore and Van Dyne (2015).

Developing a Global Mindset

Assessing your global mindset is an important first step. Engaging in a global project is a good second step. Seek opportunities to travel to a foreign land or to collaborate with a diverse team at home, face-to-face, or online. These experiences help you further develop your global mindset. You need to be intentional with these experiences so you can be reflective in action.

Expand CQ Drive

Challenge biases. Most of us feel comfortable with people who are like us. Social scientists believe children acquire prejudice as toddlers so that inherent biases can seem automatic. The goal is to be honest with ourselves. Being aware of hidden biases enables people to monitor and attempt to amend hidden attitudes before displaying that behavior. To take a free implicit biases test, visit https://implicit.harvard.edu/implicit/takeatest.html.

Get out of your comfort zone. Try new ethnic restaurants, visit neighborhoods catering to unique cultures, and talk with colleagues from different backgrounds. Take a service-vacation in a new country. Global Volunteers, founded in 1984, is the oldest and one of the largest international human and economic development organizations engaging short-term volunteers on long-term community projects. To date, more than 33,000 volunteers of all ages and from all walks of life have served in 34 countries on six continents. Learn more about Global Volunteers at http://globalvolunteers.org. In 2001, I did my first Global Volunteers project and realized that overcoming our fear of something different can increase our drive for new and unique experiences.

Get back into your comfort zone. When we travel internationally or work cross-culturally, our brain is not on autopilot like it is when we are functioning in our normal environment. We must think about everything we say or do. We might be sleeping in a different time zone, eating food we are not accustomed to, or staying in a hotel with strange noises. Remember to recharge your batteries occasionally. Allow time for exercise. Bring along favorite snack foods. Download TV programs from home for an evening alone. These treats will enable you to wake up rested and ready to meet the new challenges tomorrow.

Grow CQ Knowledge

Do research. Use Google, Wikipedia, and newspapers from the region. Reading newspapers and magazines with international news will help increase your global awareness in general. Visit sites that share customs and cultural information from countries around the globe. Watching foreign films or reading a novel can also provide additional information and some enjoyment.

People watch. Observe people in action. What things do they do that are similar to your culture? What are they doing differently? How are the gestures, space between people, and other nonverbal signs different? Share your observations with a friend from that culture and ask them to explain the observations.

Cultivate CQ Strategy

Use mindfulness. Mindfulness is when you stay focused and aware in the present moment. During intercultural situations, we want to remain calm and recognize and identify our feelings, thoughts, and reactions. We must resist the impulse to speak or act until after we have analyzed the conditions.

Write down observations. Sketch what is seen and heard. I once went with a team of training volunteers from Chicago to East Africa to deliver training to NGO orphanage directors. We kept a team journal during the two-week adventure and required different members to write in it daily. Each person would share their reflections during our meetings at breakfast. We were careful not to overgeneralize about what we saw and the people we met but to discuss and question our observations.

Here's a sample journal entry: "This is a verbal picture of the ordinary routine for our training team, understanding there is nothing 'ordinary' here. The afternoon is spent delivering a practice training session. We share feedback, and everyone receives it with humility. We reward ourselves with a trip to the outdoor market. As we approach, vendors notice our nonlocal style and smile at the thought of sales. We are greeted with a song to give us a true feeling for the region. It becomes a party with both cultures eager to meet, make deals, and understand each other. In the end, we achieve cross-cultural communication, and we leave sharing goodbye hugs."

Plan, then go with the flow. Anticipate and strategize for the unexpected. Do you have the resources needed? Consider what can go wrong and expect it to go wrong. Communicate with trusted colleagues for backup support. Remember to recharge your batteries both literally and figuratively, which will give you the perseverance needed to make the right behavior choices.

Utilize Correct CQ Actions

Table manners matter. Having a meal with someone from a different culture is important not only for relationship building, but also because etiquette is highly dependent on cultural differences. Conversing during the meal is important. Ask questions about local sports and recent events. My favorite question is, "How have things changed in this country since you grew up?"

Value what they value and avoid taboos. Have a respectful, nonjudgmental attitude toward the values and customs of other cultures. Don't just focus on what not to do but plan and visualize what to do instead. Before going to India, I read that it was taboo to shake hands with the left hand. It is customary to shake with the right hand in the United States, so this was not a worrisome taboo. However, by focusing so hard on not shaking the left hand, I made three mistakes in one week. Don't just focus on gestures to avoid, but envision handling situations accurately. *Kiss, Bow, or Shake Hands* by Terri Morrison (2006) is a great resource.

Valuing differences is important, whether talking about ethnic differences or generational differences. David Brown, from Nigeria, had an opportunity to demonstrate "valuing their values" when he faced a challenging generational difference in the classroom. David was not that far off in age from the participants, so he used his typical routines to engage the class. However, some participants still were not engaged. He had to adjust his delivery plan and take a new CQ action. His response was to ask everyone to take out their cell phones and tweet about the one thing they had learned in the past hour that would change the way they worked forever! There was a hushed silence. Participants wondered if this was a trick because there was a no-phones rule. David realized he could be a better trainer by respecting the Millennials' spontaneity and love for technology and not expecting them to conform to his style. (Read more about David's experiences in chapter 2.)

Language is dynamic. Language is a means of communication, and it is a carrier of cultural distinctions. Language is central to social interaction in every society, and it reveals respect for elders, hierarchy, gender veneration, and often the culture behind the words we use to communicate. There are two best methods for learning a new language:

- Move to a country, immerse yourself in the language and culture, and slowly pick up the habits of the people around you.
- Find out about the cultural nuances of a language from someone who already knows it. You will not become fluent in a language that way, but learning how to greet people, show respect and appreciation, and ask for help may be a good place to start. There are several different mobile apps, like Duolingo and Mango, that are very helpful for learning some basic words.

Create a Personal Development Plan to Increase CQ

Cultural intelligence cannot develop accidentally; it develops intentionally with your commitment to increasing your global mindset. Here are steps you can take to create a personal development plan:

- Add "growing a global mindset" to your personal development plan for the year.
- Write down interactions you have with people from other cultures. Reflect on the success of those interactions.
- Look for opportunities to travel internationally, even if it is for vacation. Alternatively, consider a service-vacation program.
- Try new foods, meet new people, enjoy foreign films and novels, or learn a new language. Reflections on these activities, done over a year, can increase your drive, knowledge, strategy, and actions, creating a stronger global mindset. These results will benefit individuals and the entire organization.

Develop CQ Within Your Organization

There are many areas of expertise within the talent development arena. Our title does not matter. We can all influence the growth of CQ within our organizations. The first step is to demonstrate our commitment to CQ and operate with a global mindset in everything we do. Additional behaviors to influence your organization include:

- Offer to perform a talent audit to assess what cultures are represented fairly within the organization and what cultures are underrepresented.
- Suggest that leaders take a valid and reliable CQ assessment, such as the Cultural Intelligence Scale.
- Offer follow-up workshops on developing a global mindset.
- Create a gap analysis survey to see how customers view the CQ of your organization. Train employees to demonstrate a global mindset to eliminate that gap.
- Review current training materials for cultural sensitivity and diversity.
- Offer coaching and training for diverse teams. Include a 360-degree multirater assessment for CQ. Keep in mind

that multicultural teams with high CQ and increased trust are more likely to share ideas and come up with innovative solutions than homogeneous teams.

- Involve HR and training leaders about how to discuss cultural issues. Many managers are hesitant to discuss culturally related issues with staff. They may not completely understand regulations governing such discussions and therefore avoid the topic. How can we build trust and relationships if we believe we cannot discuss our differences?
- Suggest that "having a global mindset" become part of organizational values. We know that CQ is measurable, so it can even be part of performance reviews.
- Celebrate diversity and reward culturally intelligent behavior throughout the organization.

References

Livermore, D., and L. Van Dyne. 2015. *Cultural Intelligence: The Essential Intelligence for the 21st Century.* Society for Human Resource Management. www.shrm.org/foundation/news/Documents/Cultural%20Intelligence.pdf.

Morrison, T. 2006. *Kiss, Bow, or Shake Hands: The Bestselling Guide to Doing Business in More Than 60 Countries.* Avon, MA: Adams Media.

Acknowledgments

I am deeply grateful to the many contributing authors of this book. We enjoyed the sharing, camaraderie, and encouragement it took to compile this global work.

I especially appreciate Heather McMillen and Elana Centor, who have been instrumental in bringing this book to fruition. You encouraged me to find our collective voice for this book and shared in the content rewrites and edits.

Heather McMillen is a Master Trainer who also holds certificates in human performance improvement, change enablement, and instructional design. She used her knowledge and experience from many industries to elevate our writing.

Elana Centor is an award-winning journalist who has worked in print and broadcast media. For the past 20 years, she has split her professional passions between writing and corporate training, where her focus is on leadership and writing. Elana was an irreplaceable coach.

About the Editor

Donna Steffey, MBA, CPLP, and president of Vital Signs Consulting, is an international trainer, author, facilitator of the ATD Master Trainer Program, and adjunct faculty member at Lake Forest Graduate School of Management. Donna has designed and delivered programs with global audiences in 25 countries. She uses her experience to educate, inspire, and coach, helping organizations achieve their desired business results.

Global organizations have found that after Donna's workshops, people were more self-directed, open to new ideas, and mindful of their responsibilities. Donna uses a blend of information, self-discovery, fun, and story to create a vital learning experience. She is certified to deliver the CQ assessment and the EQi, as well as various DiSC assessments.

Index

In this index, *f* denotes figure and *t* denotes table.

Index

M

N

P

Index

R

S

T

U

V

Index

W